Labelle, 1974.

disco

Johnny Morgan with a foreword by **Gloria Gaynor**

STERLING
New York / London
www.sterlingpub

STERLING and the distinctive Sterling logo are registered trademarks
of Sterling Publishing Co., Inc.

10   9   8   7   6   5   4   3   2   1

Published by Sterling Publishing Co., Inc.
387 Park Avenue South, New York, NY 10016

© 2011 Essential Works Limited

Distributed in Canada by Sterling Publishing
c/o Canadian Manda Group, 165 Dufferin Street
Toronto, Ontario, Canada M6K 3H6
Distributed in the United Kingdom by GMC Distribution Services
Castle Place, 166 High Street, Lewes, East Sussex, England BN7 1XU
Distributed in Australia by Capricorn Link (Australia) Pty. Ltd.
P.O. Box 704, Windsor, NSW 2756, Australia

Produced for Sterling Publishing by Essential Works
www.essentialworks.co.uk

Publishing Director: Mal Peachey
Managing Director: John Conway
Editors: Fiona Screen, Jen Eiss
Designer: Michael Gray
Indexer: Hazel Bell
Proofreader: Tania Bissell

Printed in China
All rights reserved

Sterling ISBN 978-1-4027-8035-6

For information about custom editions, special sales, premium and
corporate purchases, please contact Sterling Special Sales Department
at 800-805-5489 or specialsales@sterlingpublishing.com

Contents

WHEN one thinks of a particular type of music, one usually pictures the young people to whom the music belongs or belonged. Depending on what music and era is being considered, at least in America, that can mean picturing young people wearing anything from overalls to nearly nothing: music is always indicative of the social climate. So what could the social climate have been that acted as a catalyst for disco music and the clothing that no designer had previously imagined? Disco music was engendered by an economic decline sweeping the world in the early 1970s. This gave rise to a deep-felt need among the general populace for relief from the drudgery of their lives in which "trying to make ends meet" was a major concern. Where was relief to be found? People couldn't afford to go out for dinner, see a show, or do many of the things that one used to do to relieve the pressures, tensions, and stresses of the day because they cost money. Entertainment venues were beginning to suffer, with playhouses having more dark nights then ever before. Nightclubs and cabarets were closing because in an economic crisis the first thing people cut back

Below: Still the Queen of Disco, Gloria performing in Italy, 2009.

"Our job as entertainers was to supply them with the best thing that entertainment can give a person: a mini vacation from the everyday. This is exactly what discotheques provided."

Gloria Gaynor

on is entertainment. But people *need* entertainment, especially as life becomes more stressful. I am glad to have been there to witness the result of someone having the brilliant idea of completely changing music entertainment venues by first putting in a dance floor, and then a makeshift booth which was more than occasionally made from a storage closet, converted by cutting off the top half of the door. A shelf to hold a record turntable was placed in the booth with one and then two decks on it and someone was hired to spin records for the patrons to dance to. The cover charge for an evening's entertainment was suspended and the patrons would entertain each other on the dance floor with the help of a few drinks and the DJ. Thus were born the first discotheques that I remember visiting.

I always felt that nothing could be more gratifying for an entertainer than to know that you are the reason that people are out on the floor not just to dance, but to shake off the worries and tensions of their day. Our job as entertainers was to supply them with the best thing that entertainment can give a person: a mini vacation from the everyday. This is exactly what discotheques provided. As more and more singers and bands began to record and supply discotheques with "boogie" inspiring music, it became infectious. Across the nation and across the world people began to get turned on to discotheques and disco music, so much so that it spawned an entire culture of its own. The culture included not only danceable music, but attire and hairstyles that changed a generation. There were new and more creative moves made on the dance floor where—lo and behold—people began to dance together again instead of just showing off in the way that the "me generation" had done.

Still, none of that is what really sets disco music apart. The most unique characteristic of disco music is that it is the first in our history to have crossed every national and international border, and transcended every nationality, race, creed, color, and age group. Since it was common ground for everyone, I for one am sorry that it was not taken more seriously and used in more significant ways.

People around the world may be familiar with the "Disco Demolition Night" which took place at Comiskey Park in Chicago in 1979, where anyone who supposedly hated disco music was asked to bring along and burn their disco records. My question has always been, if these people hated disco music, why did they have disco records to begin with? It is widely believed that this event began the demise of disco and that it died shortly thereafter. I happen to know that disco has never died though; it first went underground and shortly thereafter re-emerged to live in the hearts and minds of music lovers around the world. It has simply changed its name to protect the innocent (or the not-so-innocent) and is now called dance music. So you see, disco has not died—it will survive.

Gloria Gaynor

Summer 2010

Introduction

SATURDAY *Night Fever* was the high point and beginning of the end for the disco movement. Once the movie had conquered the world, and radio stations everywhere had switched to twenty-four-hour disco sounds, people soon became over-disco-fied. Yet, the fifteen years between the birth of the scene and its end (1970–1985) were fabulous, exotic, and funky. That period is celebrated and explored here.

Disco may have begun, like so much else, in Paris just after World War II, but it became a global phenomenon only once America had reinvented it. European disco pioneers opened commercial ventures in New York and Los Angeles in the 1950s, which bore a strong resemblance to nightclubs, only they had extended dance floors and catered to a particularly socialite clientele. At least, that was until 1964 when Los Angeles' Sunset Strip saw the opening of a club that gave a hint of the delight, fervor, and thrill of what a discotheque could be.

"Disco" in many ways began at the Whisky a Go Go in Los Angeles, when the dance floor increased in size, dancing girls were hung in cages to show off new moves, and anyone who had the (low) cover charge and will to dance was given entrance. Like a nightclub, the Whisky played host to live music, but they were so placed that the bands they gave first gigs to soon became international stars—among them The Byrds and The Doors. As first the Beatles and then the West Coast hippie scene gripped America, the Whisky's successful blueprint was copied by clubs across the country.

In New York during the late 1960s, disco found another source when a number of privately run events were held in lofts or buildings in Manhattan. The owners or occupiers of the spaces would clear a large area after handing out invites to friends and friends of friends to attend a "rent party." Once attendees were inside and dancing, they were asked for contributions toward paying the upkeep on the space. These originally noncommercial, invite-only discos were run and attended mostly by gay men, who were barred from dancing together in public places by law. The scene grew from David Mancuso's Loft to encompass other, warehouse-style clubs with names like The Paradise Garage and The Gallery in New York, and soon extended to Fire Island off the Atlantic shore of Long Island and the Ice Palace and Sandpiper clubs. Soon enough commercial premises opened in Manhattan and employed the DJs who had learned their trade—which was entirely new to everyone then—at The Loft or Garage. There the DJs played the kind of dance records not being heard on the mainstream radio stations, thus helping to spread The Sound of Philadelphia, TK Disco, and SalSoul, among others, to a new music-buying market.

In the early 1970s, non-gay clubs opened across New York and the rest of America, playing the records promoted by a loose coalition of New York–based DJs, building the market for great dance music everywhere, and setting radio stations onto the emerging sound of disco. Within ten years disco had become a truly international phenomenon, and dance steps created there such as the Hustle, the Bump, the Bus Stop, and the Stomp shook America out of the politicized, protesting, polemical sixties and danced it into the clubs, bars, and discos where a new social revolution took place. America didn't change anything on the campuses or inner-city streets in the 1960s, but it ripped up the old order on the under-lit dance floors from the East Coast to the West, and all points in between, during the following decade.

To paraphrase a poet of disco: don't blame it on the hippies, don't blame it on the politicians, blame it on the boogie. Without a single unifying march and no unfurled banners, men and women of America—whether young, old, black, white, gay, or straight—simply got together to dance, dance, dance in

Below: By the time *Rolling Stone* magazine put Village People on their cover, the last days of Disco were on their way.

1970 and didn't stop until Ronald Reagan was president and changed things forever. By the time the movie *Saturday Night Fever* had conquered box offices across the globe in 1978, the whole world was dancing to funk, soul, or disco beats and in clubs, bars, purpose-built discos, and even roller rinks, which had been converted to roller discos. In truth, the excitement of the original, spontaneous movement had dissipated and diversified, but the influence it continued to exercise on the public imagination and many aspects of life—from fashion and films to TV and politics—was enormous.

Here then is the story of the rise and rise of disco, with a focus on the clubs, the DJs, and the movers and shakers who created the phenomenon, whether record company boss, musician, fashion designer, or artist. It tells a story of madness and mayhem, happiness, joy, sex, and drugs. The bands who made the music—among them Gloria Gaynor, Donna Summer, the multiracial KC & the Sunshine Band, Crusaders, Bee Gees, Trammps, Tavares, Chic, Michael Jackson, Earth, Wind & Fire, and more—are profiled, as are the dance crazes and records that spread the Fever, the dance palaces in which it raged, and the fashions that dressed the dancers, famous or unknown. This is a celebration of the music, sights, and sounds of the disco movement during its formative, productive, and final years. By 1985, "disco" had been displaced by house, hip-hop, and rap as the street-dance sound of choice at clubs and bars. Its prime was between 1970 and 1985, as reflected in these pages.

For anyone interested in reading a more academic account of how the scene developed, there is a list of books to be found in the bibliography, many of which are academic texts. Tim Lawrence's *Love Saves the Day: A History of American Dance Music Culture 1970–1979* (Duke University Press) offers a view of how it was from the mouths of many of the DJs, dancers, and pluggers who were there, and while the author is a professor, the stories are lively, uncensored, and revealing. That there have been so many serious studies of the disco era published suggests that only now are people taking the impact that it made on society seriously. I write "only now" because, as far as I can recall, disco was about not taking anything seriously except getting the moves exactly right. There was no worrying about any effect on anything except the groove when Double Exposure's "Ten Percent" was blasting out across the dance floor, or when Eddie Kendricks was claiming that "Girl, You Need a Change of Mind" as lights flashed, the mirror ball spun, and dry ice swirled. Back then, disco dancers forgot everything except the moment and the dance, which, it seemed, would go on forever.

1

Going back to my roots

Let's Go-Go Disco

WHEN the Germans occupied Paris during World War II, one of their first actions was to close down the jazz clubs, which were seen as harboring dissident elements who glorified the degenerate music of negroes and Jews. This forced music lovers underground and a series of clandestine cellar clubs started up where jazz fans met to play the banned music. Most were in the Latin Quarter. One of them, which opened on the rue de la Huchette in 1941, called itself La Discothèque, and this was quickly adopted as the generic term for any club playing recorded, rather than live, music.

After the war the live clubs reappeared, but the discothèques did not go away: in 1947 Paul Pacine opened the Whisky à Go-Go, which first introduced the idea of public dancing on a dance floor to recorded music instead of a live band. He had the first jukebox in France, presumably "liberated" from an American army base. In the early days the Whisky à Go-Go played nothing but jazz, the dance music of the time; nonetheless the modern discothèque was born. In an exercise of lateral thinking, the club's designer equated whisky with Scotland and lined the walls of the club with tartan except for one wall, which featured the wooden lids from cases of Dewar's, Cutty Sark, Hague, and Ballantine's. The club was tiny, housed in a cellar behind the Palais Royale on the rue de Beaujolais. There were three levels, each divided by five treacherous steps. At the top was a bar where about ten people could stand provided they crowded in on each other, on the second level there were four tables and a banquette, and at the lowest level was the tiny dance floor. The club was so successful that two years later, the French release of Alexander Mackendrick's 1949 Ealing comedy *Whisky Galore!* was renamed *Whisky a Go-Go* to cash in on the club's popularity.

In 1951, Régine Zylberberg, later universally known as "Régine," joined the staff, first working in the ladies' *toilettes* (as "dame pipi"), then as a bartender. In 1953, Pacine decided to move to larger premises on the rue Robert-Estienne and Régine persuaded him to let her take over and manage the old premises. She introduced a crucial new element: an extra turntable, which enabled the DJ to provide a seamless stream of music. The club was such a success that within three months they had knocked through to the next-door cellar. Even so, the club was always uncomfortably dark and crowded whenever more than forty people gathered there.

Régine was born on December 26, 1929, in Anderlecht, Belgium, to Polish-Jewish parents but became a French citizen. She moved to Paris, and after a brief marriage left to establish herself in Juan-les-Pins, on the Riviera. Her love of dancing earned her the nickname of "toupie tournante" (spinning top) and she quickly became the center of a "clan" of ambitious young people, including Moustache and Eddie Constantine. When she returned to Paris, this time to work for Paul Pacine, she brought her showbiz friends with her, which is why Pacine was confident enough to let her take over the old premises. Encouraged by her success, in 1954 Paul Pacine opened a second branch of Whisky à Go-Go in Cannes and sent Régine down to take charge of the launch. This too was a great success.

The next distinctive development in disco came with the opening of Castel's, a private membership club at 15 rue Princesse, off the boulevard St.-Germain-des-Prés on the Left Bank owned by Jean Castel, spokesman for "the republic of pleasures." With its distinctive fire-engine-red frontage with bottle-glass windows, its polished mirrors, plush crimson velvet banquettes and poufs, black lacquered side tables, fake tortoiseshell panels, red shaded table lamps, and gold and crimson brocade curtains it looked rather like an upmarket brothel. It was a private club for members only, with no name outside, just a small plaque announcing the street number. There was gourmet dining on the ground floor and a bar, and often an evening would begin there with a show or a film before everyone headed downstairs to the 250-seater disco in the basement. Castel's quickly became the magnet for the fashionable young Paris set. One of the leading members was Roger Vadim who claimed, in his memoirs, "It was people like me and Christian Marquand, the avant garde director Michel de Ré, Juliette Greco, and the singer Annabel, who created a new style and launched the idea of basement clubs. It was I who coined the term 'discothèque.' One journalist dubbed us 'existentialists.'" In fact Vadim would have only been thirteen when La Discothèque opened its door on the rue de la Huchette, but he really was at the center of a chic Parisian circle that included Jean Cocteau, Edith Piaf, Maurice Chevalier, Boris Vian, Jean Genet, and Jacques Prévert. In 1949 he met Brigitte Bardot, whom he married in 1952, and soon Castel's copper and steel checkered dance floor vibrated to the jiving couple accompanied by Alain Delon, Porfirio Rubirosa, and Jean-Paul Belmondo, sometimes watched over by Jean-Paul Sartre and Simone de Beauvoir. Even future prime minister and president of France Georges Pompidou became a regular. It was all très chic! Many of the elements for a classic disco were now in place.

Worried by the competition, Whisky à Go-Go owner Paul Pacine set Régine up in her own place on the rue du Four on the Left Bank. Chez Régine opened in 1956, and she never looked back. Money was short so she decorated the place with trees purloined from the Bois de Boulogne and upholstered stolen park benches as banquettes. Her road to success was carefully thought out: supported by her clan, a small group of friends who didn't mind that the place was almost deserted, she opened the doors at 10:30 and almost immediately closed them again with a sign on the door reading "Disco full." All through the first month she turned away most of her potential customers, who could hear the music but could not get in. It appeared to be the hottest ticket in town. When she finally opened the doors, the place was mobbed.

> # "There's just something about dance. It's like a primal thing in all of us."
>
> Patrick Swayze

In 1961 she discovered the musical *West Side Story*, then playing Paris, and invited the whole troupe back to Chez Régine to perform. She was intrigued by their warm-up exercises, dancing something called "The Twist," and quickly sent for some Chubby Checker records. The new dance caught on at once. She taught it to Edward VIII—"It was amusing, but a bit strenuous"—but with Charlie Chaplin she danced the tango. Régine was the twist queen as well as queen of the night. The Parisian in-crowd loved her. Filmmaker Louis Malle or François Sagan were often to be seen heading down the stairs to the cellar dance floor. Chez Régine was now an essential stop on a visit to Paris for the stars of Hollywood, and soon Ava Gardner, Gene Kelly, Audrey Hepburn, John Wayne, and Mel Ferrer were to be found perched at tables surrounding the tiny dance floor.

That same year Régine opened New Jimmy's with financing from the Rothschilds, in an old strip club on boulevard Montparnasse. Together with interior designer François de Lamothe she perfected her formula: an art deco interior with eggplant-colored walls, table lamps with pink shades to dispel the night club pallor and make everyone look healthy, and banquettes arranged around the dance floor with areas designated for "the young chic," "the older chic," the "lesser immortals," and "mere money." (Of course, her clientele did not know this was how they were being categorized when they were seated.)

Above: In 1966, nightclubs still
preferred tables to a dance
floor: Ondine's, New York.

Her favored clients were pampered and given gold membership cards. People danced and partied until dawn. There were male dancers in drag and females in gentlemen's attire. Here she reintroduced the now-ubiquitous nightclub practice of serving bottles of spirits labeled with the customer's name, a practice that originated at the Plancher des Vaches, which occupied the rue de Beaujolais premises before the Whisky à Go-Go, thus encouraging them to return to drink more of their own cellar. Every night was a party—exclusive, expensive, fashionable: it was the Régine brand.

JAM
BRO

'LI

ES
WN
'VE'
AT THE
APOLLO
VOLUME II

TWO
BIG ALBUMS
IN ONE

Left: DJs in 1969 would play the whole of each side of James Brown's second *Live at the Apollo* album in order to keep people dancing.

Funky President

H E was the Godfather of Soul, the Hardest Working Man in Show Business, Soul Brother Number One, the Funky President. James Brown was the power source and inspiration for practically the whole dance music revolution of the 1970s. Flamboyant, self-aggrandizing, exacting, and inimitable, JB took 1950s R&B music in a new direction and in the process helped to create soul music and set the ground rules for funk.

Having emerged in the late 1950s as a raw-throated, Little Richard–inspired R&B belter, James Brown and his Famous Flames scored hit singles with ballads "Please, Please, Please" and "Try Me" and began touring the USA playing both roadside bars and city theaters. During that time he developed a seamless, never-ending show in which his band played almost nonstop, segueing from one number to another, growing a groove that kept his audience dancing almost as much as it did James Brown.

A consummate showman, Brown had an MC introduce him onto the stage at the beginning of shows with a boxing-style rally, and the same MC physically drag him from the stage at the end of the show, having covered his shoulders with the kind of robe boxers wore to enter and leave a ring. At the end of his shows, Brown would collapse to his knees, sobbing but still singing; he'd then be partly led off the stage only to throw off the robe and sprint back to his microphone to continue the show. Naturally, audiences went wild.

In 1962 Brown scored a hit with his version of Jimmy Forrest's R&B number "Night Train." Ostensibly an instrumental with only a list of "destinations" sung by Brown, it gave a sample of the groove that Brown's band was building at gigs. Infectious, catchy, and fronted by funky, honking horns, it was a dance record unlike any other. That same year Brown insisted that his record label release a live recording of his show at Harlem's Apollo Theater. They didn't want to, thinking that there was no market for a live album, but JB knew better and *Live at the Apollo Vol I* became his first hit

GOING BACK TO MY ROOTS **17**

album release, reaching number 2 on the *Billboard* Hot 100 chart and remaining in the chart for almost eighteen months. At the center of the album is an eleven-minute version of "Lost Someone." At a time when three minutes was considered long for any pop song, it was a groundbreaking number that demonstrated the appeal of a groove to a live audience. The album ends with a barn-storming version of "Night Train."

As the 1960s progressed, James Brown built a superb backing band centered around baritone saxophonist Maceo Parker and his drumming brother, Melvin. Along with the tenor sax of St. Clair Pinckney, the organ of Bobby Byrd, Mack Johnson's trumpet, Bernard Odum's bass, and the horns of a handful of other players, Brown began to release a string of increasingly funky, dance-oriented singles, beginning with "Out of Sight" in 1964, and continuing with "Papa's Got a Brand New Bag" and "I Got You (I Feel Good)" in 1965, all of which registered in the Top 20 of the pop charts. In 1967 he released what many people consider to be the first true funk record, *Cold Sweat*.

The single was soon a staple in clubs around the country and its success—making number 7 in the *Billboard* charts—prompted other soul acts to add some funk to their sound. The following year Brown released "Give it Up or Turn it Loose," which is still credited by the first DJs of the late 1960s as one of their favorite records and essential at the time for getting people moving on the dance floor.

Brown began putting the term "funky" into his songs (he released "Ain't it Funky" in 1969) as the word became a part of common parlance in music. Like the rest of the country, he became politicized by the ongoing civil rights and anti-Vietnam war movement that was tearing American society apart. The day following the assassination of Dr. Martin Luther King, Brown performed a live show in Boston (April 5, 1968), which was broadcast on local television and appealed for calm, helping to prevent rioting. That summer Brown released "Say It Loud—I'm Black and I'm Proud" and firmly situated funk as protest music. The single featured the trombone of Fred Wesley for the first time, and his influence would help to make Brown's backing band the JBs even funkier than they were.

Another major musical element of the JBs was added when drummer Clyde

Stubblefield joined the band. Having provided the beat for "Cold Sweat," he contributed to Brown's key funky numbers of the 1970s, most influentially "Funky Drummer" released in March 1970. Although only a minor hit (making number 51 on the pop chart), it has since become the most sampled drumbeat in the world and provides the backbeat for countless rap and hip-hop numbers released since.

In 1970 James Brown scored an enormous international hit with "Get Up (I Feel Like Being a) Sex Machine," which was swiftly followed by "Super Bad," and both rapidly became familiar to dancers at clubs and bars around the world. Subsequent James Brown releases over the next five years became guaranteed floor-fillers, and constitute an impressive list of killer disco tunes by any one artist: "Hot Pants," "Make It Funky," "Hey America" (all 1971); "Talking Loud and Saying Nothing," "Honky Tonk," "Get on the Good Foot," "I Got Ants

> # "The one thing that can solve most of our problems is dancing."
>
> James Brown

in My Pants (And I Want to Dance)" (1972); "Think '73," "Stoned to the Bone" (1973); "The Payback," "My Thang," "Papa Don't Take No Mess," "Funky President (People It's Bad)" (1974); and "Hustle (Dead on It)" and "Sex Machine '76" (1975). "Get Up offa That Thing" (1976) was his last great funk opus and floor-filler until "Living in America" made number 4 on the pop charts in 1985, mainly due to being included in the *Rocky IV* movie. It was his last big hit, but James Brown or his funky drummer can still be heard blasting out at clubs and bars around the world.

Southern Soul

WHILE the electric blues and R&B played on the burgeoning music scenes of Chicago, Kansas, New York, and Los Angeles in the 1950s—which changed into the hard-edged, snare-drum-driven dance soul music of the kind played by James Brown and Tamla Motown artists (in Detroit) in the 1960s—down in the Southern states the country blues became a slower-paced soul music. Dotted across the South were the clubs and bars that made up the "chitlin' circuit," which in the 1960s offered the closest thing to a disco experience to be had. Saturday night on the circuit was dance night, and along with the obligatory soul food served in the joints there were performances by singers and entertainers, interspersed with records played so that people could dance. There were no fancy lights and not even a mirror ball, but the dancing had to be kept at a good pace, and when the house band took a break the records came out. Those records were often recorded, pressed, and distributed locally. R&B radio stations in different towns or states would play the local releases before they were even pressed, often creating a buzz about a track or a performer that would both help sell singles and raise attendances at gigs and dances where the records could be heard. Sometimes the records never got past having half a dozen copies pressed; at other times they proved so successful that it made the performer famous (and the label rich).

In New Orleans, producer, songwriter, and pianist Allen Toussaint began spreading a laid-back beat across records for fellow New Orleans–based performers that proved very popular in the mid-1960s among dance and soul music fans. He helped Irma Thomas ("Ruler of My Heart"), Art Neville ("Too Much"), Aaron Neville ("Tell It Like It Is"), and Lee Dorsey ("Ya Ya")—for whom he wrote and produced his biggest hit, "Working in the Coalmine"—to reach out beyond New Orleans boundaries. Toussaint also wrote and produced "Fortune Teller" for Bennie Spellman and Ernie K Doe's "Mother-in-Law," both of which were local hits, with the former becoming a song much covered by English rock bands, among them former Led Zeppelin singer Robert Plant (who included a version on his Grammy Award–winning 2007 duet album with Alison Krauss, *Raising Sand*).

In the 1970s Toussaint helped artists such as Dr. John and The Meters create a laid-back, slinking funk sound which, it was claimed, was based on the second line rhythm produced by New Orleans' mourners returning from a funeral. The Meters' album *Struttin'* (1970) contained pure second line, backbeat rhythms rebranded as Meters' "struts" and proved popular in clubs as each side offered twenty minutes of dance tunes. It was successful enough to gain airplay for the band beyond New Orleans, and they were signed to Reprise Records, for whom they wrote and recorded *Cabbage Alley* in 1970. That was so successful that Toussaint was asked to produce non-New Orleans rock acts who wanted that same funky beat, among them Robert Palmer, The Band, and Willy DeVille.

Further upcountry, in Memphis, Booker T & the MGs were producing a slightly different form of Southern Soul as the house band for a label named Stax. In 1962, piano and organ player Booker T. Jones had his fellow musicians with him at Sun Studios (guitarist Steve Cropper, bassist Lewie Steinberg, and drummer Al Jackson Jr.) to provide backing for a rockabilly singer named Billy Lee Riley. In between takes for Riley, the band began playing a riff that grew and grew until the studio engineer decided that it sounded like something and recorded it for them. The riff became "Green Onions," the band became Booker T & the MGs, and they soon became world famous because of the groove they'd hit that day. The song became not just a staple for thousands of aspiring garage bands across America to jam on, but also offered some soulful sounds to what were often otherwise rock 'n' roll records played at clubs and early discos in the late 1960s.

The band also recorded (without Booker T.) as the Mar-Keys for Stax and played backing for the roster of soul singers who were picked by A&R man Isaac Hayes (*see page 49*) to front a string of great soul records coming from Soulsville, USA, between 1962 and 1975. Just some of the Stax artists included: Rufus Thomas, Carla Thomas, William Bell, Wilson Pickett,

Opposite: Songwriter, arranger, musician, band leader, and purveyor of smooth Southern Soul, Allen Toussaint in the late 1960s.

Johnnie Taylor, Otis Redding, Eddie Floyd, Albert King, Sam & Dave, Staples Singers, Jean Knight, Kim Weston, Shirley Brown, and many others.

Memphis was also home to Hi Records, which made a star of Al Green, and Goldwax Records, which had both O.V. Wright and James Carr signed. A number of small labels were dotted across the Southern states, all of which turned out recordings by local soul singers (male and female) that had a slightly slower, off-beat swing to them than was being played on releases from the labels in the North. Often the recordings would be local hits, played on radios and jukeboxes across the states of Tennessee or Mississippi or Louisiana, and not make much of an impression north of the Mason-Dixon Line—at least not until decades later when they'd be rediscovered for the CD generation and released on numerous "Deep Soul" compilations. In the 1960s and early 1970s, however, singles by Betty Washington ("Breakfast in Bed"), Betty Lavette ("Let Me Down Easy"), Bessie Banks ("Go Now"), Larry Banks ("I'm Not the One"), and countless others became the closing numbers for bars, clubs, and discos everywhere. All of them big ballads oozing sensuality, heartache, and a booming bass line along with an impassioned vocal—the perfect last dance number.

Above: Former New Orleans studio backing band The Meters' solo album.

Right: The M.G.'s eighth album release (in six years), 1968's *Soul Limbo* was the first release on the newly independent Stax label after severing their ties with Atlantic Records.

BOOKER T. AND THE M.G.'S
SOUL LIMBO

LA LA MEANS I LOVE YOU
OVER EASY
ELEANOR RIGBY
AND OTHERS

Whiskey & Peppermint Twist

N America, disco's progenitors were rather more prosaic and can probably be dated back to WINS DJ Alan Freed's Rock 'n' Roll Easter Jubilee,
held at the Brooklyn Paramount and Fabian-Fox on April 12, 1955,
which pulled in 97,000 dancers and took an astonishing $107,000,
but this was really more of a radio road show than anything resembling
a discotheque.

The history of disco in New York up until Studio 54 can be told
through the stories of a small number of DJs and clubs: Terry Noel,
Francis Grasso, David Mancuso, Larry Levan, Nicky Siano, Frankie Knuckles,
Richie Kaczor, and Robbie Leslie; Le Club, Peppermint Lounge, Arthur, Aux
Puces, Salvation, Salvation II, Sanctuary, The Loft, Paradise Garage, and, of
course, many, many others that hold powerful memories for those who frequented them.

The first American equivalent to a Paris disco was Le Club, and it owed more
to Castel's than to the Whisky à Go-Go. It was started by a Frenchman from a
wealthy hotel-owning family, Oliver Coquelin, who had become an American citizen. His backers included Henry Ford and the Duke of Bedford. Le Club was
located in a converted garage at 416 E. 55th Street in East Midtown near
Sutton Place, next door to Coquelin's apartment. It was designed to look like
an alpine hunting lodge: there were wood-paneled walls painted with eigh-
teenth-century Italian allegorical figures, a seventeenth-century Belgian tapestry of the crowning of the Queen of Sheba, golden chandeliers, and fresh
flowers. In the double-height main room, the dining tables—each set with floral
centerpieces and thick white linen—surrounded a small dance floor, only about
eighteen by twenty feet. Opposite the tapestry was a huge Louis XV marble
fireplace with a real fire, and several large comfortable settees beside it. There
was a marquee leading to the curb and coaching lights on either side the door.
It opened on New Year's Eve, 1959–1960, and ushered in the new decade. It
cost $150 to join and the annual subscription was $35, ensuring that only a
certain type of person belonged. The club was so luxurious that the ladies'
room contained a gallon flask of Arpège, discreetly secured by a golden chain.
Oliver Coquelin asked society bandleader Slim Hyatt if he could recommend
a DJ. He did, and soon Hyatt's butler, Peter Duchin, who hadn't been paid in
a while by Hyatt, was in charge of a system installed by Alex Rosner, who was
later responsible for cutting-edge sound systems at The Loft and The Gallery,
but it must be said it was never turned up very loud.

YES! I'M A PEPPERMINT LOUNGER

THIS CARD NOT VALID FOR SPECIAL EVENTS

Left: A member's card
for The Lounge.

Right: Lining up
for entry to New
York's premier
nightclub in 1961.

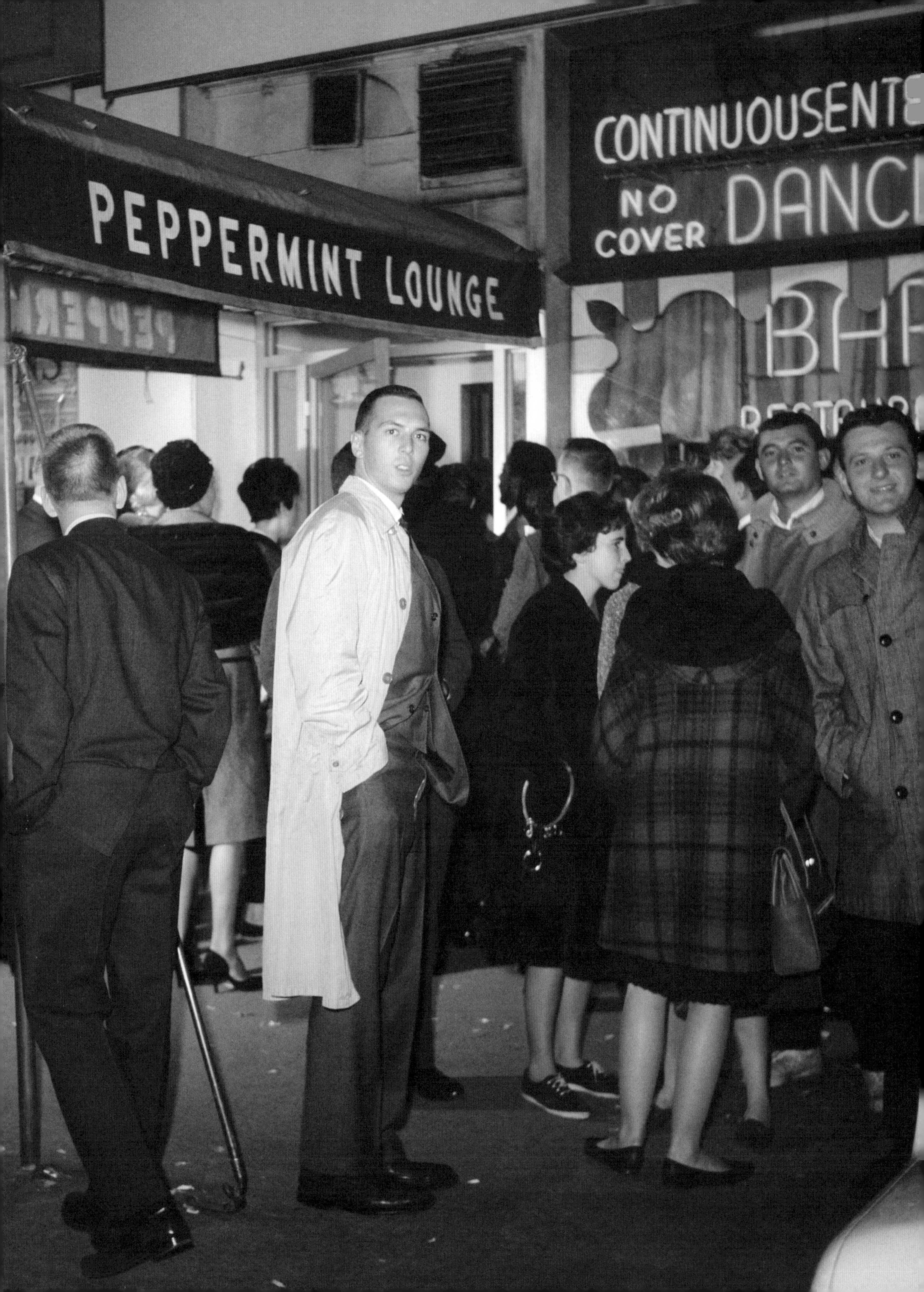
PEPPERMINT LOUNGE
CONTINUOUSENTE
NO COVER
DANC

Ringo Twists and Shouts

The Beatles revolutionized every aspect of teen culture in 1964 when they invaded America. A quip from George about his appearance—Q: "What do you call that haircut?" A: "Arthur"—gave a club owner the inspiration to name her joint "Arthur's." When footage of the Fab Four doing the Twist at London's Ad Lib Club and New York's Peppermint Lounge was screened around the world that same year, clubs became Twisting hotspots once more. Girls across America adopted the beehive hairdo shown here, and clubs cleared tables from dance floors to allow more movement.

The Peppermint Lounge at 128 West 45th Street was an altogether more democratic place: there were big neon signs on the window saying "No Cover," "DANCING," "No Minimum," and another identifying the place as a "BAR," as if you couldn't guess from the marquee and the throng of people crowding the sidewalk. Located just off Times Square, it was quite a rough place, filled with sailors and servicemen, gay hustlers, out-of-town businessmen looking to pick up someone, and leather-jacketed juvenile delinquents left over from the fifties leaning against the usual long mirrored mahogany bar, which ran down the length of one side. What made it special was the music, which was provided by a New Jersey combo called Joey Dee & the Starliters. They were originally hired just for the weekends but, fortuitously, actress Merle Oberon and Prince Serge Obolensky chose to spend most of one night on the small dance floor in the back, dancing the Twist. The gossip columnists ran the story and the next night there were mounted police and wooden barricades down the street to control a crowd that stretched all the way to Broadway. Taking no chances, owner Shirley Cohen appointed Joey Dee & the Starliters as the house band. The Peppermint Lounge was in the middle of the theater district and celebrities flocked to join in. Soon columnists were reporting sightings of Shelley Winters, Jackie Kennedy, Audrey Hepburn, Frank Sinatra, Tallulah Bankhead, Noel Coward, John Wayne, Judy Garland, Tennessee Williams, Nat King Cole, Shirley MacLaine, and even Liberace and the reclusive Greta Garbo. One paper ran a picture of Marilyn Monroe and Truman Capote dancing together. The

Left: In 1966 *LIFE* magazine focused on the emerging "discotheque" scene.

Above: Although Marilyn Monroe would not live to see the glories of Studio 54 (she died in 1962), her dance partner here, author Truman Capote, would become a celebrity fixture at the club for most of its brief existence.

Peppermint Lounge became the hot spot to be seen at; the sailors and the JDs were soon banished and a new, richer, chic crowd was ushered in.

One night in 1961, the then-unknown Ronettes waited in line to get in and were mistaken for the new Go Go dancers and told to get up on stage. They danced and sang along with Joey and the boys and the crowd loved them. They too were hired, and from then on they performed at the Lounge every night. The Twist craze showed no sign of abating so Joey Dee penned a tribute song to the club. Called "Peppermint Twist," it reached number 1 on the charts in early 1962, sold over a million copies, and earned him a gold disc. The club's high point came when the Beatles visited during their first U.S. tour in 1964. As frenzied fans clamored to get in, Paul said, "It was good to be out with real people for a change."

A New Utopia

The New Utopia Lodge in Greenfield Park, New York, was a members-only club. It boasted a swimming pool, private lake, and entertainment room which served meals along with live music and dancing. Unlike the crowded Manhattan nightclubs with their tiny, cramped dance space and segregated areas, the Utopia Lodge allowed serious dancing to truly funky sounds for all (African American) members. Similar clubs were to be found across the northern and Midwestern states, the Hampton House in Miami being a rare Southern example in 1963.

Love's Theme

BARRY White, a Texan-born, former L.A. gang member who served time in prison for stealing tires at age seventeen, decided on a career making music after hearing Elvis Presley singing "It's Now or Never" while in jail in 1961. Or so the legend goes. Whatever his original inspiration, in the midsixties White was employed as an A&R man at Bronco Records in L.A., where he worked with Viola Wills ("Lost without the Love of My Guy") and Felice Taylor ("It May Be Winter Outside") before the label went bust in 1969.

Going solo as a producer, he began working with a trio of female singers (among them his future wife, Glodean James, along with her sister Linda and Diane Taylor) whom he dubbed Love Unlimited. In 1971 White signed them to a division of MCA called Uni Records. The following year, they scored a worldwide hit with "Walking in the Rain with the One I Love." Although ostensibly a Supremes or Ronettes-style ballad, White added a string section and sound effects of falling rain and a telephone being dialed, plus telephone dialogue—between White and Glodean—to create a mini-opera out of the four-minute-plus song. After moving to 20th Century Recordings, White managed to get Love Unlimited "loaned" to him for his new label and set about recording their second album, *Under the Influence of . . .* for release in 1973. White was also persuaded that his voice would work as a lead instrument, and he used the Love Unlimited sound for his debut album, *I've Got So Much To Give*, also in 1973. He co-opted the orchestra made up of old-time film musicians he'd used for Love Unlimited and laid down lush, string-laden tracks that were used as backing over which he added wah-wah guitar, tinny hi-hat, and snare mixed way up high alongside a staccato guitar melody line to create what was a truly new soul sound.

THE LOVE UNLIMITED ORCHESTRA
Rhapsody In White
Arranged & Conducted by BARRY WHITE
FEATURING "LOVE'S THEME"

Opposite: The originally reluctant singer Barry White learns to love the camera.

Left: Barry with Love Unlimited at home on the cover of the Orchestra's debut album, 1974.

Never, Never Gonna Give You Up

White's debut recording owed something to Isaac Hayes (*see page 49*) and instead of packing it full of classic, poppy, three-minute numbers as was customary at the time, several songs were stretched into a minimum of five minutes. Just as Hayes had turned Bacharach/David's "Walk on By" into an eight-minute mini-opera, and Jimmy Webb's "By the Time I Get to Phoenix" into an eighteen-minute epic on his sophomore album *Hot Buttered Soul*, so White took the Four Tops' "Standing in the Shadow of Love" as his opening track and stretched it out to eight minutes. The first single to be taken from the album, "I'm Gonna Love You Just a Little More, Baby," was a 3:58 minute edit of the original 7:11-minute-long album track, and it made number 3 on the *Billboard* pop charts. It was also a great dance floor hit. With Ed Greene's snare and hi-hat to the fore and the kind of repetitive piano riff Frankie Knuckles would in the 1980s use so effectively in creating Chicago House music, White's growling, breathy vocals over Wah-Wah Watson's guitar, Wilton Felder's bass, and a swirling violin section, the album version kept dancers moving on the floor.

White was happy to create an album's worth of tracks with the Orchestra following the unexpected club success of "Love's Theme," which had been the opening track for Love Unlimited's *Under the Influence of . . .* in 1974. When released as a stand-alone single, "Love's Theme" was not only a number 1 pop hit, it also became the first record to earn a Gold Disc Award (marking a million copies sold) for a club DJ. Bobby Guttardo, while working at New York's Le Jardin, received the award from White's label 20th Century Records because he had played the song, along with fellow DJ Nicky Siano, late in 1973 in his club, where it proved hugely popular. Subsequently, radio DJs who had been regulars at Le Jardin began spinning the track on air and the song's popularity spread rapidly over the airwaves.

In 1973 White scored another hit single with "Never, Never Gonna Give You Up" taken from his album *Stone Gon'*, which didn't sell as well as his debut, but was quickly followed by *Can't Get Enough* in 1974. That album made number 1 on the album chart and featured the number 1 pop single "Can't Get Enough of Your Love Babe" as well as the number 2 pop hit, "You're the First, the Last, My Everything." Both songs were also huge dance hits, and ensured that Barry White became a vital part of what would become the essential disco sound for years to come.

Left and Right: The media seemed perplexed at Barry White's success, especially with his mostly female fan base.

> "Barry White hit in 1974, and that was a major change, because that was a sound that hadn't been around before. Love's Theme was one of those records that was a huge, huge club record for about six months before it went to a radio station and became No. 1."

Vince Aletti

AMERICAN EDITION (INC. STARS & STRIPES) JUNE 1975 $1.00

BLUES & SOUL

No. 161   May 27-June 9, 1975   INTERNATIONAL MUSIC REVIEW   UK.: 30p

arry White

Society Hop

I N Britain, London's first discotheque was started by a Frenchwoman, actress Hélène Cordet, born in 1917 in Marseilles, who was, from early 1950, the glamorous presenter of *Cafe Continental*—the first British television variety show, which ran from 1947 until 1953—and star of a number of fifties British films. She had known Prince Philip, the Duke of Edinburgh, since childhood, and in 1955 he pulled a few strings to get her a job as a cabaret singer at the Society Club on Jermyn Street; the cocktail bar was named Chez Hélène Cordet. Accompanied at the piano by Robin Douglas Home, her act became all the rage with everyone from Princess Margaret to the Aly Khan and Errol Flynn attending. Together with her business partner, Major Peter Davies, formerly of the Grenadier Guards, she soon opened a place of her own, a restaurant called the *Cercle Français* on Hamilton Place off Piccadilly. But it was on a short lease and a few months later, in 1961, she and Major Davies opened a club next door: The Saddle Room, at 7 Hamilton Place. In a reference to the Whisky à Go-Go, she decorated the walls with tartan but was very fond of fox-hunting, which became the club's theme, with saddles, bridles, and old brown oil paintings of Masters of the Hunt in gilt frames hanging from the walls. There was a gallery above the small dance floor with its mirror ball where couples could look down on the dancers and the more daring of them might smooch discreetly; this was not, after all, Studio 54.

On the opening night, Major Davies got them a lot of gossip column inches by having the horses, hounds, and riders of the Garth and South Berkshire Hunt assemble in the Mews behind the Saddle Room. There was always a horse and carriage parked outside. The dance that summer was the Twist, and Hélène, like Régine in Paris, got out on the dance floor to show everyone how to do it. She even got Chubby Checker, visiting Britain to cash in on his record, to dance with her and show the upper classes how to move their hips.

As this was Britain, Hélène got into immediate trouble with the Musicians Union which insisted that even though she was only playing records, the union should be paid fees for a six-man band. The Union Secretary was horrified and proclaimed, "Records in a nightclub are like serving food without knives and forks." But while the union maintained its stranglehold on the BBC for many more years to come, they could not control the clubs.

The Saddle Room was immediately fashionable and attracted all the young debutantes and guards officers as well as members of various royal families including Princess Alexandra and the Duke of Kent, Crown Prince Harald of Norway, and King Hussein of Jordan. Senator Lyndon Johnson, then American Vice President–elect, arrived one night with a party of fifteen, and he at once cut in on Major Davies to dance with Hélène. "I spent that dance pushing him away," she said. "He was a big bear of a man who clasped me far too close."

> ## "Dancing, apart to music with a beat, is my legacy. Britney Spears, all the rappers, they're doing my dances and they're making billions doing it. When they do that little thing with their hands that's The Fly and The Pony."
>
> Chubby Checker

Left: After becoming internationally famous with the dance craze hit "The Twist" in 1960, Chubby Checker continued to seek out dance hits. He visited Great Britain in 1965 to promote "The Freddie." It didn't take off and his recording career ended.

Left: A former cabaret artist-turned-television presenter, Hélène Cordet (pictured here in 1954 when she was thirty-seven) opened the upper-class members-only Saddle Room in 1961. It played records and didn't have a live band, which was then considered unusual.

When the Beatles moved to London in 1963 they always used to bring acetate copies of their new singles to play and sometimes, after a long night, used the horse and carriage outside to get home to their flat in nearby Green Street.

The façade and portico of the present Lyceum Ballroom at 21 Wellington Street, in London's Covent Garden, date from 1834, but everything else was rebuilt in 1904. As a theater, it went dark in 1939 and was converted into a giant ballroom in 1951. During the first week of August 1961, Jeff Dexter, then a fourteen-year-old schoolboy, signed the membership forms to join the Sunday Club and lied about his age—he said he was sixteen—and entered the ballroom for the first time. He was astonished by its size. Following the instructions on the record sleeve, he had practiced how to do the Twist at home, but when he hit the floor at the Lyceum, the management banned him on the grounds of lewd behavior; the Twist was not just another foxtrot or samba. But within weeks, reports in the newspapers about the dance craze sweeping America and the continent made them reverse their decision. Jeff told Bill Brewster and Frank Broughton: "This thing, this *obscenity* that I'd been ejected for, became popular and I got offered a job at the Lyceum. As a dancer!" Jeff became an instant celebrity and footage of him twisting the night away appeared on Pathé newsreels in cinemas across the country.

Ad-Lib

PROBABLY the most significant of the London "in-clubs" was the Ad Lib, in that it had a profound influence on the development of discotheques in New York City as well as inspiring imitators at home. It opened in February 1964, on the top floor of a building in Leicester Place off Leicester Square, and was the first to cater to the newly emerging class of young rock 'n' rollers—actors like Michael Caine and Lawrence Harvey, and the new breed of photographers like David Bailey—that constituted "Swinging London." Previously, London nightclubs had either catered to the older supper-club crowd, or were bare, no-frills dance halls with no liquor license or even, as in the case of the Flamingo, a place to sit down. It began life as WIPS, a jet set club owned by Lord Willoughby and Nick Luard from The Establishment Club. The walls were lined with fur, and there was a large tank of carnivorous piranhas, but the jet set were already well catered for in

Below: Soho, London, 1963.

Tamla Motown

THE artist roster of Tamla Motown reads like a members list for the soul and funk Hall of Fame (if such a place existed). Beginning in 1960 with their first million-selling single, Smokey Robinson and the Miracles' "Shop Around," the Motown sound and status was firmly established among music fans in 1961 with their first number 1 pop hit, The Marvellettes' "Mr. Postman." That song, like the first Motown hit single—1959's "Money (That's What I Want)" by Barrett Strong—was covered by The Beatles, who were as desperate to meet the Motown all-girl group The Supremes in 1964 as they were Bob Dylan or Elvis Presley.

Tamla Motown records were known for their trademark sound, driven by a boxy, tight snare and tambourine accenting the backbeat, while a melodic bassline shadowed the four-part harmonies backing the lead vocal. Motown songs, written by in-house songwriting teams Barrett Strong and Norman Whitfield or Holland-Dozier-Holland (with performers such as Smokey Robinson, Marvin Gaye, and Stevie Wonder writing their own material) were spread among the artists by label boss and founder Berry Gordy. An in-house band who later adopted the name Funk Brothers played on all Motown recordings, often putting in sixteen-to-twenty-hour days at the Tamla recording studio, which bore the title of "Hitsville USA" and stood at 2648 W. Grand Boulevard in Detroit, Michigan.

Tamla Records was begun and run as a family business. Gordy borrowed initial funds from his family to begin the company and went on to employ various Gordy family members, and had Smokey Robinson as vice president from the beginning. His band, originally called The Matadors, had worked with Gordy, writing songs for them, and were the first act to sign for Tamla, where they changed their name to The Miracles. Robinson went solo in 1972, and the band would score a big disco hit in 1975 with "Love Machine (Part 1)," which made the top spot on the *Billboard* singles charts, becoming their best-selling record and one of Motown's last big international hits.

In the 1960s Motown made international stars of The Supremes, The Four Tops, Martha and the Vandellas, Stevie Wonder, The Temptations, Marvin Gaye, Jimmy Ruffin, Gladys Knight and the Pips, Jr. Walker & The Allstars, and the Jackson Five. Their hits sold around the world and were played on radio and performed on television constantly wherever soul and pop music was to be heard and seen. At first Motown records were concerned with the familiar topics of all pop songs of the day: love, heartbreak, and reconciliation. However, as the decade wore on and other soul and pop acts began to politicize their lyrics, so too did writers such as Strong and Whitfield. They pushed the Funk Brothers to make a funkier, harder, and more extended groove for acts such as The Temptations, particularly. Marvin Gaye and "Little" Stevie Wonder (who dropped his nickname in 1968) started to write songs about spiritual and political renewal. Even The Supremes, a pure-pop phenomenon of the midsixties, embraced socially relevant material and scored their eleventh U.S. number 1 single with "Love Child" in 1967 (it's not about hippies, but an unmarried mother).

Aware of the growing dance club scene in major North American cities at the end of the 1960s, where a growing African American middle class would gather to eat and dance, Strong, Whitfield, and Gordy

Below: Formerly known only as Smokey Robinson's backing singers, in 1975 The Miracles scored an enormous disco hit with "Love Machine" taken from this album.

knew that there was a music market to be tapped. The Temptations were the chosen band to "experiment" with, and they released "Cloud Nine" in 1968, which was similar to the recently successful Sly & the Family Stone's "Dance to the Music" in mixing rock guitars with a dance beat and funky feel. It went to top 10 in the pop charts (and won a Grammy), and sent the Temps into "psychedelic soul" territory, setting off a run of extraordinary single releases that went on to become staples at the newly emerging dance clubs and nascent discos across America: "Runaway Child Running Wild," "I Can't Get Next to You," "Psychedelic Shack," "Ball of Confusion," "Superstar (Remember How You Got Where You Are)." In 1972 the Temptations released the six-and-a-half-minute-long "Papa Was a Rolling Stone," and before release it became a staple floor-filler at every disco where DJs could get a copy of the disc. A bass and wah-wah guitar-driven mini-opera, it built in intensity and drive as the record spun, putting dancers into an ever-growing groove.

After Berry Gordy moved Motown away from Detroit to Los Angeles in 1972, the company lost some of their spirit and roster. Despite signing Lionel Richie and the Commodores, Rick James, and others in L.A., the success of the company's first two decades couldn't be sustained or repeated, and in 1989 Berry Gordy sold his label to MCA Records.

Because Tamla Motown records had a shared beat and rhythm, they would blend easily into one another when played for dancers. Keying up a Four Tops number while the Supremes played was relatively easy for even a novice DJ. As Motown acts began recording longer numbers, DJs could fill time more easily with their releases. Even when Marvin Gaye and Stevie Wonder insisted on recording alone, at different studios, and without the Funk Brothers as a backing band, their output still bore the Motown sound—at least to begin with—and contained guaranteed dance hits. Well into the late 1970s disco DJs were spinning Motown singles made in the mid-1960s. Some clubs had Motown-themed nights held midweek in order to guarantee attendances on a slow night, with all music coming from the Tamla Motown studios. Forty years later, it's impossible not to dance when a Motown single is played at a club, bar, or party.

Above: Tamla Motown's superstar singing Temptations in 1972.

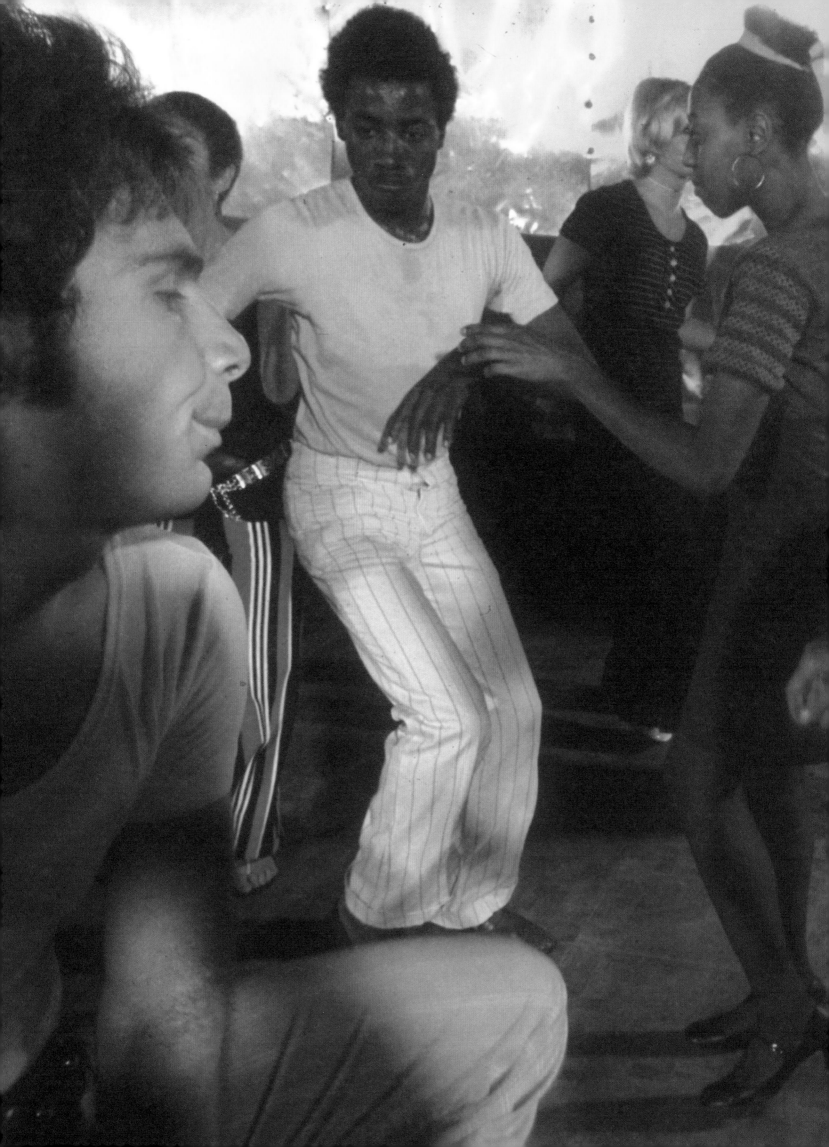

London, and not enough of them were prepared to venture into Soho and take the rickety elevator to the penthouse. It was soon sold and the new owners installed Brian Morris as the new manager. Out went the fish and the fur and, knowing that his clients loved nothing better than looking at themselves, he covered the walls with huge mirrors. Chairs were replaced with stools, and banquettes lined the walls. He chopped down the legs of the tables to coffee table height. The ceiling was low, with inset-colored lights, but it was not claustrophobic because there was a huge window looking out over the nighttime rooftops of Soho and the theater district. He sold drinks as miniatures, twenty-five shillings for the first and ten shillings after that; ice, a coke, or soda was included. A steak and fries was about a pound. John Lennon was the first Beatle to try it out; the next time he brought Ringo, and within seven weeks it was the in-place to be. There was a state-of-the-art sound system, cranked up really loud, which played mostly Motown and Stax, which meant that all conversation was conducted as a shouting match. Paul McCartney said, "They had a chef who used to come out about 11:30 and bang a tambourine and everyone would cheer and dance the conga. I'd see people like the Hollies down there and Ringo and the other Beatles, the rock 'n' roll crowd . . . there'd be a mate in one of the little alcoves, at one of the tables, so you'd just sit there and it would just build, you know. It was a nice social scene." The sexual tension in the Ad Lib ran high with all the pop singers competing for the "dolly birds" and the models eying up the fashion photographers. McCartney: "I realize it was about pulling birds because if you're not pulling birds they are very boring places. It's lovely across the room, to be looking at some gorgeous bird and giving her the eye all evening, I mean, that's something to do. But if you're sitting there with your wife, it's a completely different matter."

Members Only

WHILE the Beatles were busy breaking down class barriers in England, there were still some parts of the aristocracy who didn't want to mix with hoi polloi, and they fought against the democratization of nightlife. There would always be Brits who considered themselves to be above anyone who did not go to the same schools as them. The invention of the luxurious, exclusive, by invitation, members-only nightclub was inevitable. The first in London was Mark Birley's Annabel's at 44 Berkeley Square, housed in the basement beneath John Aspinall's Clermont gaming club. Builders had to excavate 6,000 tons of London clay from the basement of the 1745 townhouse to give enough headroom in the club. That still left forty-three pillars holding up the building which rather got in the way. Architect Philip Jebb, chosen because he had never been in a nightclub, solved the problem by introducing a series of false, transverse barrel vaults and wrapping the square pillars in polished brass, making the place look, in the words of a *Daily Mail* correspondent, like "a cross between a lap dancing club and the palace of an Arab sheikh." The oak-paneled alcoves were filled with a mixture of oriental statuary, vegetation, and Mark Birley's collection of rather dull, very conservative paintings.

After two years in the planning, it opened its exclusive doors on June 4, 1963. Birley named the club after his then-wife, Lady Annabel Vane-Tempest-Stewart, who later had an affair with Sir James Goldsmith who became her second husband. It claimed to be London's first members-only club, because that way they could control who they allowed in. This was obviously not the case: David Tennant's Gargoyle Club on Dean Street, Soho, which had run

Below: Italian designer Cerruti sold aspiration and class by posing his model alongside an expensive Lamborghini car. The jacket was designed by Giorgio Armani.

The car: Lamborghini Urruco
The suit: Nino Cerruti's Royale
by Society Brand, Ltd.

during World War II, was one of many precursors of this type of club. But it may have been the first to be so exclusive as to exclude all but the very rich and well-connected. Ex-wives were also not allowed in.

Initially they catered almost entirely to aristocrats and royalty, but aristocrats don't like parting with their money. They claimed to be introducing new money to old, but the standing joke was that it was more like introducing the middle-aged to the Middle East. The club was very dark, to disguise the advanced age of most of the members. It was here that Richard Nixon and Ted and Robert Kennedy hobnobbed with Frank Sinatra, arms dealers, shipping tycoons, and conservative politicians. It was the venue for Sarah Ferguson's hen night when she and Diana, Princess of Wales, dressed as policewomen. It is the only nightclub known to have been attended by the queen. The club was breathtakingly expensive, with guests entertained by the likes of Ella Fitzgerald, Diana Ross, Tina Turner, and Ray Charles. Birley turned the club over to his son and daughter, but then returned to the helm, banning his son from the club because he disapproved of the class of member that Robin was allowing in (his son married Bryan Ferry's daughter). One of Robin's innovations was to introduce a guest DJ night on Thursdays; naturally he chose people like old Etonian club mixer John Lycett-Green. The snobbery and elitism of Annabel's was much admired and copied across the planet—Doubles in the basement of the Sherry-Netherland hotel, Olivier "I invented disco" Coquelin's Le Club, and his later venue, Cachaca, being just three in New York to use that template.

Thankfully the English class system wasn't to be found in many spots around the world. In more egalitarian societies—such as America—clubs would take anyone's money, pretty much regardless of who they were or how they earned it. No one had to fight for their right to party with the upper classes in New Jersey or Queens. Although not many of the upper class would travel that far.

The Hot 100 Disco Trax Part I (1968-1976)

James Brown: Give It Up or Turnit a Loose (running time: 3:10/Format: single/Label: King Records/January 1968)

Sly & The Family Stone: Dance to the Music (3:00/single/Epic/January 1968)

The Supremes: Love Child (3:0/single/Tamla Motowenm/September 1968)

Marvin Gaye: I Heard it through the Grapevine (3:16/single/Tamla Motown/October 1968)

Isaac Hayes: Hyperbolicsyllabicsesquedalymistic (9:55/album track on *Hot Buttered Soul*/Stax/August 1969)

The Temptations: Ball of Confusion (That's What the World Is Today) (4:06/single/Tamla Motown/May 1970)

Curtis Mayfield: Move on Up (8:50/album track Curtis/Curtom/June 1970)

James Brown: Get on Up (I Feel Like Being Like a) Sex Machine (5:15/single/King Records/July 1970)

Booker T & The M.G.'s: Melting Pot (3:50/single/Stax/February 1971)

Isaac Hayes: Theme from Shaft! (4:37/single and album title track/Stax/July 1971)

The Temptations: Papa Was a Rolling Stone (6:58/single/Gordy Records/September 1972)

Bobby Byrd: Hot Pants—I'm Coming, I'm Coming (3:27/single/Brownstone Records/1972)

Manu Dibango: Soul Makossa (4:30/single and album title track/Fiesta [France]/March 1972)

Eddie Kendricks: Girl You Need a Change of Mind (7:30/album track on People . . . Hold On/May 1972)

War: City, Country, City (13:18/album track on *The World Is A Ghetto*/November 1972)

The Intruders: I'll Always Love My Mama (Part I) (3:04/single/Gamble Records/June 1973)

Love Unlimited Orchestra: Love's Theme (4:08/album track on *Under the Influence of Love Unlimited*/20th Century Records/September 1973)

Herbie Hancock: Chameleon (15:34/album track on *Head Hunters*/Columbia/October 1973)

Kool & The Gang: Jungle Boogie (3:08/album track on Wild & Peaceful/De-Lite Records/October 1973)

The O'Jays: For the Love of Money (7:14/album track on *Ship Ahoy!*/Philadelphia International/November 1973)

Barry White: Never, Never Gonna Give You Up (7:58/album track on *Stone Gon'*/20th Century Records/November 1973)

MFSB: TSOP (The Sound of Philadelphia) (3:29/single/Philadelphia International/December 1973)

George McCrae: Rock Your Baby (3:14/single/TK Records/May 1974)

The Commodores: Machine Gun (single, Tamla Motown/July 1974)

BT Express: Do It ('Til You're Satisfied) (3:09/single/Scepter Records/September 1974)

The Fatback Band: Keep on Steppin' (4:21/album title track/Event Records/November 1974)

Gloria Gaynor: Never Can Say Goodbye (2:55/single/MGM Records/November 1974)

Blackbyrds: Walking in Rhythm (2:54/single/Fantasy Records/December 1974)

Below: Former Temptations singer Eddie Kendricks recorded one of the great early disco numbers, "Girl, You Need a Change of Mind."

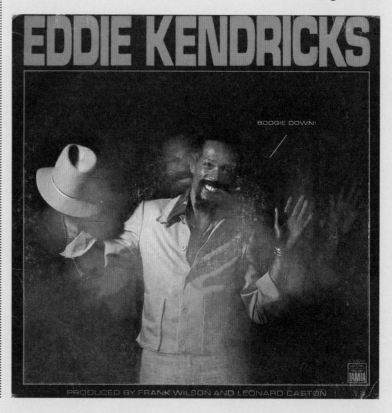

Ramsey Lewis: Sun Goddess (8:29/album title track/Columbia/1974)

Lonnie Liston Smith and the Cosmic Echoes: Expansions (6:04/album title track/Flying Dutchman/February 1975)

Consumer Rapport: Ease on Down the Road (6:27/single/Wing & A Prayer-Atlantic/April 1975)

Earth, Wind & Fire: Shining Star (2:50/single/Columbia/January 1975)

Shirley & Co: Shame, Shame, Shame (3:34/single/Vibration/January 1975)

Harold Melvin & The Blue Notes: Bad Luck (6:29/album track on *To Be True*/Philadelphia International/February 1975)

Isley Brothers: Fight the Power (Part 1 & 2) (single/5:18/T-Neck/May 1975)

Van McCoy: The Hustle '75 (4:10/single/Avco Records/May 1975)

War: Low Rider '75 (3:111/single/United Artists/June 1975)

The Ritchie Family: Brazil '75 (3:14/single/20th Century Records/July 1975)

Donna Summer: Love to Love You Baby (16:50/12" single/Oasis–Casablanca/August 1975)

Double Exposure: Ten Per Cent (9:50/12" single/SalSoul/March 1976)

Andrea True Connection: More, More, More (6:15/12" single/Buddah Records/March 1976)

Boz Scaggs: Lowdown (5:18/album track on Silk Degrees/Columbia/March 1976)

The Trammps: That's Where the Happy People Go (5:24/12" single/Atlantic/April 1976)

Candi Staton: Young Hearts Run Free (4:08/single/Warner Bros Records/May 1976)

Tavares: Heaven Must Be Missing an Angel (6:32/12" single/Capitol/June 1976)

Carol Douglas: Midnight Love Affair (6:20/12" single/Midland International Records/September 1976)

Dr Buzzard's Original Savannah Band: Cherchez la Femme (5:46/12" single/RCA/June 1976)

The SalSoul Orchestra: Nice and Naasty (5:22/12" single/Salsoul/October 1976)

The Undisputed Truth: You + Me = Love (11:10/12" single/Whitfield Records/December 1976)

Rose Royce: Car Wash (5:06/album title track/MCA/December 1976)

Above: Lonnie Liston Smith was a pioneer jazz-fusion musician.

Below, left: War's 13-minute-long "City, Country, City" track on 1972's *All Day Music* was a DJ fave.

Below, right: Curtis Mayfield's "Move on Up" was a very early disco hit (1970), and several tracks from the *Superfly* soundtrack (1972) became dance floor fillers.

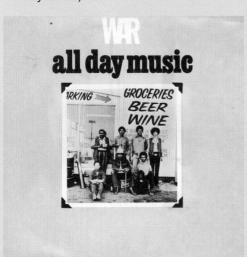

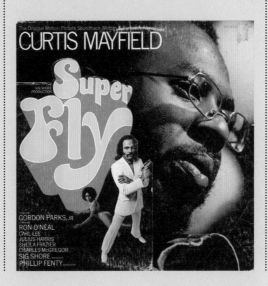

Isaac Hayes

FOR many people, Isaac Hayes' "Theme from *Shaft*" was the first true disco hit. Released in September 1971, the 3:15-minute version (the album track being 4:34 minutes) climbed the *Billboard* singles chart slowly but surely until reaching the number 1 position in November. In 1972 it won an Oscar, making Hayes the first African American to win the award for anything but an acting role. The song begins with Willie Hall's sizzling hi-hat for two bars before Michael Toles' wah-wah guitar cuts in, and two bars later Hayes' piano lands a resounding minor chord. The single-note bass adds depth to the sound before the horns begin to enter, playing three and four-note refrains, closely followed by a flute playing a melodic six-note ascending riff; Charles Pitts adds thundering guitar chords and everything builds to the entry of the violins, which raise the tempo and intensity of the groove. At 2:40 Hayes' vocal asks, "Who is the man . . .?," with vocalists Pat Lewis, Rose Williams, and Telma Hopkins chanting "Shaft" and "John Shaft" in answer.

The success of the movie, starring Richard Roundtree as a detective determined to bring violent justice to the mean streets of New York, employing Black Power rebels in his fight against drug dealers, both helped the single to sell, and vice versa. The soundtrack was released as a double album at the same time that the movie opened in July 1971. It was the first double release by a Stax—or any soul artist—to reach the number 1 spot on the *Billboard* Hot 100 charts on November 6, 1971. The hit single undoubtedly helped to drive people into cinemas, and started a trend of soul artists writing, performing, and releasing soundtrack albums (Curtis Mayfield's *Superfly* reached the number 1 spot in 1972, and Marvin Gaye's "Trouble Man" made the Top 10 in 1973).

Hayes had begun his musical career as a (self-taught) session player at Stax Records in the 1960s, where he co-wrote a number of hit songs for the label's roster, most notably Sam & Dave's "Soul Man" and "Hold on I'm Coming." He turned front man

in 1968 and recorded an extended studio jam with house musicians including M.G.'s Donald "Duck" Dunn, Steve Cropper, and Al Jackson accompanying him. The *Presenting Isaac Hayes* album wasn't a hit, but it set the template for future Hayes releases, in that it mixed middle-of-the-road pop songs with extended funky jams (one of only two original compositions on *Presenting*, "Precious, Precious," lasted over eighteen minutes in the original mix). His second album, 1969's *Hot Buttered Soul*, was recorded over the summer of 1968 and included a 12:03-minute version of Bacharach/David's "Walk on By," an 18:42-minute version of Jimmy Webb's "By the Time I Get to Phoenix," and, most importantly, a 9:38-minute version of a Hayes original titled "Hyperbolicsyllabicsesquedalymistic." The

"I felt what I had to say musically could not be said in two minutes and thirty seconds . . . So I did my thing. If it was a hit, great. But I just did what I wanted creatively."

Isaac Hayes

trademark wah-wah guitar and half-spoken, raw vocals over a determined beat showed a unique talent at work and is the only up-tempo number on the otherwise slow album. Hayes' version of the Jimmy Webb song features eight minutes of him "rapping" over a ponderous build-up before the melody, verse, and chorus begin. Both "Walk on By" and Hayes' "One Woman" are also performed as slow-tempo love ballads, played out in a jazzy, jam-like way with a string section added for impact. While it reflected musical developments in the rock world, it was completely new for a soul and R&B artist. Where he led, others soon followed, and soul numbers began to

Left: From backroom boy to superstar: Isaac Hayes went from being a record company A&R boy in the 1960s to Stax's biggest star man in the early 1970s.

C HAYES

MGM's

stax

Left: The double album soundtrack to *Shaft!* was an international smash, making the top of album charts around the world on the back of the similarly successful title track single release.

be longer than the usual three to four minutes long. Severely edited versions of both "Walk on By" and "Phoenix" made the Top 40 pop charts in 1969, but the album made the Top 10 in the *Billboard* Hot 200 chart and Hayes became an established recording artist.

The follow-up album, *The Isaac Hayes Movement*, was released in March 1970. It repeated the same formula and included another Bacharach/David song, "I Just Don't Know What to Do with Myself," George Harrison's "Something," and Jerry Butler's "I Stand Accused" as extended jams (backing was provided by Stax Records' house band the Bar-Kays). Again, the album made number 8 on the pop album chart. Six months later . . . *To Be Continued* was released and was similar to both previous albums (this one features Bacharach/David's "The Look of Love"), but included a Hayes original, "Ike's Rap," a slow number over which Hayes raps a "confession" and "apology" to the woman he's wronged. The dramatic monologue was soon copied by other soul singers (most notably on Harold Melvin and the Blue Notes' "Be for Real" in 1973) and the song extensively sampled by 1990s rappers.

And then came *Shaft*. Almost as soon as DJ Bobby Guttadaro heard the theme he began playing it at The Ice Palace on Fire Island. He was the first (as he was with many other tracks; *see Barry White, page 33*) but it was soon being played by rival DJs at other Fire Island clubs, most of them spinning the longer album track, months before the single was pressed. From there the word spread and clubs across the USA and then Europe were filling dance floors with the "baddest mother . . . ." Hayes followed the soundtrack with another double album release, *Black Moses*, in November 1971, the cover of which was engineered to fold out into a full-length image of the singer/producer in a suitably biblical-style robe (and gold-rimmed sunglasses). The album made number 10 on the album chart, and the single taken from it, "Never Can Say Goodbye"—previously a hit for the Jackson Five—made number 22 on the singles chart. Hayes would never again be as successful as he was with "Theme from *Shaft*" in the pop charts, but his records would be disco hits for years to come— particularly the lengthy tracks in the days before the 12" extended play single was introduced to the disco scene.

MOST of the elements for what would come to be known as disco were now in place: disc jockeys spun seamless dance records as lightshows flashed around the room, sound systems were powerful, and dance floors larger. The only thing missing was that scourge of nightclubs, the velvet rope. This soon originated at Arthur, a New York nightclub named after a line about George Harrison's hair in the Beatles' film *A Hard Day's Night*:

AMERICAN JOURNALIST: "What do you call your haircut?"
GEORGE HARRISON: "I call it Arthur."

The club was started by Sybil Burton, using the divorce money she received when her husband Richard Burton dumped her for Elizabeth Taylor. She had been a regular at the Ad Lib in London, and she sought to repeat the atmosphere in New York. Eighty of her friends, including Leonard Bernstein, Julie Andrews, Rex Harrison, and Mike Nichols (who came up with the name) shelled out $1,000 each and in May 1965, Arthur opened its doors at 154 E. 54th Street in Midtown Manhattan on the site of the defunct El Morocco. Though you could find Rudolph Nureyev, Tennessee Williams, or Lee Remick doing the frug or the watusi on the dance floor, Arthur was open to all—from shop girls to European aristocracy—as long as you had the right look; style and attitude was as important as money, a formula later copied by Studio 54. Sybil called them the PYPs, the Pretty Young People. To achieve this mix, she introduced the velvet rope. At Arthur it was manned by Mickey Deans, who certainly knew how to pick them. One of the people he let in was Judy Garland, and he married her just twelve weeks before she committed suicide.

The club was painted black, with smoke-tinted mirrors around the entire room. There were banquettes and little padded stools and the lighting was minimal, just small, colored spots on bars down from the ceiling. Arthur introduced another innovation, the celebrity DJ. Up until now, DJs were hidden in booths or horse carriages, or in alcoves where they watched the dance floor through a hole in the decorated screens. What made Arthur special was Terry Noel, the first DJ to match the records with the mood of the crowd, carefully building the momentum until the floor was packed; then he would hit them with a series of perfect dance tunes to drive them wild with excitement. Noel began as a professional twister at The Peppermint Lounge but worked at Arthur from its second day of opening. He redesigned the lights and brought in Chip Monck—who later did the stage lighting at Woodstock—to install speakers with independent frequency controls to give him greater stereo scope: he could move a wall of sound around the room, astonishing the patrons.

Most importantly, Terry Noel was the first DJ to mix records, and demonstrated his expertise in manipulating vinyl records by dropping a solo from a different record in here, a couple of choruses from an R&B record there, a shout or a yell, a whisper or groan. The dancers didn't know if they were listening to Fontella Bass or the Marvelettes; they all merged seamlessly together into one, big rolling ocean of sound. It was primitive, but he was the first and it worked. He told Bill Brewster and Frank Broughton: "I didn't want people to even know that the song changed. Many people would come up to me and say, 'I was listening to the Mamas and the Papas and now I'm listening to the Stones and I didn't even know.' I used to try some of the wildest changes without losing a beat." Arthur was also the first of the true sixties clubs, decorated in huge primary-colored Mondrian-style Plexiglas panels and featuring Go Go dancers in Op-Art dresses; it was modern and young. Here the drinks were sloshed into huge goblets, not served by a sommelier. With the exception of actual disco music, everything was now in place for dance halls to sweep the western world, but then came psychedelia, and sadly, lovable as they were, hippies were useless dancers.

Left: Leopard-print- and pop-art-clad revelers enjoy Arthur's first birthday bash in May 1966.

Bigger, Longer, Louder

WHILE some soul artists were recording long, five-minute-plus numbers and cramming as much of them as possible onto seven-inch vinyl singles, those singles were invariably created for the radio market. Although Isaac Hayes and Barry White had by 1973 produced unconventional hits for both radio and club DJs, few other artists had

> **"The whole thing about disco is the sound. The few times I wrote songs with emphasis on the lyrics, the record company told me to stop it because the words just interfered."**
>
> Cerrone

Left: Once record companies had started to press 12" records for discos, they began to produce generic, company-stamped sleeves for them rather than commission new artwork for what they thought would be a club–DJ release only.

done much more than create songs based on the verse—chorus—verse—chorus—middle eight—verse—chorus—end structure. Club DJs liked the middle eight section, because it was often instrumental and featured a key and/or tempo change, allowing some variation in dance moves for their audience. Club DJs had begun spinning one disc into another as seamlessly as possible, by running together tracks with similar (preferably identical) beats and tempos. Motown records were particularly good for this.

Album tracks, being longer, were being played in clubs to great effect; Eddie Kendricks' 7:32-minute-long "Girl You Need a Change of Mind" from 1972's *People* . . .

Hold On was a big hit at David Mancuso's Loft (*see page 102*), prompting other DJs to play it too. Other DJs were playing two copies of the same track and switching between each on the middle eight, so extending it and keeping the beat going. DJs who had their decks playing through a mixing desk were able to enhance aspects of a single's sound above others, bringing up the bass, treble, or adding echo and so on. It was fairly basic, but added to the novelty and originality of sounds to be heard at any particular club.

Tom Moulton began his career as a record plugger in the early 1960s, before becoming a model. After discovering Fire Island (*see page 94*) in the early 1970s,

he came up with the idea of seamlessly blending tracks together on a reel of tape, which could play forty-five minutes of non-stop music. The Sandpiper took his first tape and played it to great reaction from the crowd, prompting them to ask Moulton to make more for them. While compiling his tapes, Moulton "mixed" the recordings to push up bass, extended drum breaks, and recreated the original songs in a different form. The success of his tapes at the Sandpiper (having been rejected initially by The Ice Palace) led to his being asked by other clubs for similar tapes, and it wasn't long before record companies who were beginning to cater for the club market asked his advice on record releases,

Below: Some releases were destined for chart success and the 12" release for those did have specially-designed sleeves. Band images were not considered sexy enough though.

and increasingly through 1974 and '75 Moulton was asked to remix a track before the seven-inch record was released.

Often Moulton would remix songs in a cutting studio by directing engineers with ideas of what he wanted to hear from the record—which often the artist knew nothing about. He'd play the original recording from a seven-inch vinyl pressing and the desk would separate out all the elements of sound. Then he'd flatten drum sounds, bring up the snare, and extend sections as far as he could—which was never far enough on vinyl for him, because the seven-inch single was limited as to how much time each could run for.

While he is usually credited with "inventing" the twelve-inch single, Moulton has always insisted that its evolution was the result of circumstances. In 1975 he took a seven-inch copy of Al Downing's "I'll Be Holding On" into the studio to create a new mix for Chess Records. Because the studio had run out of seven-inch blank discs on which to press Moulton's mix, the engineer, Jose Rodriguez, used a ten-inch one instead, but in order to make the track fit, pushed up the levels to expand the groove—Moulton thought that the huge run-in that dwarfed the sound band looked "silly" on the first pressing. The result was a very loud single, which New York's leading DJs of the day absolutely loved. The next track to get the Moulton/Rodriguez mix was Moment of Truth's "So Much for Love," which they cut as a twelve-inch vinyl rather than the ten-inch, and in doing so began a

trend among New York club DJs. Not only were the twelve-inch singles louder, but of course they could be much, much longer, too.

Moulton then discovered by accident how stripping everything back to just drums could stretch a number perfectly. Because Don Downing's "Dream World" stepped up a key toward the end of the record, Moulton felt that he couldn't just bring the original chorus straight back in to repeat the number seamlessly—it would sound odd. So he took all the instruments out of the mix in the middle of the track, and then added them back in, one by one; it came in at almost six minutes long and fit onto a twelve-inch vinyl easily.

MGM records had Moulton mix the whole of Gloria Gaynor's debut album, *Never Can Say Goodbye* in 1975 (*see page 107*) into a 19-minute medley, and it was constantly played by club DJs—the track's length being particularly useful for when they wanted a break from their booth. Apparently Gloria wasn't too pleased at first, but after it became an enormous hit, she was happy. Two years later, Moulton did the same thing for Grace Jones's debut album, *Portfolio*, for which he was credited as producer. He went on to produce her next two albums, too (*Fame* and *Muse*), both of which are now considered disco classics, even if they didn't sell particularly well in their time. It took until the following decade and a switch to Island Records for Ms. Jones to become as big an international star as she was a Disco Diva.

For the Love of Money

It took the O'Jays almost ten years to make it. After a bunch of regional hits in the 1960s (they were big in Cleveland), in 1972 they recorded "Backstabbers," produced by Gamble & Huff, who were about to launch the Philadelphia label. Following international success with the song and album of the same name, and after signing with Philly, the O'Jays produced a string of socially aware, dance-driven soul records which began with the international number 1 hit "Love Train" and includes the epic "For the Love of Money" (1973) and "Give the People What They Want" (1975).

The Sound of Philadelphia

BY the time that Ken Gamble and Leon Huff decided to pool their talents and create Philadelphia International Records in 1971, they had several years' experience of working in the music industry. As well as being musicians, songwriters, and producers, they had run small, local Philly labels. They joined forces as songwriters and producers in the late 1960s, and worked with The Intruders ("We'll Be United," 1967), The Soul Survivors ("Expressway to Your Heart," 1967), Archie Bell & the Drells ("I Can't Stop Dancing," 1968), Wilson Pickett ("Get Me Back on Time, Engine #9," 1970), and, most importantly perhaps, Jerry Butler (in 1968). Gamble and Huff were responsible for creating the sound and songs for Butler when the former Impressions front man became an international star. "Only the Strong Survive" became Butler and Gamble and Huff's first million-selling single in 1969, and made number 4 on the *Billboard* pop chart. The song was so successful that Elvis Presley covered it the following year, for his *Elvis from Memphis* album.

Butler's records were released on Mercury, but their sound was what would come to be known as TSOP—The Sound

Below: One of the Philadelphia International label's biggest, earliest stars was Billy Paul; this sophomore release from 1972 contained one of his greatest ever hits.

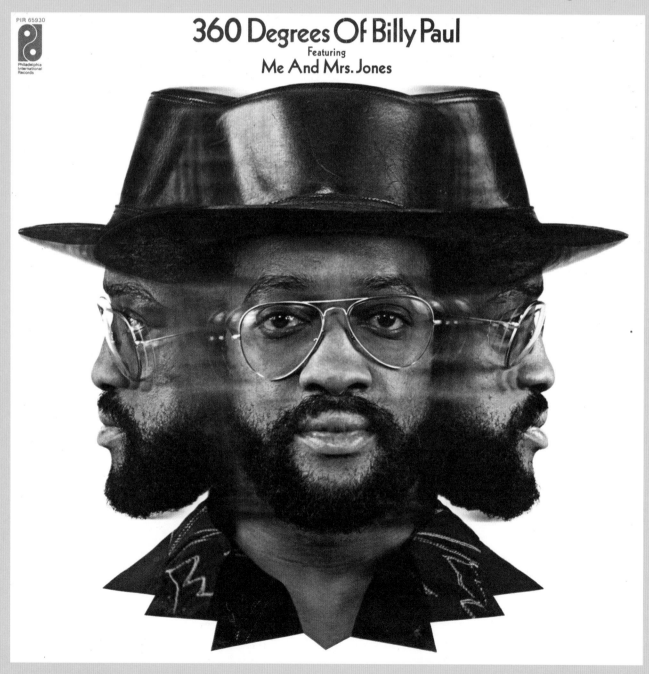

PIR 65930

Philadelphia
International
Records

360 Degrees Of Billy Paul
Featuring
Me And Mrs. Jones

Left: Messrs. Gamble and Huff share the chair in their office at Philadelphia International Records.

of Philadelphia. The success of the Butler single and subsequent albums (*The Iceman Cometh* in 1968 and *Ice on Ice* in 1970) prompted Gamble and Huff to form their label and release records by acts that they'd worked with for years: The Intruders, Billy Paul, and The O'Jays. Their first year was slow, with Billy Paul's debut album *Going East* proving an able start, but it didn't break him—or TSOP—out of the soul and R&B market. However, in 1972 Philadelphia International went truly international and scored number 1 hits around world with Billy Paul's "Me and Mrs. Jones" (which also won a Grammy), the O'Jays' "Backstabbers," and Harold Melvin and the Blue Notes' "If You Don't Know Me By Now." Gamble and Huff's string-laden, hi-hat heavy sound soon replaced that of Motown as the preeminent dance style among club (and soon after, radio) DJs, particularly after the six-minute-plus album version of "The Love I Lost" by the Blue Notes proved to be a big dance hit in 1973.

Although "The Love I Lost" was planned to be a ballad, drummer Earl Young upped the tempo during the recording, after a day spent trying to get a groove going. The result was one of the first perfect "disco" songs to be recorded, even if the term was still to be invented. It sold over a million

copies and set the style for not just Harold Melvin and the Blue Notes but other Philly acts, too. Led by Harold Melvin, the act featured the lead vocals of Theodore "Teddy" Pendergrass, and while he enjoyed a string of hits with the group—"Bad Luck," "Wake Up Everybody," "Don't Leave Me This Way"—he would become one of the great solo disco stars of the 1970s, albeit one whose records usually ended the night with a slow dance. Teddy specialized in creating sensual ballads, winning a Grammy for "Close the Door" in 1978, and out-moaning even Barry White on "Turn off the Lights" (1979).

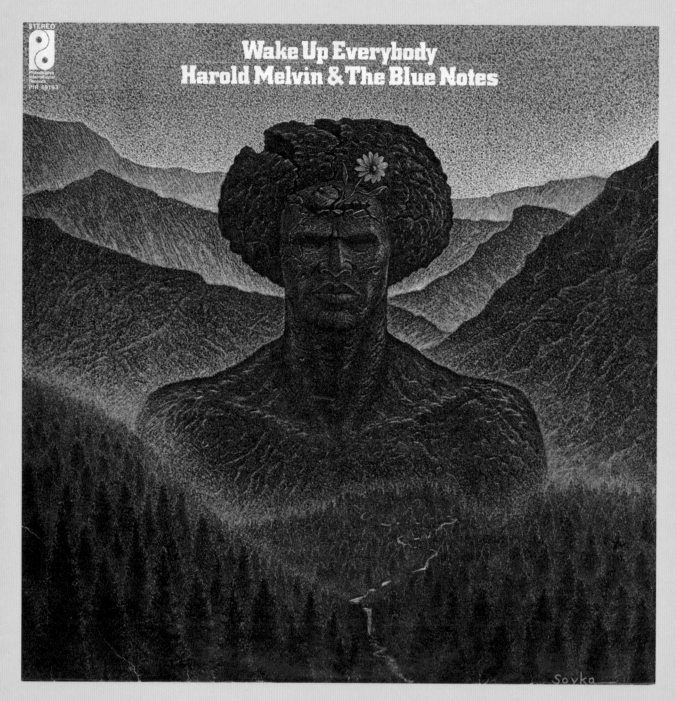

STEREO

Philadelphia
International
Records
PIR 69193

Wake Up Everybody
Harold Melvin & The Blue Notes

Sovka

Ain't No Stopping

When the makers of the influential TV music show *Soul Train* asked Gamble and Huff to write and record them a new theme tune, they used their house band—the same people who created all of their backing tracks in Philly's Sigma Studio—to create "TSOP," and credited it to MFSB. Featuring vocals from the all-girl trio The Three Degrees, "TSOP" made number 1 on the *Billboard* pop charts in March 1974. The lyrical refrain of "People all over the world" in the song was a reminder of the O'Jays' biggest hit at the time, "Love Train," a funk number with lyrics that contained a political message. Ever since Edwin Starr had hit the top of the pop charts with the anti-

Vietnam war song "War" in 1970 (the original by The Temptations was never released as a single for fear of it tarnishing their reputation), the use of political messages in lyrics had become almost a rule for soul acts. "Love Train" preceded the release of the O'Jays' *Ship Ahoy* album, which was filled with political songs: "For the Love of Money," "Don't Call Me Brother," "This Air I Breathe." The title song about slaves arriving in America begins with the sound of chains, a cracking whip, cries of pain, and crashing waves. After Marvin Gaye's groundbreaking *What's Going On* was a huge hit in 1971, Gamble and Huff had realized the potential of making funky dance music that was socially and politically pointed.

Above: Harold Melvin & The Blue Notes not only sold vast numbers of singles, but albums, too.

The 7:14-minute album version of "For the Love of Money" by the O'Jays was arguably the epitome of what made a perfect Philly dance record, and the 3:42-minute edit, a Top 10 pop hit.

In 1972 Philadelphia International missed out on an unlikely international hit with The Trammps, when they hit with a version of "Zing! Went the Strings of My Heart." Despite featuring Philly house drummer Earl Young, they had their debut album and single released on Buddah. However, in 1975 Philly put out their second album, *Trammps*, which featured a song titled "Trammps Disco Theme." Released in 1975 the track, along with Hamilton Bohannon's "Disco Stomp" and Hot Chocolate's "Disco Queen," both released in May 1975, mark

the beginning of the emerging mainstream recognition of disco music. In 1976 The Trammps would release their biggest hit (on Atlantic Records; *see page 117*)—although it didn't become a hit until two years later, when it was included on the soundtrack to *Saturday Night Fever* (*see page 172*).

Philadelphia International—by the mid-1970s—was regularly releasing 12" disco mixes of tracks from their roster of stars, one of the last being McFadden & Whitehead's "Ain't No Stopping Us Now" in 1979. Their rise to prominence in an industry used to such flash-in-the-pan occurrences was not surprising, but it was certainly deserved. The label continued to exert an influence on dance music well into the next decade.

Below: After considerable success as the voice of Harold Melvin & The Blue Notes, Teddy Pendergrass began a successful solo career.

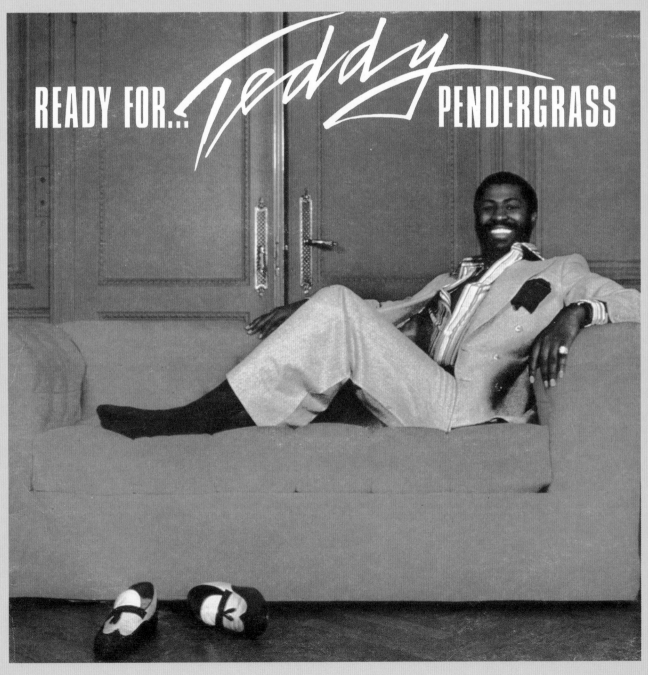

READY FOR... *Teddy* PENDERGRASS

2

Let's start
the dance

Pride!

ON the night of June 27–28, 1969, a new subculture emerged as a spin-off from the Stonewall riots, where members of the gay community had finally retaliated against persistent police intimidation during a raid at the Stonewall Inn, a private members club at 53 Christopher Street in Greenwich Village. At that time, New York State law prohibited men from dancing with each other in public unless in the presence of a woman; it also required that people wore at least one "gender defining" item of clothing, which effectively made it illegal to appear in drag. Carefully controlled private clubs were the only way that gays could legally fraternize, but the police raided them anyway. The Stonewall paid $2,000 a week to the police in order to be given advance warning of a raid, but on this occasion the warning had not been given. (The club had no liquor license, no running water behind the bar, and contravened numerous other ordnances.) There had always been gay clubs, but they were necessarily secretive, often illegal, and more like social clubs than dance halls, though they often had a dance floor, as the Stonewall did. A number of lobby groups emerged from the Stonewall riots; foremost of which, the Gay Activists Alliance (GAA), brought a legal challenge to the law, which was changed in less than two years. After Stonewall a network of openly gay clubs began to materialize.

It started slowly, with clubs like Aux Puces, at 70 E. 55th Street, between Park and Madison, where you had to look right to doorman David Smith or else you could not get in. Often cited as the first of the new gay discos, this had previously been Billy's Club but opened as Aux Puces in July 1966. It remained upmarket with gourmet French food—the onion soup and sole Kathleen were cooked at home by the owner, Nilo dePaul, and reheated on demand—and had an open mirror-framed fireplace and expensive drinks. Low mirrored coffee tables were painted with signs of the zodiac, there were velvet curtains and banquettes, a few fake palm trees, and wire birdcages and chandeliers hanging from the low ceiling. After Stonewall it became the first of New York's gay discos. One of the DJs there was Cherry Vanilla, who later became David Bowie's publicist and released two albums of her own on RCA as well as appearing in Andy Warhol's stage show *Pork*. She played mostly Motown, the Philadelphia sound, R&B, and soul at Aux Puces. Aretha and Carolyn Franklin were always on the turntables along with Otis Redding, Marvin Gaye, Junior Walker, Lee Dorsey, and Lorraine Ellison. Later she added Janis Joplin, The Doors, and Jimi Hendrix. She told Chris Parcellin, "It was the late sixties and what we know now as disco music didn't really exist yet. I also mixed in French pop, U.S. and UK rock, a waltz here and there—James Taylor, Leon Russell, Ken Nordine, some crazy stuff . . . I played 'In-a-gadda-da-vida' by Iron Butterfly at least once a night, 'cause it was long enough for taking a joint-break!" From the street it looked like an unexceptional fake Paris bistro, but those in the know lined up, desperate to get through the big wooden door. Cherry Vanilla told Peter Shapiro, "Getting in depended on your being known, beautiful, sexy, famous, a drug dealer, a madam, whatever David had decided was going to make the night divine."

"I have tasted freedom. I will not give up that which I have tasted. I have a lot more to drink. I know the rules of their game now and how to play it."

Harvey Milk

Chapter opener: Dancers enjoy a normal Saturday night out in Chicago, 1978.

Left: Twenty years after the riot at Stonewall it was still being celebrated as a momentous event. Gay Pride marches past in 1989.

Donna Summer

BOSTONIAN LaDonna Adrian Gaines moved to New York in 1967 when she was eighteen to join the cast of *Hair*, and a year later she moved to Munich to play Sheila in the road company show of the musical. She moved to Vienna where she starred in *Showboat* and *Porgy and Bess*. While touring in a production of *Godspell*, she married fellow performer Helmuth Sommer, but they were together only two years. In 1974 she was signed to producers Pete Bellotte and Giorgio Moroder's tiny Oasis label in Munich, and her first single on the label, "The Hostage," went to number 1 in France and charted in Holland and Belgium (she had previously released a cover of the Jaynettes' "Sally Go Round the Roses" in 1971). A spelling mistake on the label led to her becoming known as Donna Summer. Her next single, "Lady of the Night," did not fare so well, but she had a couple more minor hits in Germany and established something of a reputation as a *Schlager* (soft pop) singer.

Then one day, early in 1975, while talking about the European charts with Giorgio Moroder, he mentioned that Serge Gainsbourg and Jane Birkin's 1969 "Je t'aime . . . moi non plus" had reentered the British charts. "Oh, really?" Donna said. "Well, why don't we make our own?" Bellotte and Moroder protested that it was not her image, but Donna was brought up in a large family in an overcrowded house and knew how to make her point. "What do you mean, it's not my image?" she asked. "Who are you to say I can't make a song?" Two days later she showed up at the studio with the lyric "I'd love to love you" and left it with a delighted Moroder, who then stayed up all night turning it into a fully fledged disco number. Next morning, Moroder's girlfriend went to get Donna—who had no phone—in order to record the vocal track. He had to use all his powers of persuasion to get her to moan. She drew on her skill as an actress to find the right voice and imagined she was Marilyn Monroe, singing in "that light and fluffy but highly sensitive voice of hers, and hers was the image I used when I laid down the first vocal track

for the song." It was the only take they did; the song was finished before noon.

Though she had spent time as a hippie in Greenwich Village, Donna was very religious, and after she heard the song played back she had a change of mind about her change of style. She suggested that perhaps her version be used as a demo to give to some other artist because the explicit lyrics and moans might cause offense among her church community. Moroder, though, persuaded her to release it under her own name. Initially, perhaps because it was not her style, "Love to Love You Baby" only did well in Holland.

Meanwhile Bellotte and Moroder were looking for someone to distribute their records in America, and at the January 1975 MIDEM music convention they met Neil Bogart, president of Casablanca Records (*see page 98*) who bought "Love to Love You Baby" to release in the States. He did nothing with it for several months, then at a party at his house he put it on the stereo. The mood changed, everyone started dancing and touching. "Play that again" his guests demanded—and again three minutes later. It was then Bogart realized what had bothered him about the record; it wasn't long enough. Even though it was 2 a.m. in Europe, he called Moroder in Munich, waking him up. "It's the greatest dance record! But I've got to have a twenty-minute version," Bogart told him.

"I think maybe you call me back later,"

"Neil Bogart saw dollar bills flying out of my pockets when I said I wanted to sing rock 'n' roll."

Donna Summer

Moroder said. "I don't think I understand too well." They spoke again the next day and Bogart insisted on at least a seventeen-minute version, long enough "to get the job done." Moroder explained it was only a demo, and they would need to find another singer, but Bogart insisted that whoever was on the demo was the only one who could sing that song. Donna was called back into the studio to add a further fourteen minutes of vocal. They had no more lyrics and so had to improvise. They dimmed the lights, lit some candles, and Donna lay back on a rug. In her autobiography she wrote: "I'd never intended to sing the song that way. I'd only intended to give Giorgio my idea for the song. When it came time to expand it to seventeen minutes, Giorgio left all those oohs and aahs in . . . I had to do something to fill up the time." According to the BBC, which banned it, there were twenty-three orgasms on the track. American stations (some of which also banned it) found only twenty-two, as did *Time* magazine.

Casablanca released it as the whole of one side of an album of the same name and promoted it by encouraging radio stations to play it at midnight. The album sold 40,000 copies in New York in the first week, mostly to discos. Six weeks later, 400,000 albums had been sold, and by December 1975 it had reached number 2 in the *Billboard* charts. Disco had gone mainstream, and Donna was a star, going on to have three consecutive number 1 platinum albums, the only artist ever to do that.

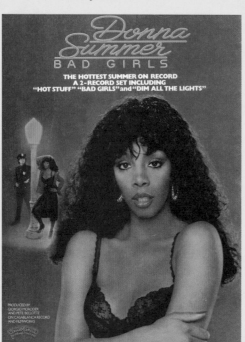

Right: Released before Studio 54 opened its doors and showed off their Man in the Moon With a Spoon, Summer's disco take on the four seasons was released in 1976.

Below: Playing up to her sexy image to promote "Bad Girls."

Following pages: Donna Summer and Giorgio Moroder in 1976.

DONNA SUMMER

R·SEASONS·OF·LOVE

Splish Splash

AUX Puces was not strictly gay, even though gay men made up the majority of the clientele: it was more a forerunner of Studio 54, with an eclectic mix of party people, uninhibited sexual activity, and a lot of drug-taking (mostly quaaludes and cocaine). The only all-gay venue in Manhattan at the time of Stonewall was The Continental Baths. (There were two more on Fire Island: The Ice Palace and the Sandpiper.) The Continental Baths operated in the basement of the giant beaux arts Ansonia Hotel at 230 W. 74th Street on Broadway on the Upper West Side. It was opened in September 1968 by Steve Ostrow, a former cantor, as The Continental Baths Club and was for "men only, open day and night all year round." It was appointed as a luxurious men's health club, with rattan wing chairs, glass columns, and palm trees. Derek Jarman gave a detailed description of it in *The Last of England*. It cost $11 to enter, but as it was open twenty-four hours, there was little reason to leave; it was much cheaper than a hotel. Derek met one young man who had lived there for three months, only leaving the building a couple of times. The dance floor was next to the Olympic-size pool, which featured fountains and a waterfall, and was surrounded by beach chairs. There were sauna rooms, a games room, a restaurant, bar, hairdressers, and a hundred bedrooms. The Baths aimed to cater to 1,000 men a day. The showers had glory holes in the walls and a supply of A200 lice-killing shampoo. The candy machines dispensed condoms and K-Y Jelly, and there was an in-house VD clinic. Derek wrote: "Off to one side was a labyrinthine white-tiled Turkish bath whose corridors ended in pitch black. The scalding steam took your breath away; in the darkest recesses a continuous orgy was under way, but the heat was so searing only the most intrepid could get it up." There were pitch-black orgy rooms, a sunroof, and backrooms fitted out with bunks. Derek continued, "The handsomest were the drug dealers, sprawled out on their bunks, gently masturbating, their doors slightly ajar to trap the unwary, and if you swallowed their bait, inhibitions cast aside, you'd be making love in that swimming pool, packed with naked bodies." The Baths also featured a cabaret lounge and a disco dance floor.

The performance area, next to the pool, was where singer Bette Midler began her career in 1970 accompanied by Barry Manilow who, like the audience, sometimes wore only a white towel. She became known as "The Divine Miss M" or "Bathhouse Betty" because of it. The cabaret entertainment included many of the artists associated with the later disco scene: Melba Moore, Labelle, the Pointer Sisters, Freda Payne, and Melissa Manchester, as well as DJs Nicky Siano, Larry Levan, and Frankie Knuckles who all got their start there and provided a steady diet of soul and R&B.

The Baths was not immune from police harassment. Twenty-two patrons were arrested during a raid in February 1969 (before Stonewall), and three patrons and three employees were arrested in another raid in December of that year and charged with "committing lewd and lascivious acts and criminal mischief." After that the Baths installed an advance warning system to tip off patrons in the event of a police raid.

Gay men provided the most important constituency at The Loft and The Sanctuary, but both were mixed in terms of sexual orientation. It was not until The Tenth Floor opened, in December 1972, that an exclusively gay disco venue emerged (The Continental was foremost a bathhouse and secondarily a disco, even though so many disco figures got their start there). By this time the New York State laws prohibiting gay couples from dancing had been changed. The sociology of these clubs has been studied intensively as it is generally recognized that they were significant in the development of gay identity. Tim

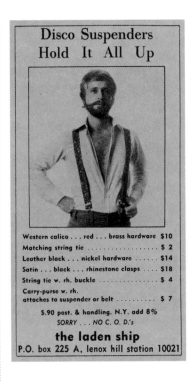
Above: As disco caught on among the hip and trendy of New York and other major U.S. cities, independent retailers exploited the term to sell anything they could get away with.

Below: The Pointer Sisters emerged from the gay bath scene and adopted a 1940s-style look and released blues, R&B, and even country songs until 1975, when they made #1 on the R&B charts with "How Long." The following year they appeared in *Car Wash* and became disco stars.

Lawrence from the University of East London writes, "To varying degrees, these members-only gay nightspots became incubators of gay identity, and by the end of the decade nightspots such as Flamingo were even being referred to as 'finishing schools'— environments in which gayness was not simply expressed, but actively taught. Disco, according to Gregory Bredbeck, was not just a space in which gay men expressed an already-formed identity. It was also a key site for their interpellation as gay men." In the early days, disco was primarily gay, primarily underground, secret, subversive. It was dangerous. It was fun.

Bathhouse Bette Midler

New York's Continental Baths gave Bette Midler her first gig and subsequent break in the music business. Performers were hired to provide cabaret and entertainment for the sweating audience; those who became favorites built an important fan base. As Midler says, "I'm still proud of those days. I feel like I was in the forefront of the gay liberation movement." When she released her debut album it bore her bathhouse nickname, The Divine Miss M, and the first single to be released from it, a slow dance version of "Do You Want to Dance," became a huge hit.

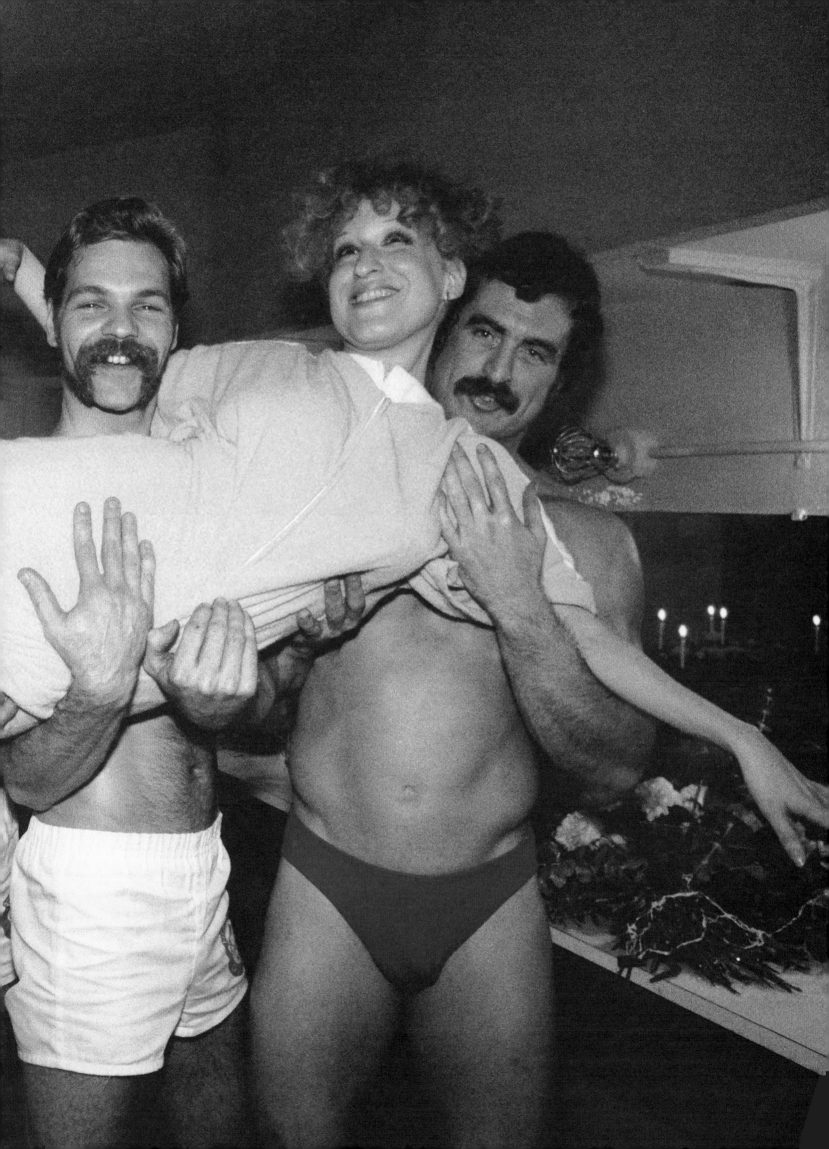

Giorgio Moroder

GIORGIO Moroder was born in Val Gardena, in the Dolomite Mountains of Northern Italy, in 1940, and left home at nineteen to play guitar in a dance group, touring Europe and even playing at the Savoy Hotel in London. After five years of this, he stopped playing and concentrated on writing. "I was quite lucky. I had my first hit as a composer about six months after I started writing all the time, with a German song in '68." (It was a version of the Sir Douglas Quintet's American hit, "Mendocino," translated into German.) Then came bubblegum music, and in 1969 he recorded "Lookie, Lookie," his first song as both composer and producer, which did well in France, Italy, and Spain. In 1970 he met Pete Bellotte, and they began to write together. One of their first collaborations was "Son of My Father," which became a smash hit in England for Chicory Tip, spending three weeks at number 1 on the charts in 1972.

Then, late in 1973, Moroder and Bellotte met Donna Summer, at that time living in poverty in Munich as a single mother, when she answered an advertisement for a black female vocalist (*see page 69*). Two years later Moroder, Bellotte, and Summer had created "Love to Love You Baby," the world's first disco hit. It was not the only breakthrough number he produced with Donna Summer. "I Feel Love" introduced a whole new sound to listeners. He told the *NME* that he had already used one of the original Moog synthesizers: "I contacted this guy who owned one of the large early models. It was all quite natural and normal for me. I simply instructed him about what programmings I needed. I didn't even think to notice that for the large audience this was perhaps a very new sound. We did the whole thing in a day."

Problems developed between Moroder and Summer as she reacted to fame by becoming very religious. Moroder told Vince Aletti, "She wouldn't sing about this, she wouldn't sing about that. Having her biggest hit with a sexy song, she was suddenly saying that she wouldn't sing that type of song anymore, and then she insisted on having a song about Jesus on her album." Fortunately she was not his only act. "I Feel Love" got him into the movie business, and he won his first Oscar for the soundtrack to Alan Parker's 1978 *Midnight Express*. When the backlash against disco came, he had already diversified and was working in both pop music and the film business. In 1980 he not only produced Blondie's "Call Me" but combined both careers to write the score and the songs for Paul Schrader's *American Gigolo*. Though he is best known for his electronic disco productions, he was not a victim of disco's downfall because, working from Europe, he was never that close to it and was able to move on. He told Anthony Haden-Guest, "Certainly disco killed itself. And there was a terrible backlash. Too many products, too many people, too many record companies jumping on this kind of music. A lot of bad records came out. I guess it was overkill. Everybody started to come out with disco and it became . . . what's the word? A cussword."

Moroder went on to establish a career as a writer of film soundtracks.

Left: Moroder in his favored position, working the desk at a recording studio.

Below: An ad for Moroder's solo album *Knights in White Satin* (1976), which plays up his work with Donna Summer, and uses a "bathhouse scene" as artwork—neither made much impact, and the record flopped.

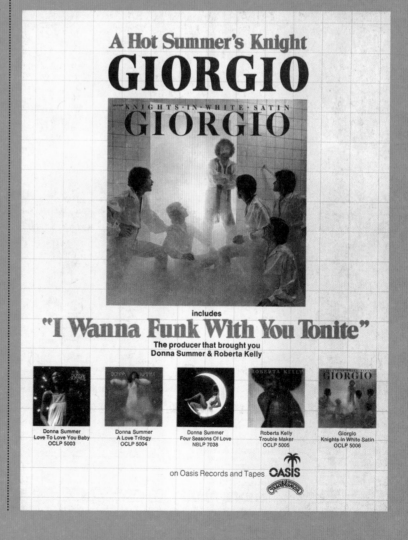

Sanctuary

SANCTUARY was opened by Arnie Lord at 407 W. 43rd Street at Ninth Avenue and was housed in a former German Baptist church where the pews had been arranged around the walls as banquets, and where the DJ had his equipment installed on the large marble communion table where the altar once stood (testament to the importance of the DJ who now directed the proceedings like a high priest). It opened in 1969, just after Stonewall, and Leigh Lee, one of Robert Mapplethorpe's models, told Peter Braunstein, "It was supposed to be a secret, but I don't know how secret it could have been when faggots and lesbians can come out of a church from midnight till sunrise." The club was originally called The Church, but within two weeks of opening, the Catholic Church brought an injunction against them (even though it had previously been a Baptist church) and got them closed down. One of their objections was to a large mural featuring a well-endowed devil surrounded by a flock of angels engaged in every possible sexual position. DJ Francis Grasso described it as "unbelievably pornographic." The owners changed the name to Sanctuary and stuck plastic fruit over the offending parts of the anatomy, a bunch of green grapes here, some red grapes there. Now the club was owned by a gay couple who went only by the names of Seymour and Shelley. Sanctuary's importance lies in this: for about a year it was where Francis Grasso spun his discs.

Whereas Terry Noel at Arthur was the first to build excitement with records and manipulate and control the crowd, he still did it as if he were a substitute for a live band. Francis Grasso knew from the beginning that he *was* the main act. He began his career at Salvation II on Central Park South in New York in 1967 when the regular DJ Terry Noel took an acid trip and failed to show up

Below: Although this ad is from a gay magazine (*After Dark*), its overt use of gay models and risqué T-shirt slogans offered proof of how far the disco "revolution" had disseminated gay culture.

Right: The opening night of
Sanctuary in 1969. The dancers
were the club's "performers."

until 1:30. By then Francis had his job. This became his first regular gig. He
next worked at Tarots on 14th Street, but was head-hunted by the doorman
from Sanctuary. Grasso continued to play at other clubs, however, and during
the Stonewall Riots he was spinning records at Haven on Sheridan Square, a
few doors down from the Stonewall Inn.

Among the new innovations introduced by Grasso was the use of head-
phones, which enabled him to preview the next record while one was already
playing. He invented the technique of slip-cueing to enable him to match up the
time signatures of records in order to perform a seamless switch from one to
the other, often without the dancers even knowing that one record had ended
and another had begun, such as transforming Chicago Transit Authority's "I'm
a Man" into Led Zeppelin's "Whole Lotta Love." This was only possible on belt-
driven turntables, not the motor-driven Reco-Cuts that Salvation II had. For this
he pioneered the use of Thorens turntables, which quickly caught on among
DJs at that time. To get a perfect match he sometimes speeded up or slowed

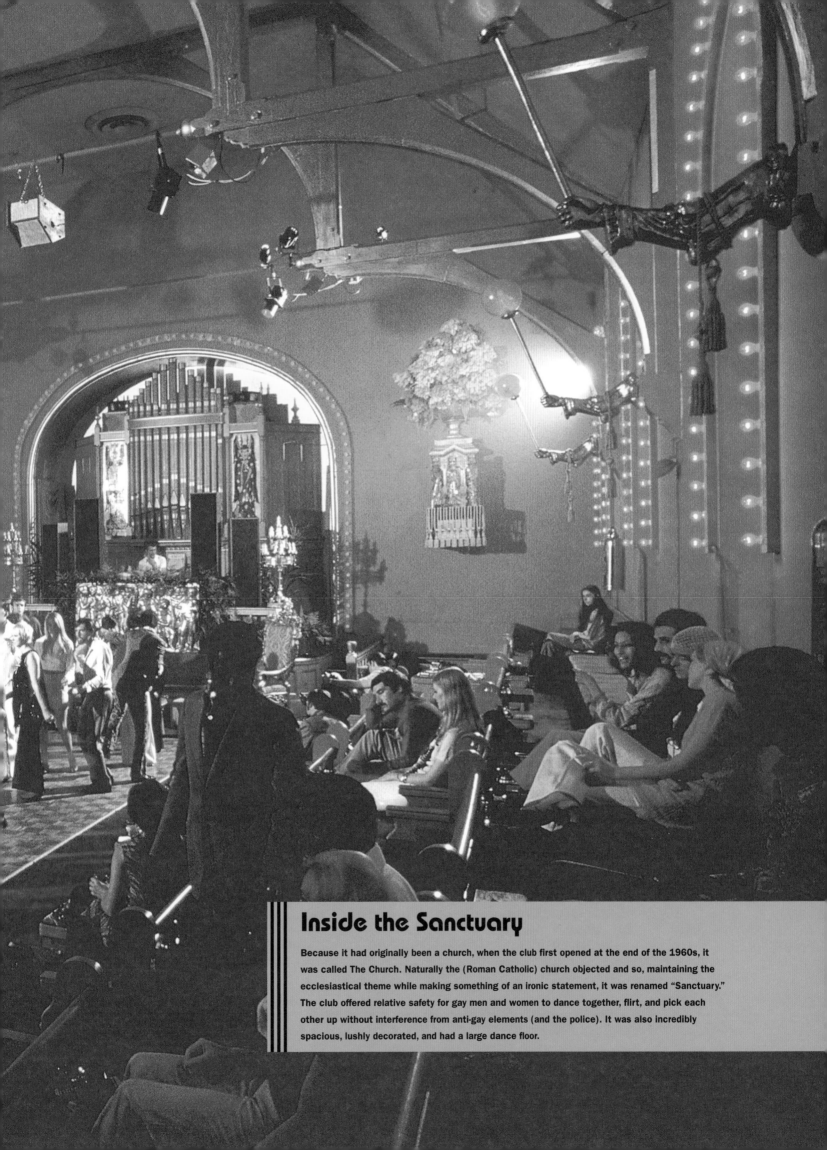

Inside the Sanctuary

Because it had originally been a church, when the club first opened at the end of the 1960s, it was called The Church. Naturally the (Roman Catholic) church objected and so, maintaining the ecclesiastical theme while making something of an ironic statement, it was renamed "Sanctuary." The club offered relative safety for gay men and women to dance together, flirt, and pick each other up without interference from anti-gay elements (and the police). It was also incredibly spacious, lushly decorated, and had a large dance floor.

down the next record imperceptibly—beatmatching, as it came to be known—cueing them up in a matter of seconds. The fact that in the late sixties Grasso was dealing with live drummers, not drum machines, is a tribute to his mixing skills. He would play records for extended periods without losing a beat, and even then only because he sensed the dancers wanted him to up the tempo.

Francis told Frank Broughton from *DJ History*: "I found with the two slide faders, that I had gotten so good, 'cos you see the reflection off the record, you can see the different shades . . . of black. And I got so good I would just catch it on the run . . . The record's spinning, you put the needle in it, right into it. And you just practiced. I guess I practiced live. You start out with records like, say, The Staple Singers' 'I'll Take You There'—now that's a slow beat, and you build slowly and slowly, till you get them dancing fast."

Other popular tracks on his turntables were Creedence Clearwater Revival's "Proud Mary" and Question Mark and the Mysterions' "96 Tears," as well as tracks by The Temptations, The Four Tops, The Supremes, Brian Auger and the Trinity, and Julie Driscoll. When he needed to go to the bathroom he put on *James Brown Live at the Apollo Volume II* which was 25 minutes and 32 seconds. He told Broughton, "There wasn't really guys before me. Nobody had really just kept the beat going. They'd get them to dance, then change records; you had to catch the beat again. It never flowed. And they didn't know how to bring the crowd to a height, and then level them back down, and to bring them back up again. It was like an experience . . . And the more fun the crowd had, the more fun I had."

Sanctuary was featured in Jane Fonda's 1971 movie *Klute*—Grasso played the DJ and had to do three weeks' work for a few seconds on screen. Fonda had a big argument with the club's owners because, even though it was a gay club, they wouldn't allow lesbians in. After that there were more women around, including straight ones, which pleased the DJ enormously.

Grasso said, "I was caught so many times getting oral sex in the booth it was disgusting. I would tell the girls bet you can't make me miss a beat. Gave them a little challenge and away they go! In fact one time the manager walked in. Michael Krenne. He walks into the disc jockey booth, in the Sanctuary, and he sees this girl on her knees, and I says, don't bother me now. If you're gonna yell, yell later." His job was not in danger; he was the main attraction. He estimated that about 500 girls took the challenge, but as the club was overwhelmingly gay they must have been relieved to find a straight man there. Apparently, whenever any female asked if there were any straight men there, the management would point to him and say, "Sure, there he is over there." As for the gay dancers, there was no sex allowed on the dance floor. However, you could do what you liked in the toilets and every cubicle was constantly engaged, with the action frequently spilling out into the washroom, and if there was no room in the toilets, it would happen in the hallways, stairs, and vestibules.

In the first two years of their existence, the predominantly gay discos became places that "straights" would get to hear about through rumor and gossip. Because of the sense of freedom and abandon engendered by the sexual liberality in such places as the Sanctuary, there was an excess of libidinous public behavior. The musical beat which drove the dancing—and fucking—was chosen for its high-tempo repetitiveness, more than for any overtly political message. Unlike the hippies or civil rights movement of the 1960s, disco dancers didn't need anyone to carry their message anywhere outside of the walls of their dancing sanctuaries as long as they could dance.

"Disco is a form of liberation."

Frank Floyd, Consumer Report

WAR/PSYCHE

YOU NEED LOVE

Three Black Designers

Photography: Gordon Parks

If this season's fashions tend to be tailored and just a bit broad of shoulder, you'd never know it looking at the feminine, sexy designs of three of our foremost young designers: Stephen Burrows, Willi Smith and Scott Barrie. All are gifted, black and in their early 30s. All make clothes best worn by a woman with the body—and the bravado —to carry them off. Each began his career poking fun at the fashion establishment "look," and while their collections have become more sophisticated, they still have great verve. Each man has a distinctive style. Burrows' clothes have a fiery brilliance. Barrie's are the most subtle, and Smith's low-cost sportswear is the kind women collect. None has had any significant trouble making it in a predominantly white industry. As Scott Barrie puts it, "Whatever prejudice there is, I'm too busy to notice."

Stephen Burrows was the first black ever to win a Coty Award, the fashion industry's top honor. That was in 1973. Last year he won it again. Despite the recognition, the New Jersey-born designer at age 34 still considers clothes nothing more, he says, "than toys for adults." His sensuous evening dresses, cut to move with the body, have earned him the title "the King of Cling." Other Burrows specialties include a zigzag edging called the lettuce stitch, thigh-high slits and a playful mismatch of colors. The Burrows customer—his New York-based company is called Stephen Burrows for Pat Tennant—can be any age but better have a good figure; his slinky creations go up only to a size 12 and camouflage nothing.

80

Chamois cinches Burrows' T-shirt dress (left) of rayon matte jersey ($250). Below, spaghetti straps hold up what little there is of this $225 matte jersey dress, which has cascading ruffles back and front and deep sexy slits.

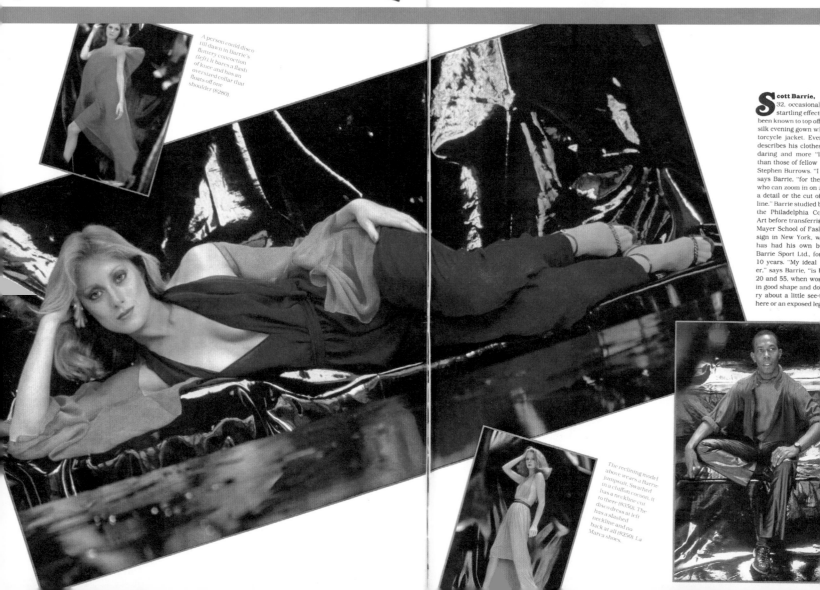

A person could disco till dawn in Barrie's fluttery concoction (left). It bares a flash of knee and has an oversized collar that floats off one shoulder ($280).

Scott Barrie, 32, occasionally startling effect been known to top off silk evening gown with torcycle jacket. Even describes his clothes daring and more "I than those of fellow Stephen Burrows. "I says Barrie, "for the who can zoom in on a detail or the cut of line." Barrie studied the Philadelphia Co Art before transferri Mayer School of Fash sign in New York, w has had his own b Barrie Sport Ltd., fo 10 years. "My ideal er," says Barrie, "is b 20 and 55, when wor in good shape and do ry about a little see-t here or an exposed leg.

The reclining model above wears a Barrie jumpsuit. Swathed in a chiffon cocoon, it has a neckline cut to there ($350). The disco dress at left has a slashed neckline and no back at all ($250). La Marca shoes.

Fashion

HEN British writer Nik Cohn wrote the article that would eventually become the basis for *Saturday Night Fever* (*see page 172*), he based most of it on his own past life in London as a Mod. In the early 1960s, a new teen cult sprang up among young working-class men who spent their money on clothes. Often with their first paycheck Mods would commission a suit from a tailor, using a photograph torn from an Italian fashion magazine as a template. Mods bought shirts, ties, and boots from the few men's clothing boutiques that had begun to import their stock from Italy and France, and that were usually situated in the Carnaby Street area of London. Determined to look smart but different from their fathers (and the Teddy Boys who'd adopted an Edwardian style of clothing), instead of tweed jackets or double-breasted blazers and baggy pants, they wore two-button box jackets (no side vents) with flat-fronted, razor-sharp-creased, tapered trousers often in a two-tone color, worn above pointed leather ankle boots. Mods also adopted the Italian motor scooter (either Vespa or Lambretta models) as their mode of transport, and covered their beloved suits with ex-U.S. Army issue parkas while riding them.

London Mods cared more about the way they dressed than anything else. They also made a ritual of dressing up and going out to be "seen" at dance clubs, where they would show off idiosyncratic dance moves to one another, often ignoring the women in the clubs—whom they were also there to impress, of course. Ex-Mods and one of the premier early 1960s Mod bands The Who (then known as the High Numbers) captured the world of a working-class Mod perfectly in their 1973 "rock opera" *Quadrophenia*. Nik Cohn was an old friend of Pete Townsend of The Who and was writing a novel about a female pinball wizard ("Arfur") at the same time the musician was working on *Tommy*. Cohn knew all about Mods. He guessed that all young men who'd grown up in the West in the wake of World War II were pretty much alike, with the same concerns, likes, and dislikes, and so he made Tony Manero, the central

CADILLAC SEVILLE
designed by
GUCCI

Matching five piece set of luggage included in each SEVILLE designed by GUCCI.

Seville
designed by **GUCCI**

I.A.D.
INTERNATIONAL AUTOMOTIVE DESIGN INC. | 20™ And Biscayne Boulevard
Miami, Florida 33137
Toll Free 800-327-7874
305-576-7010

character of his article, an American Mod. Cohn had been confirmed in his opinion that U.S. males were dedicated narcissists while watching them dance, in line, in sequence, ignoring the females, at a club in New Jersey.

The scene in *Saturday Night Fever* when Tony gets dressed to go out dancing was enacted in millions of American homes every Saturday night in the 1970s. Not everyone was wearing what the Italian Americans of New York, New Jersey, and the Eastern seaboard were, but as major fashion stores such as J.C. Penney caught on to the predominantly Italian styles being favored by the men and women who danced at the big clubs in New York, Chicago, Miami, and L.A., they began to import versions of the hip labels, among them Cerruti (for whom Giorgio Armani was chief designer until 1974), Valentino, Gucci, and particularly Fiorucci—or create versions of them for themselves. American designers Ralph Lauren and Calvin Klein began to gain reputation and sales as they moved into the kind of lightweight, easy-

Opposite: *LIFE* magazine focused on disco designers in their November 1978 edition.

Above: The rise of imported designer labels meant that even Cadillacs got the Gucci treatment.

moving clothes that the Italians had been creating since the late 1960s. Especially as the scene moved away from formal eveningwear—suits and evening dresses—to more relaxed and workable clothes, with both labels reinventing the denim look in the midseventies.

Cool Cuts

Because dancers wanted to look good as well as dance, they chose outfits that were lightweight and allowed ease of movement. Women liked the kind of halter tops and swirling skirts or flapping trousers that flowed but didn't drag as they moved. Men's shirts had to be open-fronted (unbuttoned) and made of light fabric (cheesecloth was briefly fashionable). While the hardcore dance clubs such as David Mancuso's Loft filled up with serious dancers who showed more skin than cloth as they moved (sparking off a trend for sports shirts, sneakers, and headbands on the dance floor), upper-class crowds, such as would frequent Studio 54, went for more upmarket outfits.

The first American fashion designer to become essential at Studio 54 was a Warhol associate named Halston. Later, a former factory worker named Betsey Johnson would break into the mainstream after making a name for herself as a designer of rock star–favored outfits via her Alley Cat label, but in the mid-to-late 1970s everyone who was anyone and wanted to get past the door at 54 had to wear something by Fiorucci or Halston. The American milliner who created Jackie Kennedy's

Right: A fabulous, full-page ad for Fiorucci shoes from a fashion magazine in 1975.

Left: Warhol and Studio 54 darling Halston sells rayon disco fashions in 1979.

FIORUCCI

"Disco is a major influence in the world of fashion. It is a dynamic factor in contemporary advertising. It is a message from every consumer that there has been a rediscovery of America's greatest by-product: fun."

Neil Bogart

pillbox hat in 1961, Halston turned his hand to women's wear at the end of the sixties, and soon became a firm favorite with Hollywood's elite. As fashion entered a radical chic phase along with every other aspect of American culture from music to art, literature, and movies in the 1970s, so Halston designed caftans, used leopard prints, and put women into "men's suits" and hooded tops that tied at the waist. His clothes were elegantly cut, sexy, easy to wear, and easy to dance in. He set up one of the first licensing deals with J.C. Penney for his lines and enabled wannabe Studio 54 dancers who lived in Ohio to at least dress like Bianca Jagger, Grace Jones, or Elizabeth Taylor as they were photographed going in or out of the club.

Italian Elio Fiorucci established his eponymous label to sell in his shop of the same name in the late 1960s, taking London's emerging fashion scene for inspiration (he sold Ozzie Clark dresses alongside his own) and transporting it to Milan. He sought inspiration from street fashions around the world and added his own take on radical chic by creating multicolored caftans, using rice bags from India for handbags, and selling his own version of the monokini after a trip to Brazil. In 1975 Fiorucci opened a store in London and the following year moved to New York and a site next door to Bloomingdales. It soon became a place for the Studio 54 crowd to be in seen during the day. Within two years Fiorucci stores were dotted across America; in 1981 they signed the first fashion licensing deal with Disney and produced Mickey Mouse T-shirts, and in 1982 added Lycra to denim and created stretch jeans. Fioruccci ceased to be a cutting-edge disco designer at about the same time that disco ceased to be anything more than a joke.

While the fashionistas of New York sashayed in originals, the disco dancers of Des Moines, Pleasantville, Springfield, and every American town with a discotheque danced in the knock-offs of those originals. Everyone had to look good on the floor.

Above: Ralph Lauren's preppy East Coast look soon became a disco staple look.

Right: Two years before *LIFE* magazine discovered it, *After Dark* magazine focused on disco fashion, in November 1976.

Left: Former fashion model and Disco diva Grace Jones' second album, from 1978.

FASHION:
RUNAROUNDS

by Louis Miele
photos by Francis Ing

You'll see them all over, uptown and downtown, east and west. Clothes that do the trick for running around can be found in New York designer Andrew Downs's new menswear collection. The look is clean, but with the right touch of accessories you can transform any of Downs's outfits into a personal fantasy trip. Downs's moderately priced line is definitely designed for the young at heart.

Below:
Keep on trucking with this superlooking outerwear: a red quilted vinyl waterproof jacket, a black vinyl raincoat, and a brown-and-white plaid wool pullover. Outfits are worn by Jerry Fargo, Adam Ladny, and David Gibson. Jeans are from the French Jean Store, New York City. All footwear is by Frye, from Stitching Horse, New York City. Sunglasses are by Riviera.

Opposite page:
Andrew Downs's jumpsuit look is great from dusk till dawn, proven by this fun-loving quartet. Polly Yau wears a design from Downs's women's collection. Handkerchiefs are by the Leather Man, New York City.

At left:
For those posh evenings out, Andrew Downs has designed a black-velvet evening suit with a drawstring waist, pull-on trousers, and a washable satin shirt. The slinky black evening dress is worn by Willa Scott.

Opposite page:
For those evenings of fun and games at home, it would be hard to beat this wrapped kimono robe of white satin quilt lined with terrycloth over pull-on washable satin drawstring pants. Polly sports a washable satin nightshirt.

Below:
A standout in any crowd are these sterling silver eyeshields and necklace worn with a hooded zipped-front sweatshirt jacket. All jewelry designed by Robert Lee Morris from Sculpture To Wear, Plaza Hotel. Hairstyles by Deborah Tomasino of Cinandre. Make-up by Polly Yau of Cinandre.

Bottom:
Get down and boogie in pull-on sweatpants and T-shirt with insignia. Our lovely lady is decked out in Andrew Downs's peppermint-striped cotton jumpsuit. Photographs at Twelve West, one of New York's hottest discos, were taken with the cooperation of Tony Martino and Alan Harris.

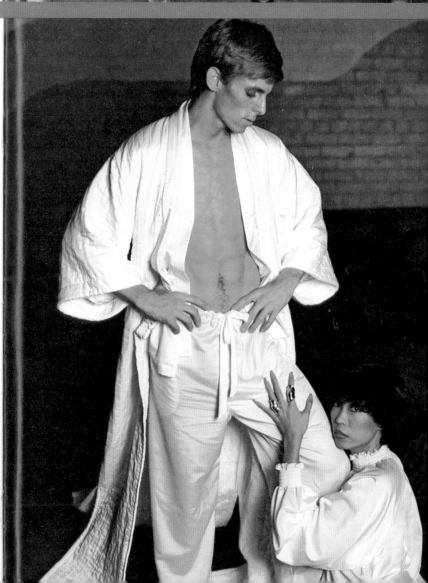

THE MEN IN THE GLASS BOOTH

by Vince Aletti

*He's there each night from ten to closing time
With sights and sounds to help the crowd   unwind
And from his booth each night, he blows your mind
With his mix and his tricks* *

Forget—for the moment at least—Donna Summer, Silver Convention, Brass Construction, Gloria Gaynor, Bohannon, Love Unlimited—that endless, ever-changing, slippery starstream of names shooting through disco heaven. The *real* stars of the seventies disco boom aren't on records. They're spinning them. Discotheque DJs are no longer mere human jukeboxes—they've become tastemakers, record-breakers (several have received gold records in recognition of their influence on sales), mood magicians, performers with personal styles. The new DJ doesn't just change records, he creates a "total evening," a musical "journey," blending records into "one continuous song, one

Dirty Business

FRANCIS Grasso told Frank Broughton that his proudest moment was when Michael Krenne called him and asked if he would look at some equipment, which someone had fooled with. Grasso said he would stop by on his way to Haven, where he was working that night, and when he walked in, the customers saw him in the booth and began applauding and cheering a big cheer, thinking he was going to play for them. Francis taught a number of other DJs their craft, including Michael Cappello and Steve D'Acquisto, and got the idea of setting up a DJ school called Club Francis. He was working at a Mafia-owned joint at the time, and they didn't want him to leave. "The guy in the corner had instructions not to hit me, but to *scare* me. Only the guy they sent got carried away." They systematically beat his face to a pulp, and he was off work for three months of reconstructive surgery. At least he survived to spin another record. His boss, who recruited his lovers from among his waiters and rough trade cruising Times Square, turned up dead on his bathroom floor, having been shot in the chest and stomach and had his skull beaten in. By that time the club had deteriorated badly and was overrun by drug dealers. It could also house only 1,500 people and often more than 3,000 were out in the street, giving each other blow jobs in hallways and lobbies, buying and selling drugs, shouting and having fun. The club finally closed in April 1972 when the police and fire department staged a combined raid. They came armed with a complaint list containing 78 separate charges.

Disco and drugs went together like sex and rock 'n' roll. Though most of the patrons—and management—were not averse to a toke on a joint, the main stimulant was found in pills. Speed sold well as the clubs didn't usually open until midnight so people needed something to combat tiredness, but the drug of choice in the '70s disco was methaqualone: downers such as quaaludes—the standard Rorer 714 capsule contained 300 milligrams of the drug—or the more popular Paris 400 (aka blues), which contained 400 milligrams and rendered one helpless. Also on sale were Seconals (aka reds) and Tuinals which, when mixed with alcohol, could be deadly. Albert Goldman described the effects of downers: "Ludes produce an intense sense of euphoria and a tingling feeling all over the body; that's why they're called 'the love drug.' They also destroy your motor coordination, turning your arms and legs to rubber and making it hard to articulate words. Lude heads are always making jokes about bumping into things ('wall bangers' is another name for the drug), but you never get the point of the jokes because the speaker is so mush-mouthed that he sounds like an idiot."

> "The best discotheque DJs are underground stars, discovering previously ignored albums, foreign imports, album cuts, and obscure singles with the power to make the crowd scream and playing them overlapped, non-stop so you dance until you drop."
>
> Donna Summer

Left: Penned by Vince Aletti, a sometime DJ who wrote the first article on disco for *Rolling Stone*, this rare photo of all the top New York DJs of the day appeared in *After Dark* in 1976.

Boom Boom

THE impact of the post-Stonewall gay wave on disco cannot be overemphasized: without it disco would not have existed. One of the first clubs to open was the Ice Palace, named after Tarjei Vesaas's novel of that name. It was situated on Fire Island, a long thin spit of land, only a block wide in some places, that parallels the southern shore of Long Island about fifty miles up the coast from New York. There had been a bohemian and gay community on the island ever since the twenties, mostly centered around the Sea Shack Hotel and restaurant in the tiny village of Cherry Grove, which in the forties was probably the most famous gay resort in the world. When the island got electricity in the sixties, the hotel added a dance hall, known to locals as The Boom Boom Room. In the late summer of 1969 the Sea Shack was bought by Ted Drach and Tiger Curtis, who transformed the dance hall into a modern disco, complete with a state-of-the-art sound system and mirror-tiled walls and ceiling. The Ice Palace opened in May 1970 ready for that year's summer season, and it was a sensation.

Within two weeks of the Palace opening, the owners of the Sandpiper restaurant in The Pines, another, larger gay community just a sand dune away from Cherry Grove, copied the format and suddenly Fire Island was the gay resort center of the United States. The Sandpiper was more upmarket, less bohemian, whiter, and in direct competition, but to anyone but the owners it didn't matter; it just made them bid to outdo each other with outrageous theme parties and the newest records. Another rival—Botel—opened in The Pines, owned by John Whyte. As the new decade began, Fire Island was the place to be: a visual paradise by day—with one of the longest, most beautiful stretches of beach in North America—it was a gay paradise by night and returning revelers could make their way home watching magnificent sunrises. It was on Fire Island that Love Unlimited Orchestra's "Love Theme" broke, months before

Above: The entrance ticket to Fire Island's Ice Palace.

Below: Love Unlimited, featuring Mrs. Barry White, Glodean James (right). Love Unlimited were early disco faves on Fire Island.

Right: The entrance to Fire Island's Ice Palace, guarded by a friendly doorman.

Following pages: *After Dark* magazine depicted the state of disco across America in 1976, including the interior of Ice Palace.

it reached the radio late in 1973, because the DJs at both clubs—Bobby DJ Guttadoro at the Ice Palace and Barry Lederer at Botel—had acetate copies.

Miles from straight society, supported by their own sympathetic village community, it was a case of anything goes on the island. Naked and half-naked men danced all night in the summer heat. At the Ice Palace, the steam rising from the dancers would collect on the silver Mylar ceiling, condense, and drop as disco rain on their sweating bodies. From time to time they would go outside to visit the Meat Rack, the wholly appropriate name given to the path across the dunes that leads from Cherry Grove to The Pines. Most people got no further than the bushes. Thus was established a pastime that was exported to New York City by returning vacationers, with bushes replaced by trucks parked under the West Side Highway, abandoned warehouses, and piers on the old West Side docks. Dancing was done in the new gay bars that were springing up along neighboring Christopher Street.

At left:
Donna Summer, whose latest release is "The Four Seasons of Love"(Oasis), tapped the disco phenomenon for her leap to stardom.

Below:
The action in some discos, such as Fire Island's Ice Palace, gets steamy. (Photos by Jeff Tennyson)

Opposite page, clockwise beginning top right: Every night, one thousand disco babies crowd into Studio One, California's most popular disco. The club's percussive beat gives a special underlying rhythm to Studio One's Backlot Room, where top acts draw sellout crowds. Some of the artists creating that percussive beat are the Spinners (Atlantic); Double Exposure(Salsoul Records); Carol Williams(Salsoul); KC and the Sunshine Band(T.K. Records); Van McCoy, doing the hustle with his grandmother on her 101st birthday; the Trammps(Atlantic); the Tavares(Capitol); the Silver Convention(Midland International); Carol Douglas(RCA); and(center) Betty Wright(CTK Records).

Casablanca, West End, Prelude

BROOKLYN-BORN Neil Bogart (formerly Bogatz) made a name for himself in the music business at the end of the 1960s when he worked at Buddah Records and signed a large part of their bubblegum roster, among them Ohio Express, the 1910 Fruitgum Company, and The Lemon Pipers. In 1973, along with three other Buddah executives, Bogart established Casablanca Records with a loan from Warner Brothers and promptly signed on a glam rock band named Kiss. Although now best known as one of the biggest and best disco record labels of its time, Bogart didn't plan it that way. He wanted to have as many successful acts playing whatever music sold best. The label's first release was by Canadian singer-songwriter Bill Amesbury in February 1974, a folk-tinged number titled "Virginia (Touch Me Like You Do)." That was followed by singles from the Bob Crewe Generation, Gloria Scott, all-girl rock band Fanny, and an attempt at a comeback by former Herman's Hermits singer Peter Noone, none of which scored on the Top 40 charts. Neither did the first Kiss album or the great funk album, Parliament's debut *Up for the Down Stroke*—at first. It took until almost the end of 1974 before Casablanca scored a hit—when the Hudson Brothers' "So You Are A Star" made number 21—and until summer 1975 for Kiss to finally crack the singles charts, with "Rock 'n' Roll All Nite."

Casablanca's huge success with disco music happened almost by accident. Desperate for turnover, Bogart began distributing a European label called Oasis, run by record producers Giorgio Moroder and Peter Bellotte (*see page 79*). The success of "Love to Love You Baby" (number 2 on the pop charts in January 1976) prompted Bogart to bring Moroder and Summer to America and to distribute a number of other Euro-Disco labels in the USA. The electronic beat and backing of the Euro disco sound wasn't a big hit with the New York clubs, but it worked everywhere else.

In 1977 Bogart signed Village People to Casablanca (*see page 220*) and they,

along with Donna Summer, proved to be disco superstars around the world, despite not being included on the soundtrack to *Saturday Night Fever*, which would mark the mainstream explosion of disco music. In 1978 Bogart's film arm of Casablanca (cofounded with Peter Guber) made the pre-*Saturday Night Fever* film *Thank God It's Friday* (*see page 219*) with some success. But by the end of the decade, after spending millions of dollars promoting his acts, and not always in the most ethical manner, Bogart was bought out of Casablanca by Polygram Records, a European company taking their first steps into the American market. Bogart founded a new label, Boardwalk, and signed Joan Jett, but sadly died of cancer in May 1982.

Do It ('Til You're Satisfied)

As if to counter the mass popularization of disco music and its embrace by the mainstream, New York DJs and clubbers set about establishing their own record labels. As a former A&R head to Scepter Records, Mel Cheren had earned himself the nickname of Godfather of Disco when he took BT Express from the clubs he frequented in New York into the pop charts with "Do It ('Til You're Satisfied)" in 1974. When Scepter closed in 1976, Cheren set up his own New York–based label, West End Records, in partnership with Ed Kushins. At the same time Cheren loaned former lover Michael Brody enough money to open the Paradise Garage in New York (*see page 192*), which opened with Larry Levan as DJ. Cheren employed Levan as a remixer and producer for his West End label releases. The Garage also helped Cheren and Kushins find new acts, since independent producers and unsigned performers would often drop demo recordings into Levan's booth, and if he liked them, they'd get a spin—and some great market research from the dance floor. Many of the West End releases were local hits only, in that they were played in NYC clubs and local dance radio stations, but they didn't have a chart hit until 1978 when Karen Young's "Hot Shot" broke into the *Billboard* Hot 100 singles chart at 67 (it reached number 1 on the dance chart). In 1979 Taana Gardner's "Work that Body" made number 10 on the *Billboard* Dance charts. However, acts such as Bombers had proved enormously successful in clubs (particularly with 1979's "Everbody Get Dancing")

"Hey, if I can, through Casablanca, create a fantasy for people, give them a couple of hours of music with which to dance their asses off, to make them forget that they have a payment to make tomorrow, then I think I'm doing a public service. If I can make money by doing it, that's fabulous."

Neil Bogart

Left: Originally the Brooklyn Trucking Express, as BT Express the band made a succcess of West End Records in 1974 with "Do It ('Til You're Satisfied)" and then "Express" in 1975.

by mixing elements of the Philly sound with Euro Disco and R&B vocals. As it entered the 1980s, West End began working with Arthur Russell and the Larry Levan–remixed "Is It All Over My Face," credited to Loose Joints, became a formative influence on Chicago House music.

Another ex-Scepter Records employee, Marvin Schlachter, started a New York-based disco label in 1976. Prelude Records began when British label Pye closed its American office, run by Schlachter for three years. Prelude launched with German band Jumbo's "Turn on to Love," but scored their first hit with Musique's "In the Bush" and "Keep on Jumping" in 1978. Musique's leader Patrick Adams, a New York-born producer, employed Jocelyn Brown as a singer with the band and thus launched her career. In 1979, Prelude scored a number 1 disco hit with the Canadian performer France Joli's "Come to Me" and continued their disco success with Sharon Redd ("Can You Handle It") in 1980.

Nothing Going on but the Rent

AVID Mancuso's loft parties began soon after he moved into 647 Broadway, near Bleecker Street, in 1965. It was a big space, 100 feet long with double-height ceilings and a wooden floor. He was not technically allowed to live there, and his bedding had to be hidden in case of a surprise visit from the building inspectors. He loved hi-fi and, after a year or so, invested in two pairs of Klipschorn speakers, which he combined with a pair of AR turntables. He opened his loft to friends on a regular basis, providing food, drinks, and superb music all night, but by 1970, he found that he could no longer afford the rent on the loft and had to ask his friends to chip in. His first pay party was on Valentine's Day that year; the party invites were inscribed with "Love Saves the Day" and illustrated with a picture of a children's party with balloons. It was a reference back to his own fond, if somewhat idealized, memories of his childhood at an orphanage where he was brought up by a kindly nun. At first he held pay parties twice a month, but after six months, Mancuso began to hold them every Saturday, from midnight until 6 a.m.

These became known as rent parties. They were private, by invitation only. His close friends all held numbered cards that entitled them to admission and to bring in a specified number of friends. It was not a membership club and the 200 guests were all invited by David or by his friends. Then in 1972, his landlord allowed him to knock through and double the size of his loft. Now he could invite 300 people. Among his regulars were Frankie Knuckles, David Morales, François Kevorkian, Larry Levan, and Nicky Siano, all of whom went on to become celebrity DJs. Admission was $2.50. For this you had your coat checked, and there was fresh squeezed orange juice, organic nuts and raisins, bowls of fruit and fresh popcorn, bowls of candy and gum. There was no alcohol, but there were times when the punch was spiked.

The Loft had a huge mirror ball that the dancers themselves spun, plus an illuminated Christmas tree that stood by the dance floor and was often the only light in the vast space. The décor was retro-children's party, with streamers and balloons; it felt like it might have been your birthday party when you were ten. Near the entrance was a giant snake pillow, where people sprawled to chill out. Frankie Knuckles described his first visit to The Loft: "There were church pews on the left side of the dance floor and people dancing on top of them beating tambourines and cowbells. The energy just pulled you in automatically . . . Behind the snake pillow was a small closet-like structure with a man inside with a flashlight between his legs. As we got closer, the man inside looked at us. It was David Mancuso, looking very Jesus-like with his long dark hair and beard. He had the most piercing eyes."

Mancuso was never the kind of DJ that fades and mixes. He told Danny Krivit, "I don't want to interfere

"DJs became the stars, because the records came and went. There were one-hit wonders, there were major stars, there were records like Manu Dibango's [Afro-jazz] Soul Makossa, but the DJs were the ones who found a way to mix all this very disparate stuff and create a whole evening."

Vince Aletti

RECORDS

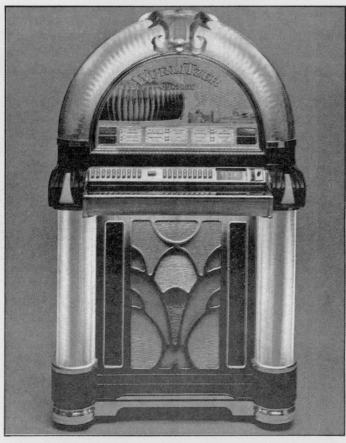

Discotheque rock '72: Paaaaarty!

BY VINCE ALETTI

Paar-ty! Paar-ty! You hear the chant at concerts, rising like a tribal rallying cry on a shrill wave of whistles and hard-beaten tambourines. It's at once a call to get down and party, a statement that there's a party going on and an indication that discotheques, where the chant originated, are back in force after their virtual disappearance with the flashbulb pop of the Sixties.

Actually, discotheques never died; they just went back underground where the hardcore dance crowd—blacks, Latins, gays—was. But in the last year they've returned not only as a rapidly spreading social phenomenon (via juice bars, after-hours clubs, private lofts open on weekends to members only, floating groups of party-givers who take over the ballrooms of old hotels from midnight to dawn) but as a strong influence on the music people listen to and buy.

The best discotheque DJs are underground stars, discovering previously ignored albums, foreign imports, album cuts and obscure singles with the power to make the crowd scream and playing them overlapped, non-stop so you dance until you drop. Because these DJs are much closer to the minute-to-minute changes in people's listening/dancing taste, they are the first to reflect these changes in the music they play, months ahead of trade magazine charts and all but a few radio station playlists.

Records like the O'Jays' "Love Train," Eddie Kendricks' "Girl You Need a Change of Mind," the Intruders' "I'll Always Love My Mama," the Pointer Sisters' "Yes We Can Can" and the Temptations' "Papa Was a Rolling Stone" were broken or made in discotheques but, with few exceptions, their acceptance above ground was nothing compared to their popularity with the dance crowd. Other records—many of those noted here—live and die in discotheques, like exotic hothouse flowers. Typically, the music nurtured in the new discotheques is Afro-Latin in sound or instrumentation, heavy on the drums, with minimal lyrics, sometimes in a foreign language, and a repetitive, chant-like chorus. The most popular cuts are usually the longest and the most instrumental, performed by black groups who are, frequently, not American.

One of the most spectacular discotheque records in recent months is a perfect example of the genre: Manu Dibango's "Soul Makossa." Originally a French pressing on the Fiesta label, the 45 was being largely undistributed by an African import company in Brooklyn when "a friend" brought it to the attention of DJ Frankie Crocker. Crocker broke it on the air on New York's WBLS-FM, a black station highly attuned to the disco sound, but the record was made in discotheques where its hypnotic beat and mysterious African vocals drove people crazy. Within days, "Soul Makossa" was *the* underground record and when copies of the original 45 disappeared at $3 and $4, cover versions (many unlicensed and one a pirated copy put out under another group's name) were rushed out. Atlantic Records stepped into this confusion, bought the US rights and had both the single and an album out on their own label days later.

The album, *Soul Makossa* (Atlantic SD 7267), far from being a package of waste filler cushioning the title single, is one of the best to emerge from the new discotheque scene. Recorded in Paris, Manu Dibango and his group of expatriates from formerly French West Africa put together a heady Afro-jazz blend, using horns and electric guitars but in an utterly African way. Their "Soul Makossa" is still the gutsiest, most compelling of all the versions that followed and no one has matched the strange, slightly echoed quality of the lead vocal. The other cuts are more instrumental than vocal and several are at least as good as dance music, particularly "New Bell" and "Oboso." Perfect for a subtropical evening in the jungle of the cities.

The only group to get a version of "Soul Makossa" on the charts before Atlantic picked up Dibango's original was a 13-man congregation of studio musicians called Afrique. Their "Makossa" is exactly as long as the original (4:30) but has a hard-edged, over-slick feel and vocals that sound somehow more Latin than African. Their album, *Soul Makossa* (Mainstream MRL 394), features guitarists David T. Walker and Arthur Wright and Chuck Rainey on Fender bass and is about as Afrique as the Temptations. Not for dancing.

A third *Soul Makossa* album (Paramount PAS 6061) is considerably more interesting, if only as the first LP from African drummer Babatunde Olatunji in four years. At nearly seven minutes, his version of "Soul Makossa" is the longest I know of, but its length is its undoing. It lacks the concentrated energy of the original and though far from boring, it's entirely too rambling and overworked. But it's only a minor disappointment in an otherwise fine album. Being much more drum-based, the sound is denser than Manu Dibango's, but the structure of

the cuts is looser, more improvisatory. The horns are not as integrated into the texture of the music as they might be and most tracks don't achieve any tightness or intensity until they are halfway through, yet the music is always rich and exciting. Though it's hard to sit still for any of this, "Takuta" and "O-Wa" are especially good for dancing. Still largely undiscovered, this album could be very big once the word gets out.

The following albums form a sort of basic discotheque library—supplemental to the selected works of War, Eddie Kendricks, the O'Jays, Earth, Wind & Fire, the Temptations, James Brown, Stevie Wonder et al., but vital to any house party for the moment at least. Several of these records are fading fast or have disappeared from the turntables at clubs, but they all revive rather remarkably given the right atmosphere at home.

Doing It to Death, the J.B.'s (People PE 5603). James Brown & Co. in another one of their many permutations. The title cut is a little more than ten minutes, twice the length of the 45, and *smokes* from Brown's opening words, "Hit it!" to a fade-out on flute. *The* funk band at their best. The remainder of the album is less exciting, even a little laidback. Nearly the entire lyric content of the repeated theme track, "You Can Have Watergate Just Gimme Some Bucks and I'll Be Straight," is right there in the title, and much of the rest is basic black jazz and very loose.

Composite Truth, Mandrill (Polydor PD5043). The third and most successful album by a seven-man New York group, *Composite Truth* focuses a wide range of black, Latin and rock influences into several tracks. Side one, with "Hang Loose," "Fencewalk" and its Latin extension "Hagalo," is the party side, a hard-whipped combination of horns, nervous guitar, organ and Latin percussion with tough, deep vocals. Side two is in a different mood, cooled down but, after a few listenings, quite pleasant, capped by a sweet breeze of an instrumental called "Moroccan Nights."

Barrabas (RCA APL1-0219). On the basis of two tracks, "Wild Safari" and "Woman," *Barrabas* broke in discotheques when it was still an import record. The group, oddly enough, is from Spain, including among its six members one from Cuba, one from Portugal and two from the Philippines. Where they got such a hard Afro-rock sound, I don't know, but at their best they're fantastic. "Wild Safari" crackles with electricity and Latin percussion that makes it impossible to sit down. The rasp-

---

with what the artist intended or the integrity of the recording 'cause that's the artist's message, so I play the record from the beginning to the very end." Mancuso played dance music, mixing it with classical and jazz, but in such a way that it all carefully segued to build a mood. The music was not deafening; in fact, it was just below being loud so people had to really listen.

360.047

SOUL
MAKOSSA

MANU
DIBANGO

◆ FIESTA ◆

In the Pool

DAVID'S next move was to acquire much larger loft space at 99 Prince Street, in Soho, which took him a year and a half to bring up to a standard that allowed him to invite the public in. While the work was going on, he and DJ Steve D'Asquisto organized the Record Pool, a non-profit venture set up because, although DJs were often responsible for breaking new records, it was proving very difficult for some of them to get publicity copies from record companies: there were accusations of racism, discrimination, preferential treatment, and other irregularities that the Record Pool sought to rectify. Frankie Knuckles described how only a handful of black DJs in New York could get free press copies of new records: "There was only a small contingent of black DJs playing in Manhattan that was given this access; Me, Larry Levan, Tee Scott, and David Todd. But when The New York Record Pool opened all of this changed. And for the better." At first, about two dozen of the most important DJs in New York joined together to lobby records to provide press copies to all the members of the collective. Mancuso financed it himself for the first two years, and the Pool operated from 99 Prince. All they wanted to do was get the music and share it. As he said, "We did it for the music." Many of the DJs were only getting between $20 and $50 a night, and yet they had to buy all their own records. Their influence over the buying power of the public was evident in, for example, Consumer Rapport's 1975 single "Ease on Down the Road" on Wing, which sold more than 100,000 copies in New York City in just two weeks before it received any radio play. Mancuso himself "discovered" numerous classics, including Third World's "Now That We've Found Love," D-Train's "Keep On," Chuck Mangione's "Land of Make Believe," "Girl You Need a Change of Mind" by Eddie Kendricks, Manu Dibango's "Soul Makossa" (which became so popular that in the end there were twenty-three different cover versions recorded in New York alone), and a recording of the *Missa Luba* by Les Troubadours de Roi Baudoin from the Congo. Browsing through record bins in Amsterdam while on holiday, he came across "Wild Safari" by the Spanish group Barrabas that became hugely popular with the dancers at The Loft, so much so that David made arrangements with the Spanish record company to press up a few copies for sale at The Loft.

David Mancuso operated his parties from 1974 until 1985 from 99 Prince, by which time rising gentrification, and consequent rent hikes, forced him out of the building. Much of that time he spent battling against the New York City Department of Consumer Affairs over his right to party without a cabaret license. After protracted hearings he won his case; as he was not selling food or beverages to the public he was exempt from the need for an NYC cabaret license. This model was adopted by many other famous dance clubs including The Saint, The Gallery, and The Paradise Garage. David said, "It was basically a rent party. Private: by invitation only. It was NOT a club, there was not a membership needed, none of that stuff. I made it very clear; this was an invitation and you made a contribution. The money only came into it because I had to do it. When the money came into it, I didn't want it to spoil it. I wanted to maintain the integrity of the party and provide as much as I could and it worked."

For many people, David Mancuso's Loft was the epitome of the early private dance clubs—nowhere else ever felt so like a family affair, so like home (if a loft filled with half-naked dancing people, out of their minds on drugs at 4 a.m., felt like home, that is). It was clearly welcoming and had the sexual and racial mix that made for a great disco: about 60 percent black or Puerto Rican and 70 percent gay, rich and poor, all united by the music. But the music always came first at The Loft.

DISCO

Record pools: disco DJs beat the system

By Martha Hume

NEW YORK

NEW YORK HAS had a genuine, certifiable musical counter-culture since 1975 and nobody's noticed. The culture is disco and the club disc jockey is at its heart. The most interesting part, however, is that DJs—the ones in New York, at least—have been organized for four years. These organizations are called record pools, one of the most influential marketing tools in the skyrocketing disco industry.

At the outset of the disco phenomenon, though, disco DJs—the people who have the power to break hits from the dance floor—were largely ignored by record companies, who were more concerned with distribution and radio airplay. Record pools were formed not only as places where DJs could

meet to discuss the records they were playing, but also as a vehicle to attract the recording industry. Today, there are disco pools around the nation, and their potential impact on disco marketing could challenge that of Top Forty radio DJs. That is, providing internecine rivalries don't get in the way.

The first pool in the country was the New York Record Pool (NYRP), formed by David Mancuso, Steve D'Asquisto and Eddie Rivera in the summer of 1975. Disco was still considered an underground market at that time, and in order to get records to play at their clubs, DJs had to visit each company individually. Soon, the need for organization became apparent.

"It got too crazy in offices," says Judy Weinstein, president of For

For the Record's Judy Weinstein

for the reco

PHOTOGRAPH BY BONNIE SCHIFFMAN

I Will Survive

NEW Jersey–born Gloria Gaynor began her career in the mid-1960s as a singer with the Soul Satisfiers, a gospel group who recorded half a dozen songs for Savoy Records in 1964. When a solo single of 1965 proved unsuccessful, Gaynor worked as a backing singer while trying to make a name as a solo performer. In 1973 she was signed to the Disco Corporation of America, a band of producers named Meco Monardo (who would enjoy a huge hit as Meco on releasing a disco version of the *Star Wars* theme in 1977), Tony Bongiovi (cousin to Bon Jovi), orchestrator Harold Wheeler, and Gaynor's manager Jay Ellis. They produced a disco version of the Jacksons' hit "Never Can Say Goodbye" with Gaynor singing, and MGM put it out early in 1974 after it had won support in the hippest New York clubs. It took almost a year between the recording and the single's success, but in December 1974 "Never Can Say Goodbye" made the Top 10 pop chart.

The following year Gaynor's debut album *Never Can Say Goodbye* was released, after having been remixed by Tom Moulton (*see page 56*) so that the three tracks on side one became a nineteen-minute nonstop medley. Gaynor didn't know about it until the record was pressed, apparently. All three tracks—the title plus "Honey Bee" and "Reach Out, I'll Be There"—were edited for radio and issued as singles but didn't sell anywhere near as well as "Never Can Say Goodbye." Her follow-up album *Experience Gloria Gaynor* had the same construction but failed to produce any hits. Despite a change of labels (to Polydor), Gaynor failed to score any more hits until 1978 when she made number 1 around the world with the now classic disco anthem "I Will Survive," taken from her sixth album *Love Tracks* (which made number 4 on the Hot 200 chart). It was her crowning moment.

Left: Gloria Gaynor's 1975 debut album, the title track of which made her a star and began her long career in music.

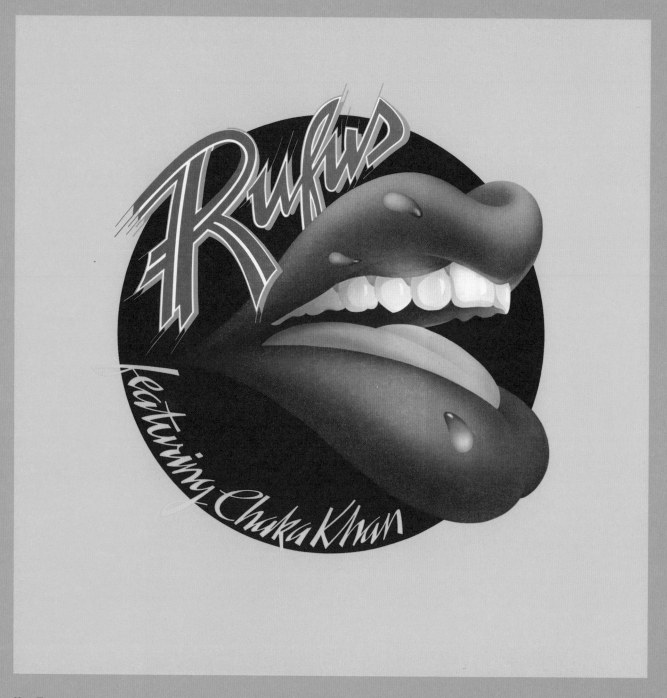

I'm Every Woman

"I Will Survive" started something of a trend for female empowerment disco anthems in America. Also released in 1978, Chaka Khan's "I'm Every Woman" took a slightly different angle to Gaynor's hit, which had the song's narrator rejecting a man who had first rejected her, and instead making omnipotent, all-powerful figures out of women. Chicago-born Khan had already enjoyed chart success with the multiracial funk/rock band Rufus, which had sprung out of the American Breed in 1970, singing the pop hit produced by Stevie Wonder "Tell Me Something Good" and "You Got the Love" in 1974, and "Sweet Thing" a year later. The band had continued to sell albums and create a renowned live show, though their singles didn't crack the Top Thirty pop charts again until a live recording—Chaka's last with Rufus—of "Ain't Nobody" made number 22 in 1983. That hit in turn helped Khan to her first chart hit since "Every Woman," with "I Feel For You" in 1984. Ashford & Simpson's "I'm Every Woman" was a dance floor hit as well as a pop one, and while it didn't allow Khan to challenge Gloria Gaynor's standing as "Queen of Disco"—she was "crowned" in a ceremony at New York's Le Jardin club at the end of 1975, which gained the club and her lots of publicity—it ensured her reputation as a great disco vocalist.

Above: Although it was their fourth album release, this was the first success for Rufus and Chaka Khan. It includes a version of the Bee Gees' "Jive Talkin'" which proved a dance floor hit.

Young Hearts Run Free

"Young Hearts Run Free" spoke directly to women from an experienced viewpoint, telling young girls not to get hung up on one man too early in life, and to "run free" instead. Singer Candi Staton knew what she was singing about; married at the age of sixteen, she was mother to four children by the age of twenty-five and divorced soon after. Her second husband, the blind R&B singer Clarence Carter, and she were married in 1970 and divorced three years later, after the birth of a son. "Young Hearts" became a disco hit on release, and soon topped the *Billboard* Soul chart, making number 20 in the pop charts in 1976. Its mix of rousing chorus, uplifting horns, and Staton's soulful voice combine with the drumbeat mixed at the fore to make a classic disco hit.

Staton would go on to enjoy more chart and disco success with "Nights on Broadway" in 1977 (making number 16 on the R&B charts), "Victim" in 1978 (number 17 on the R&B chart), and "When You Wake Up Tomorrow" in 1979 (number 13 on the R&B chart). She also married three more times, and with her third husband, former drummer John Sussewell, set up an Anglican ministry in Atlanta in 1982, recording eight gospel albums since then. "Young Hearts Run Free" continues to be played at clubs and on radio programs around the world.

Below: At the end of the 1960s Candi Staton found some succcess as a Southern Soul belle, but in 1976 she became a disco queen with the release of the title track from this, her fifth album.

Love Is the Message

**N**ICKY Siano told Frank Broughton: "I always feel like I took what David did onto a more commercial level. Ours was a club version of David's." Siano was a precocious, bisexual teenager from Brooklyn, who moved to Manhattan in 1971 at the age of sixteen with his girlfriend Robin and who, at the age of seventeen, was already running his own club, The Gallery. He began spinning records at a club called The Round Table, but he really wanted his own place, intending to make it as similar to Mancuso's Loft as possible. He borrowed money from family and friends and opened The Gallery in a loft on 22nd Street which, after a clampdown by the Fire Department, closed down for lack of fire exits (along with seven other clubs). He reopened in a huge 3,600-square-foot loft at 172 Mercer Street in Soho, cleverly timing it to coincide with Mancuso's annual holiday, passing out leaflets at the last Loft party before its summer closure.

Siano hired Mancuso's sound engineer, Alex Rosner, and used many of The Loft's innovations including the excessive number of tweeters. Siano loved a powerful bass, and The Gallery was heavy on sub-bass woofers. His greatest innovation was the introduction of a third Thorens TD125 turntable, an idea which he claimed came to him in a dream where he was mixing two records and suddenly wanted to bring in a third track. Playing on the decks were Betty Wright's "What Is Love?," "The Love I Lost" by Harold Melvin, Diana Ross's "Love Hangover," and one of the greatest favorites at both The Loft and The Gallery, MFSB's "Love Is the Message." Bill Brewster and Frank Broughton

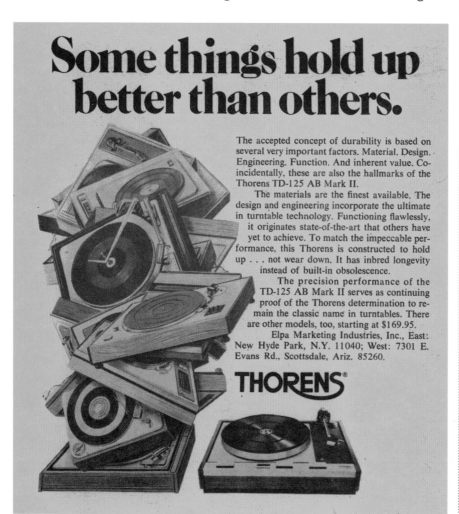

Left: Spinning records became more of a science in the 1970s, as DJs made their reputations on their ability to merge songs and cue discs so as to keep a seamless flow of sound going in discos.

MFSB: LOVE IS THE MESSAGE

Above: MFSB's *Love Is the Message* album brought politics to the dance floor.

quote journalist Sheila Weller who described her first visit to The Gallery in the *New York Sunday News*: "Furious dancing. Gentle laughter. Crepe paper and tinsel. Body energy shakes the room . . . In darkness pierced by perfectly timed bursts of light, Labelle's rousing 'What Can I Do for You?' takes on a frenetic holiness. The floor is a drum to the dancers—many of them gay, most of them black—whose extended fists and tambourines lob the balloons and streamers above at what seem to be collectively chosen intervals." The floor was run by Siano and his friend Robert DeSilva who worked the lights, which was more about timing than effects, just a mirror ball and some spots. Nicky knew how to build a mood until everyone was singing along and the dance floor was heaving and then, after a brief pause, in would come his incredible bass speakers and everyone would scream and blow their whistles. The Gallery lasted until 1978. After that Siano worked a club called The Buttermilk Room and for three months at Studio 54 until his prodigious drug intake forced him to leave. Even at The Gallery he would sometimes slump over the decks, stopping the music, but he was so loved that dancers would wait until someone righted him and got the records going again. It was all too much, too soon.

Tenth Floor

WITH the ending of the summer season in Fire Island, the Pines clientele of the Sandpiper and Botel wanted to continue the action in the city. Market forces prevailed and David Bruie, Jim Jessop, and David Sokoloff, who had put on a number of spectacular theme parties that summer (including an erupting volcano situated on a barge moored offshore from their beach house), set out to recreate a club in the city where the same degree of sexual freedom was possible. Clearly there was no Meat Rack or beach sunrises available in winter in Manhattan, so they used David Mancuso's Loft as a model and made it a members-only club to circumvent the licensing laws and to restrict the clientele to only those deemed to be good-looking and rich enough to belong. Tenth Floor opened in December 1972 at 151 W. 25th Street, in the middle of the Seventh Avenue rag trade, housed in a 1,000-square-foot loft on the tenth floor. As in The Pines, they catered to a mostly white, rich, conservative gay crowd, sometimes known as the "clones" for their identical mustaches, short hair, muscular toned bodies—the result of countless hours in the gym—and their careful choice of jeans and shoes. The club had white walls, grey industrial grade carpeting, and that staple of all seventies clubs—huge arrangements of lilies and ferns. Peter Shapiro described it as "the gentlemen's club of the gay elite . . . The Tenth Floor represented the four hundred people who 'mattered' in gay society in the early seventies." One of the few black people there was the DJ Ray Yeates, whose prodigious drug intake sometimes badly affected his performance, but who was known for his daring creativity and for discovering and breaking some particularly odd records, one of which, Area Code 615's "Stone Fox Chase," was later used as the theme tune for the BBC's *Old Grey Whistle Test*.

Fire Island rivalry resumed in December 1974 when Michael Fesco from the Ice Palace opened up his own place in New York. Called The Flamingo, he closed it down each summer when most of his customers relocated to The Ice Palace itself in Cherry Grove. The Flamingo was on the second floor of the Ayer Building at 599 Broadway, just down from Houston Street and one block over from Nicky Siano's Gallery. It was enormous, a double-height manufacturing loft running half a block with huge windows and no pillars to obstruct the view of the dance floor. The design was minimal, with mirrored panels and an ever-changing selection of artwork. The banquettes were moved around every week so it always seemed new and fresh. Fesco had a reputation for hosting themed parties: black parties, white parties, cowboy parties. Hired bodybuilders posed on trestle tables dressed as bikers, Roman centurions, or even deep-sea divers. Once again Fire Island exclusivity reigned: the club was almost 100 percent wealthy and white. It was run as a $600-a-year membership club, which automatically excluded everyone but the gay elite. Like most of the other clubs, it ran from midnight until 6 a.m. Edmund White described an evening at The Flamingo: "I saw a roomful of husky men, many

> ## "The music is a symbolic call for gays to come out of the closet and dance with each other."
>
> Nat Freedland, A&R director for Fantasy Records

Right: Former *Merv Griffin Show* "celebrity hairdresser" Monti Rock III became a camp disco star in 1974 after easy listening veteran Bob Crewe invented the identity of Disco Tex for him. The single success "Get Dancin'" resulted in this 1975 debut album.

Prime movers in a pop revolution

DISCO'S TOP THIRTY

Neil Bogart
President of Casablanca; Donna Summer's Svengali; on the strength of disco and Kiss, turned his company into one of the top three in domestic sales.

Giorgio Moroder
King of Eurodisco; Donna Summer's producer; composer of *Midnight Express* score.

Bill Wardlow
As *Billboard*'s associate publisher, pushed disco from the beginning; organizes annual *Billboard* Disco Forum.

Chic
Producers/leaders Bernard Edwards and Nile Rodgers put this show together for "Dance, Dance, Dance" and "Le Freak."

Jacques Morali
Conceptualized and produced the Village People (and before them, the Ritchie Family).

Morali (far left)

The Village People
Made disco safe for America with "Macho Man" and "Y.M.C.A."

Vince Aletti
Staunch supporter of disco, first as a writer for ROLLING STONE, then for *Record World*'s Disco File column; now vice-president of Warner Bros.' RFC Records in charge of A&R.

Richie Rivera
Disco DJ at New York's influential Flamingo; top disco mixer.

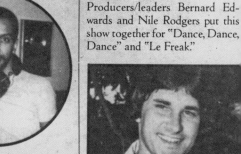

Tom Hayden
Heads Tom Hayden & Associates, a top national disco promotion company; president of Nucleus Records, a new CBS disco label.

Gloria Gaynor
Early queen of disco with "Never Can Say Goodbye"; back on top with "I Will Survive."

Alec R. Costandinos
French producer of "disco operas," including *Romeo & Juliet, Love and Kisses, Golden Tears, Sphinx.*

Tom Moulton
Invented the "disco mix" (what you hear on the dance floor); Grace Jones' producer; president of Salsoul's Tom N-Jerry label.

Voyage
French studio musicians who worked with Cerrone, Costandinos, Don Ray; hit LP (*Fly Away*) and single ("Souvenirs").

Judy Weinstein
President of For the Record, the most influential New York disco pool (record distribution center for club DJs).

> ## "The disc jockey is a creative person, an artist creating an experience in one evening. They are performing."
>
> Judy Weinstein, President, For The Record, New York record pool

of them shirtless, sipping beer or coke and casually watching the entertainment . . . The blending of the records, the estimation of the crowd's mood, the choice of music were superb—the most discerning I'd come across anywhere . . . the mirrored panels were frosted over with condensed sweat." The music was provided by Armando Galvez, but a whole succession of DJs passed through in the club's long history—it did not close down until February 15, 1981, after a celebratory Valentine's Night bash. The two most famous were Richie Rivera who joined The Flamingo in 1977 and broke a number of records like Roy Ayers' "Running Away," "Le Spank" by Le Pamplemousse, and Chocolate's "King of Clubs." The other was Howard Merritt, who had joined the year before and specialized in light, high-energy disco music like Barry White and Odyssey better suited to the dancers out of their heads on speed or cocaine.

Régine Zylberberg's nightclub formula reached New York in May 1975 when she opened up in a suite at the Delmonico Hotel at 502 Park Avenue on the corner of 59th Street (which had been the center of Beatlemania when the band stayed there in August 1964). She told *W* magazine what her new club would be like: "Andy Warhol holding court at the bar; couples making love in the ladies' room; the Social Pros—Françoise de la Renta, Mica, and Ahmet Ertegun—reigning from a discreet corner . . . the designers—Calvin Klein and Giorgio di Sant'Angelo—with a bevy of beauties." And that's how it was. Andy and Jackie Onassis and Paloma Picasso partied till 4 a.m. closing and you had to wear a jacket: no stripping to the waist to do the Frug. Régine gave Alberto Pinto half a million dollars to create an Art Deco wonderland, and Daniel Glass presided over a $20,000 sound system. But Régine's had become a chain: at her height—and the figures vary—she had between nineteen and twenty-four nightclubs on three continents, a magazine, three perfumes, and an entertainment deal with the *Queen Elizabeth II* cruise ship. It was a formula—it was still hard to get in, it was glamorous, but there was little in the way of intimacy.

Disco Radio

NEW York's WPIX-FM was originally an easy-listening station, famous for never staying with one programming format for any length of time; in fact it was derisively known as "the format-of-the-month" station by many in the New York radio industry. An example of the many formats adopted by this station came in November 1974 when it became the world's first radio station to host a disco program: Steve Andrews' *Disco 102*, which aired every Saturday night from 8 p.m. to midnight, featuring songs he had picked up at the city's discos. The *New York Times* reported: "Characterized by a strong bass, a simple melody, and terse repetitive lyrics . . . 'Disco,' as this music is called . . . is becoming increasingly popular on AM and FM radio stations. WPIX-FM recently switched several hours of its nightly programming over to 'disco.'" The station leaned toward disco the rest of the day. However, by the summer of 1976 the station was back to the adult Top 40 format popular on FM stations. Between 1978 and 1980 it became the first New York station to play punk and new wave.

Left: Six years after identifying the Disco trend, *Rolling Stone* magazine paid tribute to the prime movers of the disco revolution. Not everyone at the magazine approved of the coverage.

Burn Baby Burn

ALTHOUGH they began at Philadelphia's Sigma Studio and featured many of the Philadelphia label's best musicians and singers who had been part of MFSB (*see page 111*), The Trammps enjoyed their greatest chart success not with Gamble and Huff but on the Atlantic label. The band had been formed by Philly drummer Earl Young with singer Jimmy Ellis, guitarist Harold Doc Wade, and bassist Stanley Wade, and originally called themselves The Volcanoes. They scored a hit with their single version of "Zing! Went the Strings of My Heart" in 1972 on Buddah Records (there was an album of the same name). By 1974 the lineup had changed to include Ronnie Baker on guitar and Norman Harris on guitar in place of the Wades, plus keyboard player Ed Cermanski. The success of "Zing!" prompted Gamble and Huff to offer the band a distribution deal for their own label, Golden Fleece, and in 1976 The Trammps had a pop (number 35) and R&B (number 10) hit with "Hold Back the Night," which also gained a lot of play in clubs, helping the album it came from (*Trammps*), which also contained the "Trammps Disco Theme," to minor chart success.

The same year the band enjoyed more chart success backed up by club approval with "Where the Happy People Go," a pop (number 27) and R&B (number 12) hit, which also earned a place on DJs' best of year lists—possibly aided by the line about disco being the place to which happy people go. The next two singles, "Soul Searchin' Time" and "Ninety-Nine and a Half," also released in 1976, were less successful.

But in 1976 the band released a 3:30-minute single version of "Disco Inferno" on Atlantic Records, and it immediately became a club hit—helped by Tom Moulton's 12" version, which was originally over nineteen minutes long (so he told Tim Lawrence, for "Love Saves the Day"), and became a dance floor favorite at a club called 12 West in New York. Moulton cut it down to just over ten minutes, and other clubs began playing it, too. However, "Disco Inferno" failed to set the pop charts alight,

Left: The Trammps "Disco Inferno" single release took two years to make number 11 on the US charts. Its inclusion on the soundtrack to *Saturday Night Fever* made it an international hit in 1978.

making only the mid-50s. It seemed as if it was all over for the band, until movie producer Robert Stigwood asked for "Inferno" to be included on the soundtrack of his disco movie, *Saturday Night Fever*. The song was subsequently re-released in May 1978 and became an international pop hit (except in England, where it had been a Top 20 hit a year earlier). It can only have been helped by the fact that disco DJs had been playing it two or three times a night since the original release. The Trammps would not enjoy such a big hit again, and their career has been defined by the song, but it did get them a place in the Dance Music Hall of Fame in 2005.

"Disco is not only dancing—it's a way of life, a state of mind."

Freddie Perren, songwriter & producer

Heaven Must Be Missing an Angel

Another vocal group who began life as an R&B act—originally named Chubby and the Turnpikes—Tavares, like The Trammps, became international superstars after having a track included on the multi-platinum-selling soundtrack album *Saturday Night Fever* in 1978. Also like The Trammps, the five Tavares brothers had enjoyed chart hits before *SNF*. In 1973 they had their first Top 40 pop hit with "Check it Out." A year later they scored with a version of Hall & Oates' "She's Gone," and in 1975 had a Top 40 pop album with *In the City*, from which their first Top 10 pop hit single, "It Only Takes a Minute," was taken. That also became the band's first disco hit and a highlight of their set when they opened a U.S. tour for the Jackson Five (KC and the Sunshine Band were also on that bill; see *page 143*). In the summer of 1976 Tavares released "Heaven Must Be Missing an Angel," which made number 15 on the pop charts and, in its six-minute-plus 12" version, became a firm disco favorite. The success of "Heaven" ensured that new Tavares tracks would be given a spin at clubs across the country, and both "Don't Take Away the Music," a number 1

Right: The five musical Tavares brothers from New Bedford, Mass., became huge disco stars in 1975 with the relase of "It Only Takes a Minute Girl" and "Heaven Must Be Missing an Angel" in 1976. The title track of this, their debut album from 1973, was an R&B hit.

CHECK IT OUT

dance chart hit in 1976, and "Whodunnit," a number 22 pop hit in 1977, were big dance floor hits.

The Tavares song included on the *SNF* soundtrack wasn't one of theirs, however, but a cover of a Bee Gees song, "More Than a Woman." The Bee Gees' version was also included on the soundtrack album. The Tavares single only made it to number 32 on the pop charts—the Bee Gees' version was never released as a single—and proved to be the band's last big pop Top 40 hit. It did, however, earn the band a Grammy.

Machine Gun

Although best known as creators of slow ballads of the sort that would usually close a night's dancing with a smooch, the Commodores began life as a pure funk band. The six-piece band, who met at college in 1968, released their debut Motown album, *Machine Gun*, in 1974. It contains not only the title track—itself a funky instrumental dance floor hit—but also "The Bump," one of the first songs to induce dancers to bang hips, thighs, and behinds with a partner on the dance floor. The dance, like the Hustle in 1975, marked a return to people dancing *with* someone else instead of alongside them, as had been the fashion for the previous few years, and went on to become an international phenomenon (*see page 214*).

With a setup consisting of a horn section, keyboards, and standard guitar-bass-drums, the Commodores were originally more comparable to Sly & the Family Stone or Parliament/Funkadelic than many of Motown's other acts. "Machine Gun," "The Bump," and "I Feel Sanctified" (number 12 on the R&B chart) established the band as a dance act. In 1975, "Slippery When Wet" furthered that reputation (and seems to have inspired Wild Cherry's "Play That Funky Music" of 1976), when it made the Top 20 pop charts and number 1 on the R&B chart. It was the success of their next single, "Sweet Love," which made number 5 in the pop charts early in 1976, that changed perceptions of the Commodores, however. Featuring Lionel Richie's vocals and a synth-powered string-like backing, the success of "Sweet Love" along with the Top 10 pop placing for that year's next release, "Just to Be Close to You," and the failure of the funkier "Fancy Dancer" on the pop chart, sent the band into the

studio to record Richie's slow and country-tinged classic "Easy." It proved to be the band's biggest hit to date, making number 4 in the pop charts in March 1977, and despite the success of the funkier "Brick House" later that year (making number 5), the Commodores returned to slow songs once again. In the summer of 1978 they released the international smash-hit ballad "Three Times a Lady," and both the band and Richie became forever associated with slow, romantic songs. "Sail On" and "Still" in 1979 confirmed their international pop standing. In 1981 Richie left the band to pursue a solo career, and apart from "Nightshift" (number 3 on the pop charts) in 1985, the Commodores drifted to a stasis by the end of the 1980s.

Previous pages: The Commodores in close-up.

Above: The Bee Gees, the acceptable face of disco fever, 1978.

Right: Commodores lead singer Lionel Richie.

"We want to attract the pop and R&B markets. But we don't want to lose the disco audience. We want to bring them along with us as we evolve."

William King, Commodores

Opposite page, clockwise (beginning top left):
Artists who have had a major impact on the disco
music market are the Bee Gees (RSO / Polydor);
Isaac Hayes (ABC Records); Walter Murphy
(Private Stock); Ralph MacDonald (TK); Gloria
Gaynor (Polydor); (a dancer at Fire Island. photo
by Jeff Tennyson); D.C. LaRue (Polydor); Lou
Rawls (Philadelphia International, photo by J. Paul
Simeone); the Crown Heights Affair (Delite
Records, photo by Richard E. Aaron); and (center)
Eddie Kendricks (Motown).

At right:
Pop superstar Diana Ross began as a lead singer of
the Primettes, who later became the Supremes.
Today disco babies boogie to her hits on Motown,
of course.

Below:
Vicki Sue Robinson's second album for RCA,
"Vicki Sue Robinson," promises to be a big
success, particularly her cut of "Daylight."

Bottom:
Van McCoy, the genius behind the rock group
Faith, Hope, and Charity and song stylist Melba
Moore, achieved popularity as a performer with
"The Hustle" (Avco).

At left:
Andrea True was known in the entertainment
business as a porno star until her incredibly
popular hit "More, More, More" (Buddah)
launched a new career.

Below:
The interior effect of a disco is all-important.
Infinity has an elaborate lighting system (top,
photo by Jeff Tennyson), while Regine's is noted
for its opulence and its fashionable clientele
(bottom, photo by John Fehl).

Opposite page, top:
Dr. Buzzard's Original Savannah Band (RCA)
offers a soulful strut through a relaxed era in
American music. The album's unique blend of jazz
and rock make it an original and exciting release on
the disco market.

Opposite page, bottom left:
While the Ritchie Family's latest album "Arabian
Nights" (T.K. Records) is climbing the charts, the
girls are wrapping up an international tour.

Opposite page, bottom right:
Twentieth Century's Barry White was the first
disco artist to create a special sound with a full
orchestra and lush string arrangements, a sound
other Philadelphia groups were quick to imitate.

Warehouse Nights

N March 1977 Robert Williams opened The Warehouse in Chicago at 206 S. Jefferson Street in the West Loop below West Adams. He asked Frankie Knuckles to be its musical director and as The Continental Baths had just gone bankrupt, Knuckles took the job. He moved into the club, staying there for three years: "It wasn't like living in a nightclub. It was just like living in my home. Warehouse wasn't like a nightclub. It was a house party that grew into a nightclub as we know it today." It has to be said that this was a time when it was not fashionable to live in the West Loop. As Frankie put it, "It was pretty much like Death Valley around here."

Knuckles got his start watching Nicky Siano DJ at The Gallery, then joined his friend Larry Levan spinning discs at the Baths in New York. He had been a regular at The Loft where he was a founder member of David Mancuso's Record Pool scheme. Frankie played records at The Warehouse from day one. The club attracted an audience consisting mostly of gay black and latino men. Then they began renting the club to fraternities on Friday nights, and slowly, the students started filtering in on Saturday nights. He told *Chicago Time Out*: "At this point, it was fashionable to act gay if you were straight just so you could be at the party. The minute people heard it was a gay party, they thought it was sexual, but it wasn't. It was really about dancing . . . Musically, I played everything, because when you go to a good house party, that's pretty much what you hear: disco, James Brown, jazz, postpunk, all of it. The crowd that's hanging out now, I think they misunderstand what house music is. Once people got in there and heard the music, they began to spread the word, and it all took off. That's when they ended up giving [the club] the name the House and [called the music] house music."

There have been various theories about the origin of the word "house," but the most likely comes from Chip E, whose 1985 single "It's House" helped spread the word. Chip E used to work at the Importes Etc. record store where one of the record bins was labeled "As heard at The Warehouse" and contained records that Frankie played there. This category inevitably got shortened to "House" as customers demanded new records in that category. Another version comes from Leonard "Remix" Roy, the South-Side Chicago DJ, who put a sign in the window of the bar saying, "We play house music." He called it that because he played the kind of music you might find at home; in this instance, his set was made up of his mother's soul and disco records. Frankie Knuckles told the makers of a TV documentary titled *Pump Up the Volume* that the first time he heard the term "House Music" was when he saw that sign. One of the people in the car with him pointed the sign out and told him, "You know, that's the kind of music you play down at The Warehouse," and they all laughed.

Another definition of house is supplied by Larry "Mr. Fingers" Heard, who claims it comes from the fact that many DJs created their own music at home using synthesizers and drum machines. Frankie Knuckles himself specialized in an eclectic mix of disco and European electronic music played by such acts as Germany's Kraftwerk and the British New Romantics like Depeche Mode and Spandau Ballet.

In 1982, the owners of The Warehouse doubled the admission fee. Frankie was so indignant about it that he quit. The club closed shortly afterward. Chicago Mayor Richard M. Daley declared August 26, 2004, "Frankie Knuckles Day," and Barack Obama, then a State Senator, was responsible for the ordinance that changed the name of the street where The Warehouse once stood to "Frankie Knuckles Way" in recognition of his outstanding services to music. As he told *Chicago Time Out*: "The best thing about [that] is that Barack gave it to me . . . Coming here in 1977 was the best decision I ever made."

Left: More disco greats as defined by *After Dark* magazine in 1976.

Below: Small ads in *After Dark* reveal the increasingly open nature of gay culture.

3

Boogie nights

Tell It to The Man in the Moon

T could be that Studio 54 can be blamed entirely on party organizer and publicist Carmen d'Alessio. It was she who brought Steve Rubell and Ian Schrager in from Queens, where she had very reluctantly organized parties for them at The Enchanted Garden at 63 Marathon Parkway. They were an unlikely couple to run the world's most famous discotheque. Steve Rubell had made money on Wall Street, then started the Steak Loft in suburban Long Island, which he soon built into a chain. Ian Schrager came from a less salubrious background: his father was Louis Schrager, described by *Esquire* magazine as "a convicted felon . . . a known associate of Meyer Lansky . . . and second only to Herman Siegel in

Lansky's loan-sharking and numbers racket." Schrager himself was a lawyer and had worked in the real estate business, but his father's legacy was to plague him. From day one, Studio was set up to avoid paying taxes, and it was to be their downfall. Carmen d'Alessio very much disliked working in the outer boroughs, so she took Schrager and Rubell and installed them in Manhattan where she knew just the building for them. She took them to Barney's on Seventh Avenue and dressed them in designer suits. Now that they looked fabulous, she turned her attention to the building. D'Alessio invited architect R. Scott Bromley to come and see the raw space: a disused theater built in 1927 at 254 W. 54th Street, once used by CBS as a radio and television broadcast center. Bromley said, "I walked in, and all of a sudden it hit. I said, 'You know, everyone wants a little bit of fame. So we'll rip out all the seats and turn the stage into the dance floor.' They loved the idea. We were designing it on napkins." To get it done fast he hired a construction crew of tough local Irish kids

and they built the stage themselves. Some of them got quite excited by the idea of the club and couldn't wait to see it finished, but already Steve Rubell was showing his colors: "No way are they gonna get let in here." The interior of Studio 54 ended up being made by a mix of people. Ron Dowd, a fashionable young interior decorator, did the lounge and lobby in what was then high camp—with burgundy walls and towering mirrors, banana leaf-pattern carpets and ficus trees. Everything then changed as you entered the huge main hall with its ninety-foot ceiling and high-impact flashing lights. It was like walking into Times Square with all the neon on at once. This had been designed by the theatrical lighting team Jules Fisher and Paul Marantz; it was state-of-the-art, cutting edge, and had that all-important "wow" factor. In fact it took your breath away. It cost $400,000, virtually all of which was borrowed.

The balconies were where the action was, though. There were tables and a few settees as well as the infamous bleachers, which had been the circle when the building was a theater. These were now upholstered in a waterproof material that was hosed down daily to get rid of the evidence of the previous night's activities. On either side of the space were unisex bathrooms, used for powdering your nose by both sexes, as well as for those who preferred not to have sex right out in the open but to do it in a toilet cubicle. Although plenty of couples, and sometimes more, hetero and gay, had sex on the banquets. In the space at the center of this great hedonistic void were great silver tubes studded with lightbulbs that rose and descended over the dance floor like a fifties science fiction film. Above them hung the infamous man-in-the-moon, waiting to be lowered to a position above the stage to do his act: a huge, wooden, C-shaped cutout, almost circular with a big grin and a huge proboscis carved into it which, from time to time, was dipped into a coke spoon that made a rhythmic journey across the sky to feed his insatiable habit. As flared nostril and spoon touched, a cascade of lights ran up his nose, the music increased in volume, and cheers and screams could be heard from the dancers below. This became the symbol of the club, something that Steve Rubell, in a creative mood, originally intended on expanding upon. In an interview in the October 1977 issue of *Interview* magazine, the interviewer Bob Colacello said, "I'm always amazed when that silver man in the moon drops from the sky, and then the coke spoon goes up his nose."

Steve Rubell replied, "Next we're doing a popper with a cerebrum, a cerebellum, and all the parts of the brain. And the popper is going to shoot up the nose, which will light up the brain, and then the whole thing is going to explode."

Below the balconies was the main bar where people made contact and in the middle was the dance floor, a huge seething mass of half-naked people, many of them celebrities, most of them on drugs, all happy to be there in what to a Studio 54 regular was the center of the known world.

> # "The idea was a nightclub based upon diversity, not uniformity. To have rich people and poor people, black and white, old and young being there together."
>
> Ian Schrager

New Year's Eve 1978 at Studio 54

Schrager and Rubell might have started out with the idea of mixing the social and economic classes at their club, but as far as the world knew it was a celebrity hang-out first and foremost. Photographs such as the one above gave the impression that 54 was for the stars only. (L–R) Diana Ross greets Halston with a kiss, Bianca Jagger whispers in Andy Warhol's ear, Liza Minelli (behind) leans across her husband Jack Haley Jr. to smile at a camera which struggles to capture the object of Warhol's gaze—Grace Jones. All on New Year's Eve 1978.

Dancing Machine: Michael and The Jacksons

DESPITE being an important part of the Motown hit machine from 1969 when they made the number 1 spot on America's pop charts with "I Want You Back," "ABC," and "The Love You Save" in succession, the Jackson Five didn't become a dance floor success until 1974. The bubblegum pop appeal of the young Michael Jackson, best exhibited on "I'll Be There" (1970) and "Never Can Say Goodbye" (1971), didn't translate to any kind of funky appeal until their last two Motown albums, *Dancing Machine* (1974) and *Moving Violation* (1975). The title track of the former release was their first hit (number 2 on the pop charts) to cross over to the club scene, and at the same time give the world its first glimpse of the "robot" dance when Michael performed it on TV, miming to it. However, it was the Part 2 of the album's opening track, "I Am Love," that really got DJs into the Jacksons, with its wah-wah guitar, screaming lead line, and driving beat kicking in halfway through the 7:30-minute-long track. That and "She's a Rhythm Child" were funky enough to allow them to slip into any New York disco playlist without unsettling the mood.

Moving Violation, The Jackson Five's ninth and final album for Motown, opened with a disco version of the Supremes' hit "Forever Came Today," complete with a Philly-style string arrangement. It failed to climb any higher than number 60 on the pop charts, but was the number 1 dance hit and succeeded the huge club hit "Ease on Down the Road" by Consumer Rapport in July—which was taken from an R&B version of "The Wizard of Oz" then playing on Broadway, titled *The Wiz*. Three years later Michael Jackson starred in the big screen adaptation of the show (as the scarecrow) and sang the song in duet with Diana Ross (who played Dorothy); it made number 41 on the pop charts.

Michael's solo career had begun when he was still singing with his brothers in 1971 with "Got to Be There," which reached number 4 on the pop charts. While he'd had a number 2 pop hit with "Rockin' Robin" and a number 1 pop hit with "Ben," both in 1972, his solo career didn't really get going until 1979 with his first international number 1 hit, "Don't Stop 'Til You Get Enough." Taken from his first, enormously successful solo album *Off the Wall*, Michael's work with producer Quincy Jones helped breathe some life back into what had become an oversubscribed disco

Opposite: The Jackson Five in 1975 (L–R) Tito, Jackie, Michael, Jermaine, Marlon.

Left: Woody Allen and Michael Jackson at a fund-raising event held in Studio 54 for failed NYC Council Presidency candidate Carter Burden (owner of the *Village Voice* magazine). He lost to the council's first female president, Carol Bellamy.

"I wake up from dreams and go 'Wow, put this down on paper.'"

Michael Jackson

scene. It took the work of Chic (*see page 197*) and then Jackson to help push dance music in a new direction. With "Workin' Day and Night" and "Get on the Floor," Jones and Jackson paid tribute to Rodgers and Edwards' signature disco sound with sharp, sparse guitars, melodic driving basslines, and chanting female backing singers set against snatches of strings and tons of reverb. The album proved to be full of pop hits—"Rock with You" making number 1 while the title track and the ballad "She's Out of My Life" both made number 10.

Michael proved that he had been listening to what club crowds were dancing to during the mid-1970s with his next album release, *Thriller*, in 1982. The record's opening track, "Wanna Be Startin' Something" in its full six-minute version was an instant—and familiar—club hit. Based on African musician Manu Dibango's *Soul Makossa* record of 1972, its "ma-ma-se ma-ma-ko" refrain was lifted straight from the African record, while the beat and melody were nearly identical to the original. The African record had become an unlikely U.S. club hit when New York DJ David Mancuso began playing it at his Loft (*see page 102*), and it proved to be such a favorite that after being an import hit, Atlantic licensed it in 1973, and it reached number 35 on the *Billboard* Hot 100. Originally not given a co-writing credit, Dibango, after being complimented by acquaintances for working with Jackson, made contact and was eventually issued a co-credit. The single proved to be one of the last big, great disco hits for Jackson, and he turned more toward rock styles of music for future recordings.

Right: Andy Warhol gets his copy of the Jacksons' hit album *Triumph* signed backstage after a date on the Triumph Tour in 1981. L–R Tito Jackson, Andy Warhol, Jackie Jackson, Michael Jackson. Michael designed the costumes and set, inspired by an Earth, Wind and Fire gig he'd attended the previous year.

The New Look

The Studio 54 door policy—such as it was—didn't always favor the brave, although often the less people wore the more likely they were to gain entrance. However, as this overdressed couple demonstrate, there was a new flamboyance abroad among patrons at the end of the decade who considered themselves hipper-than-thou. Dressing up for the art crowd didn't mean fashion labels, it meant outfits from the past century. In time, clubbers at discos would look more like Dracula and Marie Antoinette than Travolta and Bianca Jagger.

WILD AND PEAC
KOOL & THE G

CONTAINS
THE HIT SINGLE:
"FUNKY
STUFF"

Stereo 2310 299

polydor

Jungle Boogie

LIKE The Trammps and Tavares, Kool & The Gang had been around for more than a decade before the inclusion of a number on the *Saturday Night Fever* soundtrack made them international disco stars. Originally from New Jersey projects, bassist Kool (Robert Bell), his brother Ronald (sax), and school friends Claydes Charles Smith (guitar), Rick Westfield (piano), Dennis Thomas (trumpet), and George Brown (drums) played a mix of soul, jazz, and R&B under a variety of names from 1964—The Jazz Birds, the Jazziacs, the Soul Town Band, and Kool & The Flames. While playing a one-off gig as backing band at a record company audition for James Brown's bus driver Wally Foster in 1968, the company man—Gene Redd of De Lite records— signed the band to the label, but not the bus driver, and became their manager in the process. They changed their name to Kool & The Gang so as not to be confused with James Brown's Famous Flames, and the following year recorded and released their eponymous debut album. Their debut single, also titled "Kool and the Gang," scraped into the *Billboard* pop charts at number 59, but more importantly it became an instant dance hit at clubs in New York. An instrumental with punchy horns, conga drums backing up a jazzy beat, and sparse, scratchy guitar, the sound was closer to that of Manu Dibango's "Soul Makossa" than any other contemporary American soul or funk band. The follow-up release, "Kool's Back Again," was not as successful, but the third single from the album—"Let the Music Take Your Mind"—was a huge dance floor hit, its drum and bass breaks and chanted (not sung) chorus presaging a musical trend that wouldn't kick in fully until the mid-1970s. Kool & The Gang's next album release was a live recording, *Live at the Sex Machine*, in 1970. While the band proved what a fabulous live act they were, the singles taken from it failed to light up the charts—although the anti-drugs, pro-ecology message number "Who's Gonna Take the Weight?" was released a few months before Marvin Gaye's similarly concerned *What's Goin' On* album and at six-

Left: Kool & The Gang's sixth and funkiest album to date (1973).

minutes-plus proved to be another dance hit. During their first extended international live tour in 1971 and '72, the Bell brothers converted to Islam, and other band members soon joined them, after which they sacked Gene Redd. Their record label put out *Music Is the Message* in 1972, and the single "Love the Life You Live" from it was another R&B and club hit, but again failed to sell in huge numbers. De Lite understood the growing power of club DJs and their ability to make a hit single, and suggested that Kool and the Gang cover Manu Dibango's "Soul Makossa." Instead the band wrote and recorded "Funky Stuff" and "Jungle Boogie." The first put them into the pop top thirty for the first time and became an essential summer dance floor hit of 1973; the latter made number 4 on the pop charts at Christmas the same year, helping their sixth album, *Wild and Peaceful*, into the top thirty album pop charts. "Jungle Boogie" proved to be the biggest-selling hit the band would have until 1980 (when "Celebration" became their only number 1 pop hit) and has since become a staple sample for hip-hoppers and R&B artists.

Deliberately not shifting their sound into a string-laden disco sound at first, Kool & The Gang released albums of spiritually concerned soul music that had a hard funk edge. "Hollywood Swinging" from *Wild and Peaceful* was a Top 10 pop hit, but their next ten single releases failed to trouble the pop charts. Even though "Open Sesame" was included on the *SNF* soundtrack, it failed to get any higher than

number 55 (although it was number 13 on the dance chart). In 1978 the band hired a lead vocalist for the first time, James "JT" Taylor. Their first album with him was *Ladies Night*, and the title track became an instant international hit and continues

> # "I wanted to make an album that would all be up-tempo. Shake Your Booty was written out of frustration, seeing people struggling with wanting to have a good time. Wanting to just feel free and be themselves. Get up off your ass and do something."
>
> Harry "KC" Wayne Casey

Below: Kool & The Gang in the early 1980s. They have sold more than 90 million records worldwide.

to be played at clubs and bars around the world. Produced by Deodato and employing a disco sound reminiscent of Earth, Wind & Fire (*see page 188*), it proved so successful that the band stuck with it for the follow-up, *Celebrate!*, as well as the hit single from it, "Celebrate." Kool & The Gang continued to enjoy enormous pop success throughout the 1980s ("Cherish" making number 2 on the pop chart in 1985) and to tour the world well into the next century.

That's the Way

Unlike Kool & The Gang, KC and the Sunshine Band formed during the first wave of disco acts to make a hit in 1973. Formed in Miami by a singer and employee of TK Records (*see page 164*) named Harry Wayne Casey (hence "KC") and producer, songwriter, and bass player Richard Finch who co-wrote the songs, they were originally called Ocean Liner and featured the musical skills of the TK house band. Casey and Finch wrote and produced George McCrae's "Rock Your Baby," which became an international hit in the summer of 1974. The legend goes, McCrae wasn't originally booked to be the vocalist but happened

to be in the studio and his vocal on what was intended to be a KC and the Sunshine Band demo was recognized as having hit potential by TK, who put it out and was proven correct.

Casey and Finch produced their first big club hit with "Queen of Clubs" (on which McCrae sang), taken from the band's debut album, *Do It Good*, in 1974, but they became multi-platinum-selling artists with their second, eponymous album release in 1975. "Get Down Tonight" and "That's the Way (I Like It)" were number 1 pop hits around the world and dance floor hits everywhere, too. The following year they had a number 1 pop hit with "(Shake, Shake, Shake) Shake Your Body," and in 1977 made number 1 with "I'm Your Boogie Man," both taken from their third album, simply titled *Part 3*.

Their contribution to the *Saturday Night Fever* soundtrack, "Boogie Shoes," failed to make the Top 30 in 1978, but in 1979 they had another number 1 pop hit with "Please Don't Go," which proved to be their last big hit—although the post-disco "Give It Up" made the Top 20 in America and number 1 in the United Kingdom.

Above: Harry "KC" Wayne Casey and his Sunshine Band performing live in the late 1970s.

Open Studio

Above: Bianca Jagger makes her entrance at Studio 54 to celebrate her thirty-second birthday on May 2, 1977.

D'ALESSIO knew that Studio 54 had to open with a bang, and it had to be fantastic. First she organized a pre-opening dinner attended by Halston, Andy Warhol, and Calvin Klein, just to set the right tone. She persuaded showbiz columnists Liz Smith, Rex Reed, and Cindy Adams to all announce it as a major event in New York's cultural history. Then she sent out 5,000 personal invites to the people on her mailing list, enclosing a gift with each one. She told Albert Goldman, "Ze backbone of any club is ze mailing list. Without zat, you end up with ze white elephant." As Goldman put it, "In the case of Studio 54, Carmen provided not only the guests but the elephant." The trouble was, Studio only held 720 people. On April 26, 1977, more than 5,000 people, all waving invites, filled the street outside, yelling and jostling for position. She had used not only her own address list, but those of Andy Warhol, Calvin Klein, Francis Scavullo, and many of her gay friends from the Fire Island scene, too.

Among those who managed to get through the door were Mick and Bianca Jagger, Salvador Dali, Liza Minnelli, Jerry Hall, Margaux Hemingway, Brooke Shields, Cher, Debbie Harry, Halston, Diana Vreeland, and the newlyweds Donald and Ivana Trump. Those who failed to make it through the crush included Frank Sinatra, Warren Beatty, and Woody Allen and Diane Keaton. People at the door went wild. Richard Turley reported to Anthony Haden-Guest that a doctor in his group arrived with a jeroboam-sized bottle of quaaludes, which he began to distribute. They took about twenty minutes to kick in, then women began to expose their breasts, men to pull down their pants, complete strangers felt each other up. There was a crazy energy in the air. Turley got in to the club around 1 a.m.

But there are celebrity openings all the time in Manhattan. What kept Studio in the news was that a week after that launch, Halston asked if they would open on the Monday night of May 2, 1977, for a private party to celebrate Bianca Jagger's thirty-second birthday. Carmen d'Alessio organized the party that went on to make the club famous. Bianca entered riding a white horse, hired from the Claremont Stables, led by a naked man, whose body had been painted to make him look as if he were clothed (unless you saw him in profile). She dismounted and cut her cake. The pictures went around the world. No expense was spared on these publicity-seeking events. For Armani d'Alessio put on a drag-queen ballet, and for her own birthday, she leaped out of her birthday cake wearing a gold lame Norma Kamali bathing suit that failed to hold in one of her breasts.

D'Alessio made certain that celebrities always received special treatment at Studio 54. Steve Rubell would get his assistant, Myra Scheer, to telephone Diana Ross, Halston, Andy Warhol, Liza Minnelli, and the other Studio regulars and invite them to one of his "backdoor parties," which were held behind the stage between 10 p.m. and midnight. At midnight the backdrop would lift and they would become part of the club, merging with the main dance floor. The club hired Joanne Horowitz as celebrity wrangler on commission, paying for any star she managed to get through the door. Pictures of Cher dancing alone at the opening night of Studio had appeared on the front page of both the *New York Post* and the *Daily News*, prompting Schrager to work out a deal with Horowitz. She was paid $250 for bringing in a major celebrity and $125 for a medium-sized one. Below that she sometimes had to negotiate, as she told *New York* magazine's Jada Yuan: "Everybody was a different price. Once in a while, Ian [Schrager] and I would argue because I thought Alice Cooper [$60] was worth as much as Sylvester Stallone [$80], but Ian thought no."

Below: *Rolling Stone* dissects the disco dance craze in 1979.

Left: Diana Ross on the DJ table at Studio 54 in February 1980.

Right: Musique consisted of three singers and musician/producer Patrick Adams, whose concept it was. Using an electronic disco beat and high-class-seeming sexy singers, he scored a big disco hit with the sexually provocative "In the Bush" in 1978. After the success of a debut album (*Keep on Jumpin'*) the same year, Adams cut this second album, from which "Love Massage" became another big club hit in 1979.

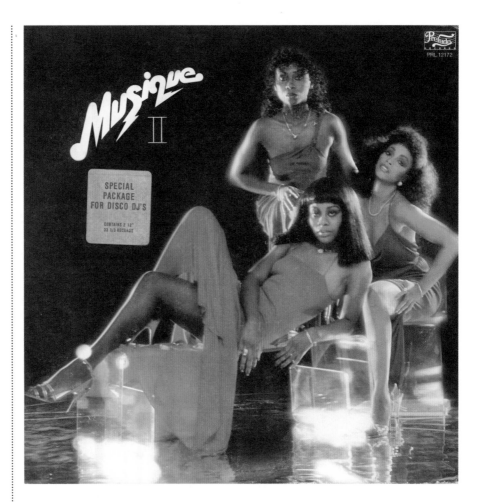

Let the Music Play

THE spectacle at Studio 54 would have been nothing without the music. The DJs were provided with the best money could buy. To be specific, the RLA company built for them a system comprising six RLA "Waldorf" horn loaded/reflex main bass boxes, six RLA "Bertha/Levan" bass horns, two "Ultima" three-way full range boxes, four "2" tweeter arrays, and an RLA X-3000 DJ crossover.

The first song on opening night was "Devil's Gun" by CJ & Co. and was spun by Richie Kaczor. Kaczor was a brilliant DJ, good at discovering new dance songs. He was the one who broke Gloria Gaynor's "I Will Survive" and made it a big hit. The DJ on the second night was Nicky Siano, who had spun the discs at Rubell and Schrager's Enchanted Garden out in Queens in 1976. They hired him for Studio 54 two weeks before opening, but he could only play weekends because the rest of the week he played his own club, The Gallery on 22nd Street—and after that at 172 Mercer Street. A roll call of the very best New York DJs played there during its relatively brief life: Tony Humphries, John "Jellybean" Benitez, Tom Moulton, and Tony Carrasco. Rubell and Schrager always hired the best.

Studio was sometimes used as the set for disco videos. The best known was probably "In the Bush" with its catchy refrain, "Push, push, in the bush," by Musique, from their *Keep on Jumpin'* album. It went on to become number one on *Billboard's* Hot Dance Club Play chart and eventually sold millions of copies across the world.

Studio flourished for a month. Then on May 21, 1977, the New York State Liquor Authority raided the club for selling alcohol without a license, as they

Steve Rubell

In an interview conducted in 2010 with Portfolio.com, Ian Schrager said of his former business partner: "Steve and I had different areas of influence. But none was mutually exclusive—there was tremendous overlap. I'll never forget the first time we opened up a nightclub in Queens. We both walked in there and Steve went to the bar to hang out with kids from Queens, and I went to the DJ booth to play with the lights. That set the tone, and that's sort of the way it went from there." Rubell died from hepatitis and AIDs-related complications in 1985 at the age of 46.

had been using one-day "caterer's permits" designed for weddings and meetings while they waited for their license to be processed. The State had denied the one-day license the day they raided. Studio had no certificate of occupancy, no cabaret license, and no public assembly license. They brought in Roy Cohn, the universally despised lawyer who damaged so many people's lives while working for Senator McCarthy, to make things right. Studio opened again the following night serving free fruit juices and sodas instead of alcohol. For the next five months they had to operate as a juice bar while Rubell's A-list people had to brown-bag the free champagne he doled out up on the bleachers. The liquor license came through in October, after much bending of the rules.

From then on Studio 54 became world HQ of hedonism. When asked about the sexual politics of Studio, Rubell told *Interview*: "It's bisexual. Very bisexual. Very, very, very bisexual. And that's how we choose the crowd, too. In other words, we want everybody to be fun and good-looking." Ian Schrager told Jada Yuan, "I hate the idea of the velvet rope. Steve and I invented that. And I'm surprised, quite frankly, that in thirty years no one's come up with something better. This may come as a shock to you, but when we did it, we thought it

Above: Studio 54's semi-legendary doorman Mark Benecke explaining why he cannot let people in on a cold night in March 1978. Or at least these people.

Left: Uncommon currency—a VIP ticket for Studio 54.

was an incredibly democratic process. It had to do with exercising the same discretion people exercise when they invite people into their home. It really wasn't elitist. It was just a couple of guys from Brooklyn rolling up the rug and saying, 'Let's have a party!'" His instructions to doorman Marc Benecke: "Just make sure you never let in someone like me!" True to his catering background, Rubell's door policy was what he called "tossing the salad." He didn't want all tomatoes; when you have a lot of lettuce you have to mix in some other ingredients. He perched on a fire hydrant to look over the heads of the crowd. People would wait for hours in the freezing cold, knowing it was hopeless. Sometimes someone would be allowed in if they took off their shirt, others if they stripped naked. He let in the male half of a honeymoon couple but not the wife. Limo drivers were let in, their hires not. Two girls arrived with a horse. Benecke had them strip naked, then said only the horse would be allowed in. It was cruel, arbitrary, and of course they had guns pulled on them, violence threatened, and occasionally meted out. But Rubell spent part of every night there with Benecke, his mouth slack, slurring his words from too much cocaine and quaaludes, eyeing up the pretty boys, acting God in his own Heaven.

SalSoul: First Choice

ALTHOUGH founded in New York by the three Cayre brothers who spent their formative years in Miami, the SalSoul record label built itself up with a recording made in Philadelphia. After successfully running various businesses, which included manufacturing hosiery, operating duty free on a cruise liner, and importing Spanish music on eight-track cartridges, the Cayre brothers started a record label called Mericana Records and specialized in Spanish-language music. They signed an English-speaking singer named Joe Bataan, whose debut album for them was titled *Salsoul*, the word being representative of Bataan's concoction of Salsa and Soul music. It was enough to get the label recognized by local New York radio stations, which started playing "Latin Strut," a track from the album written by Deodato. When CBS Records offered the Cayres $100,000 to license the Bataan album, they took the money and, inspired by the emerging disco scene, decided to invest in creating disco records. Because the Philadelphia label was at the heart of the scene, Ken Cayres approached several of the Philly label's key musicians and arrangers and recorded three songs with drummer Earl Young, bassist Ronnie Baker, guitarist Bobby Eli, vibes player Vince Montana,

"The disco beat was created so that white people could dance."

Bethann Hardison (model)

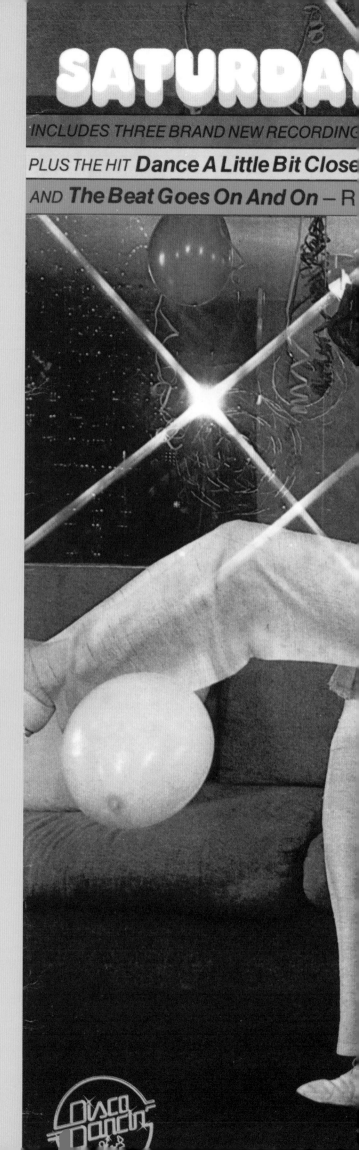

SATURDAY

INCLUDES THREE BRAND NEW RECORDING

PLUS THE HIT *Dance A Little Bit Close*

AND *The Beat Goes On And On* — R

SALSOUL
NIGHT DISCO PARTY

BY THE SALSOUL ORCHESTRA:– **Night Fever Stayin' Alive You Should Be Dancing**

– Charo and the Salsoul Orchestra

ble **Hit And Run** – Loleatta Holloway **Doctor Love** – First Choice

Salsoul
RECORDS

percussionist Larry Washington, and Bunny Sigler and Ron Kersey on keyboards in the Philly studio Sigma Sounds. Cayres called the musicians the SalSoul Orchestra and came away with the master tape of "SalSoul Hustle." When the 7" single of the song sold over 400,000 copies, Cayres got the same musicians together and recorded another seven songs to create the first SalSoul Orchestra album, *Salsoul Orchestra*, in 1975, stretching out "Hustle" by a minute and a half more than the original single version.

Later that year Cayre was in the studio with Joe Bataan as he recorded a version of Gil Scott Heron's "The Bottle," using a horn section comprising the Brecker Brothers and David Sanborn. The track became an instant club fave and gave the label access to all the top NY club DJs. Cayre hired one of the best, Walter Gibbons, to remix songs for use in clubs. His first mix, of Loleatta Holloway's "Hit and Run," was revolutionary, leaving the vocals out for two verses at the beginning, leaving in sighs, and weaving horns, drums, and guitars in and out to create an eleven-minute masterpiece.

However, it was Gibbons's edit of Double Exposure's "Ten Percent" on SalSoul in 1976 that proved to be the making of the label and the beginnings of the 12" single as staple club fare. Once clubs like Paradise Garage and The Loft had played their 12" promotional copy of "Ten Percent" a few times, the demand for that version over the shorter 7" single proved great enough for SalSoul to issue it as the first commercially available 12" single. While it is rarely remembered by the general public anyone who was a disco regular in 1976 will know every beat and word of that song: it was on constant play at discos across America.

SalSoul subsequently entered a golden period of success by releasing 12" disco singles which became hits. Among them were Instant Funk's "I Got My Mind Made Up," "Checking You Out" by Inner Life (vocals by Jocelyn Brown), and First Choice's "Love Thang." Although not signed to SalSoul directly, the Philly all-girl trio First Choice were first signed to Philly Groove where they scored an enormous hit with "Armed and Extremely Dangerous" in 1973. They then signed with Norman Harris's label Gold Mind, which SalSoul distributed. Band and label enjoyed one of *the* biggest disco hits with "Dr. Love" in 1977.

Loleatta Holloway was another SalSoul disco star who briefly crossed over to mainstream success. Her last big hit with the label, "Love Sensation" in 1980, made number 1 on the *Billboard* dance chart. However a sample of her singing "Ride on Time" from that song was integral to the hit of that title by Black Box in 1989.

Left: Former Philly Groove artists who switched to SalSoul, First Choice.

Above: A music press ad for the SalSoul roster, 1979.

Tossed Salad

WHO were the big tomatoes in Rubell and Benecke's salad? Andy Warhol, of course—his *Interview* magazine was an essential component of the hedonistic celebrity culture that Studio fed on. His close circle: Elsa Martinelli, Francis Scavullo, Truman Capote, Calvin Klein, Elizabeth Taylor, and Bianca Jagger. Then there were the usual big names, let in because they would make the gossip columns the following day: Princess Grace and Prince Rainier of Monaco; Muhammad Ali (who surely disapproved of the drugs and drinking); Gloria Vanderbilt; Fred Astaire in full evening dress; John F. Kennedy Jr.; Jackie Onassis; The Rev. Myung Moon and his extensive entourage, perhaps hoping to pick up people for a mass marriage; Pelé; Hugh Hefner; Salvador Dali, who always arrived with a huge entourage of transvestites and Euro-eccentrics in revealing costumes; and Margaret Trudeau, young wife of the Canadian prime minister, who famously slumped on a balcony settee, revealing to paparazzi that she wore no panties. The pictures went around the world and were published the day before her husband lost the election. Zsa Zsa and Eva Gabor; Michael Jackson back when he had an afro; and Lillian Carter, the former president's mother, who was taken there by party organizer George-Paul Rosell. The following day at the Russian Tea Room she described her experience in a famous quote: "I don't know if I was in heaven or hell. But it was *wonderful!*" Arnold Schwarzenegger, Vladimir Horowitz, Björn Borg, Betty Ford (perhaps screening for clients at her detox clinic), and the Hollywood crowd: Gloria Swanson, Mae West, Bette Davis, Al Pacino, Sophia Loren, Farrah Fawcett, Telly Savalas, Ann-Margret, John Travolta, cashing in on his triumph as the physical embodiment of disco here on Earth. Also, the music business crowd: Olivia Newton-John, Cher, Keith Richards, John Lennon and Yoko Ono, Rod Stewart, Alice Cooper, Giorgio Moroder, Bette Midler, Dolly Parton, Eartha Kitt, Steven Tyler, Diana Ross, and Elton John—who gathered to hear the live acts. Many of the world's most famous acts appeared at Studio, including Donna Summer, James Brown, Chuck Berry, Gloria Gaynor, the Village People, and of course the ubiquitous Grace Jones, who was both partygoer and performer; often topless, sometimes naked. She in fact arrived naked so often that people began to wish she would dress for a change. There was Dominick Montiglio, a Gambino family enforcer who had no trouble getting in, and conman Irwin Schiff, "The Fat Man."

Then there were the regular people: the septuagenarian Disco Sally, who everyone worried would have a heart attack as she twirled and leaped on the dance floor; Miriam the substitute teacher who wore a transparent wedding dress; or the Jewish couple dressed as Nazis, she with a swastika printed on her panties; André the Giant; and Rollerina, who often got to dance with Rudolf Nureyev. Rollerina was a Studio 54 regular. By day he was rumored to be a stockbroker, but by night he was a roller-skating fairy. When one of the Studio busboys, Scott Bitterman, first arrived in New York to study ballet at NYU he was greeted at Penn Station by the vision of a man on roller skates wearing

"No one knows what's going to happen after they enter this place."

Steve Rubell

Left: March 10, 1978, and Elizabeth Taylor greets Halston with a kiss to her 46th birthday party at Studio 54. A waiter helps place a chair for the designer as an enormous photo of the actress looks down on them all.

a wedding dress, a tiara, and carrying a fairy wand. He gave Bitterman his blessing as he swept past. Welcome to New York! As Truman Capote observed: "Disco is the best floor show in town. It's very democratic, boys with boys, girls with girls, girls with boys, blacks and whites, capitalists and Marxists, Chinese and everything else, all in one big mix." It was a fun crowd.

Studio 54: Steve Rubell's disco Disneyland

By Michael Segell

NEW YORK

IT'S AN HOUR BEFORE his customary nap, two hours before the doors open. Steve Rubell—disco impresario, celebrities' darling, Manhattan millionaire, social gadabout and, not coincidentally, coowner of Studio 54—lolls on an overstuffed couch near the dance floor. "Welcome to my living room," he says, his rubbery, well-tanned face flashing a warm smile. "It's beautiful, isn't it?"

There's no denying it. Virtually empty and dimly lit, Studio 54 is as impressive now as when such luminaries as Mick Jagger, Margaret Trudeau, Liza Minnelli, Halston and Andy Warhol stalk the parquet dance floor swaddled in crepe de Chine, silk taffeta and lambskin. Entrance is gained through a long, mirrored foyer with an arched, gold ceiling bathed in soft red light. The multitiered main room is expansive—half lounge, half dance floor. In the lounge area, boyish custodians brush the glittery black carpet, polish the shrinelike, chrome-plated bar, dust the sprawling couches and arrange huge urns filled with blooming calla lilies. In the DJ booth above the dance floor, a trio of technicians checks track lighting and sound equipment, raising and lowering massive neon grids, prismatic mirrors, chase poles and futuristic backdrops suspended from the great domed ceiling by thin strands of steel. There is activity in the upstairs lounge—a secluded drawing room with carved wood moldings and plush, velveteen sofas—and movement in the balcony, which in a few hours will teem with discophiles watching the nightly bacchanalia.

This is Rubell's Disneyland. Other discos mimic its opulence, but wind up with polyester imitations. Other discos follow its exclusionary policy—from charging twelve dollars for admission to keeping an anxious crowd outside the door—but have to settle for 54's overflow. Studio 54 is the international disco par excellence: a glitzy ghetto for celebrities, socialites, power brokers and parvenus, an example for enterprising foreigners, a gold mine for gossip columnists and a starry haven for

ubiquitous *paparazzi*. It's been fingered by righteous muckrakers as a laundromat for Mafia green and a cocaine palace for detached narcissists; and praised by city fathers for providing the kind of night life not seen in this town since the closing of the Latin Quarter. What it most assuredly provides is status to those who get in.

But according to Rubell, who has become the unofficial social arbiter of New York, the admissions policy is strictly democratic. "Creating the crowd is like casting a play or making a salad," he says. "You want a little bit of everything —the pretty girl, the celebrity, the guy who's a model, the kid who turns hamburgers at McDonald's. You want some straight people, some gay people—they bring a lot of energy—and some married couples who watch the dancers."

If status is accorded those admitted on an open night, nothing less than preeminence is conferred on those invited to a Studio 54 party. Ranging from modest $10,000 fetes to the $100,000 bash thrown by Fabergé to kick off its Farrah Fawcett hair products campaign, the parties have included white horses (for Bianca), white roses (for Elizabeth Taylor Warner), white ducks (for Dolly Parton), black panthers and gray elephants (for Liza Minnelli). "We try to keep it exciting and unusual," says Rubell, who oversees the party planning. "On Valentine's Day, we decided we were tired of winter, so we made the whole place into a tropical garden. We got truckloads of sod from Florida, ripped up the carpeting and laid it down. We put in palm trees and goldfish ponds and spread white Florida sand around. Part of the reason for the longevity of this place is that it's a theater; we can always change the environment."

Success is no stranger to Ru-

Steve Rubell (above) at Studio 54; doorman Mark Benecke scans the supplicants.

bell. The son of a postal worker and schoolteacher, the thirty-five-year-old bachelor ("I'm too neurotic to marry; I had too good a mother") dallied at Syracuse University long enough to avoid the draft, then spent a couple of years as an itinerant tennis pro. "I never worked a day until I was twenty-eight," he says. Work began when he opened a Long Island steak shack that later blossomed into a restaurant chain. In 1975 he converted another restaurant into a disco, which flourished for two years until neighborhood complaints about traffic congestion and noise forced it to close. In April 1977 he opened Studio 54 with Ian Schrager, his partner, lawyer and college chum. Figures on how much the club has made are not available, but to date, more than $1 million has been invested in renovations, sound equipment, props, lights and sets. Soon there will be Studio 54 jeans, a Studio 54 album and record label and a Studio 54 in Japan.

"I get calls every day from people with television, movie and product ideas," Rubell says. "I was offered $20 million to build 54s all over the world. But I'm very cautious about protecting the name and not cheapening it. Besides, I have all the money I need and, with this place, everything I want."

Later that night a mixed crowd fills the club, with the principles of Rubellian democracy clearly in effect. Robert Di Silva, the light and scene choreographer, bounces in the DJ booth like a weightless jockey, flicking switches and barking instructions over a headset while DJ Richie Kaczor mans the

turntables. A heart-shaped pendulum with an attached strobe swings down over the crowded dance floor, followed by a neon fan, cyclorama and giant, smiling man in the moon with a sparkling spoon perched beneath its nose. To complete the joke, Di Silva flicks a switch and the squealing crowd is caught in a blizzard of shredded white polyurethane, or fake snow.

Meanwhile, Rubell wends through the crowd. He stops to pat the bare back of a young waiter wearing sneakers, white socks and track shorts, then heads for the door, picking up a fishbowl brimming with candy.

"Who wants a lollipop?" he asks. His appearance on the street, where two dozen have gathered in the early morning cold, is met with supplications and bleats: "Hey, Steve. C'mon, Steve...." Others remain silent, hoping propriety will not go unnoticed. Rubell overrules his doorman, Mark Benecke, and lets in a plainly dressed couple who have queued for an hour. "It's a look they have," he says mysteriously. Rubell lets in four more and, amid many "dahlings" and wet kisses, bids good night to a departing Diane von Furstenberg.

Inside, the gregarious owner busses cheeks and shakes hands, is cornered for a minute by a fast-talking sheik, then approaches the bar, where he orders drinks for everyone within earshot. "That Arab fellow just offered me $5 million to build a disco in Kuwait," he says. "Can you imagine spending six months in Kuwait? I'd miss everything. Everything I love is right here."

He sips on a beer, nods to a sequined cat-woman who squeezes his arm. "This is like the Ziegfeld Follies. No one knows what's going to happen after they enter this place."

PHOTOGRAPHS BY CHRISTINA YUIN

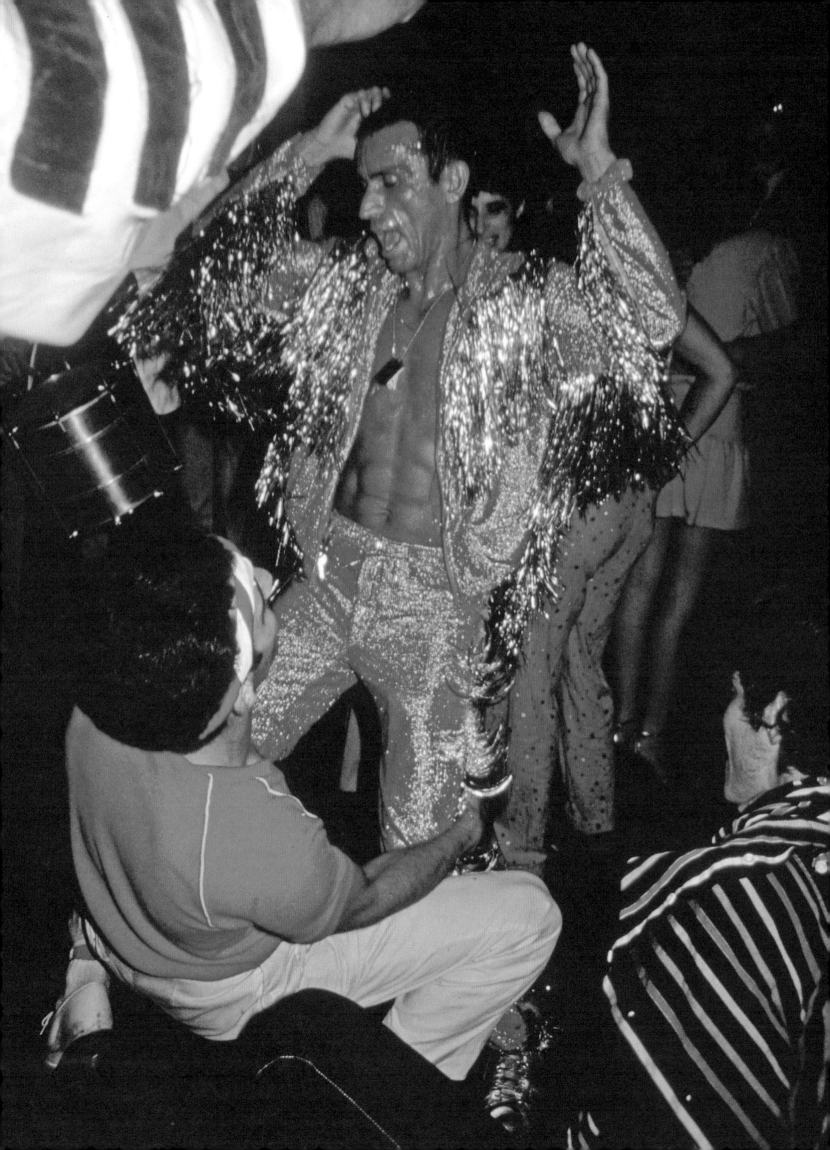

Ring My Bell

ORIGINALLY from New York, TK Disco founder Henry Stone moved to Miami in 1947 after serving in the Army during World War II (he played trumpet in a band). In the 1950s he began a record distribution company from his new home and opened a small recording studio where he worked with, among others, Ray Charles, Wilbert Harrison, and James Brown. He liked the R&B scene.

By the 1970s Henry was the distributor in Florida and the South for the Atlantic, Warner, and Elektra record labels while running a couple of his own small labels. When he enjoyed international success with a Miami local named Timmy Thomas (who enjoyed an international hit with "Why Can't We Live Together," 1972) Henry began licensing other dance tracks and releasing dance tracks on various labels he owned.

TK Disco became Henry's chosen label for distribution of 12" dance mixes of the 7" singles released on his other outlets. In 1974 TK scored another international hit with a song written by one of Henry's producers, Richard Finch, and a studio musician, Harry Wayne Casey (KC and the Sunshine Band, see page 143), titled "Rock Your Baby." Singer George McCrae became a major pop star and the song, an instant club classic. Stone then released the first KC and the Sunshine Band single, "Get Down Tonight," in the summer of 1975, and it made both the band and the label pop chart regulars.

Stone subsequently bought more soul and dance labels, among them Dash Records, which gave him the services of T-Connection, whose "Disco Magic" in 1976 became TK Disco's second 12" release (the first being Wild Honey's "At the Top of the Stairs"), and their first big dance floor hit. TK Disco released over two hundred 12" dance singles between 1976 and 1981, and while none of his other acts managed to match the pop chart success of KC and the Sunshine Band, a few, such as T-Connection, did make it to the pop charts as well as dominating the dance chart (their "Do What You Wanna Do" made

the *Billboard* Hot 100 in 1977). There was also the Ritchie Family ("Life Is Music," 1977), Dorothy Moore ("Let the Music Play," 1977), Voyage ("Let's Fly Away," 1979), and, of course, Anita Ward, whose "Ring My Bell" (1979) was an enormous international number 1 pop hit, while the album it was taken from (*Songs of Love*) became a Top 10 pop album in America.

Like many disco labels, TK went out of business as the anti-disco movement (*see page 228*) gathered pace, filing for bankruptcy in 1981. At the time, the label had a number 1 pop hit with KC and the Sunshine Band's first hit ballad, "Please Don't Go."

While TK was the first high-profile label that had built its stock on selling disco music to fold, it certainly wasn't the only one. As music tastes changed during the 1980s the small, specialist disco labels couldn't or wouldn't diversify into new areas of music. Some stuck with what they knew because they loved the sound and the scene that clung on as the "Disco Sucks" movement gained momentum (*see page 228*), but couldn't sustain their existence. Others, like TK, simply went bust.

Previous pages: Dancers on the floor at Studio 54.

Right: Anita Ward's hugely successful album featured her only hit single, "Ring My Bell."

Below: Another of TK's successful disco acts in a trade ad for their 1976 album release.

Arabian Nights.
The new LP by the Ritchie Family.

The Best Disco in Town/Baby I'm on Fire/Romantic Love/Arabian Nights/Istanbul/Lawrence of Arabia/In a Persian Market.

THE RITCHIE FAMILY ARABIAN NIGHTS
Marlin 2201

MARLIN   Distributed by TK RECORDS

ANITA
WARD

SONGS
OF LOVE

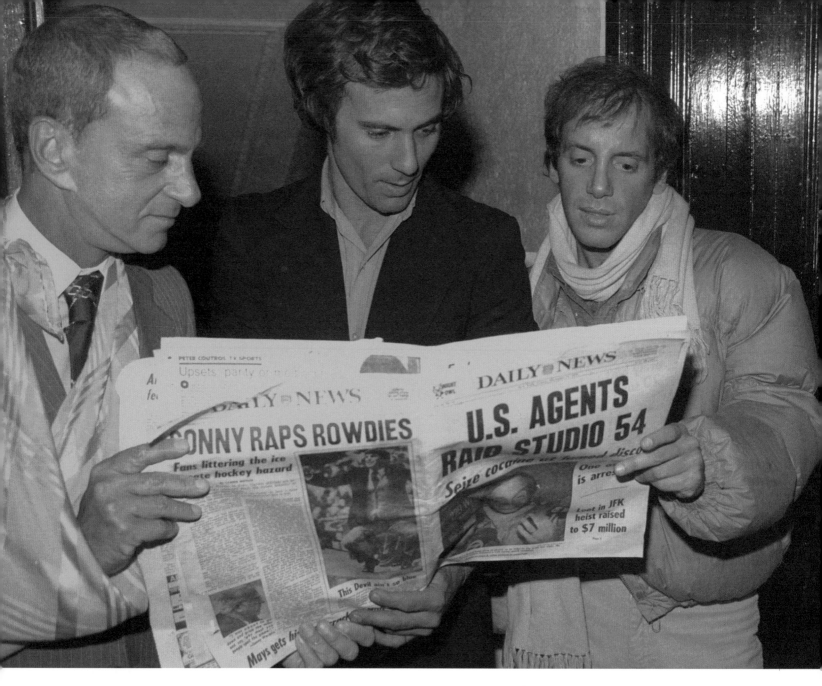

Only the Mafia Does Better

Above: The morning after the raid on Studio 54, owners Ian Schrager (center) and Steve Rubell (right) consult the news reports of the event with their lawyer, Roy Cohn.

IT could not last because, as Studio 54 security guard Bill Cunningham told *New York* magazine: "The club owners were crooks, the security company I worked for at 54 were crooked, and the clientele were crooked or at least not very straight." The intention to skim the takings was there from the very beginning. It was a system that Rubell called "cash-in, cash-out, and skim." The problem came when the IRS investigated, having been tipped off by a disgruntled employee named Donald Moon, who had originally worked for the pair at The Enchanted Garden and had moved with them to Studio 54. Rubell fired him in a particularly brutal way, so he went to the Feds out of revenge. He didn't want the reward that he was entitled to, but he did want to disappear as part of the Federal Witness Protection Program. He told them all about the secret safe containing the double set of books, and he told them where the money was kept. It was in Hefty bags, stuffed into the space between the false drop ceiling and real ceiling in the basement. The IRS began building their case. Then an article by Dan Dorfman appeared in the November 7 issue of *New York* magazine where Rubell bragged, "Profits are astronomical. Only the Mafia does better." Rubell told Dorfman, "It's a cash business and you have to worry about the IRS. . .

I don't want them to know everything." Reading the article, Schrager went crazy. Rubell had sealed their doom. But they still did nothing to cover their tracks.

The raid on Studio 54 was led by Peter Sudler, assistant U.S. Attorney, and included fifty agents from the IRS criminal investigation agency, backed up by Drug Enforcement agents. They arrived at 9:30 a.m. on Thursday, December 14, 1979, and headed straight for the basement and the metal safe containing the books. Sudler told Anthony Haden-Guest, "They [Rubell and Schrager] were arrogant and stupid. If they had been smart they would have destroyed the records." The Hefty bags were everywhere, up in the roof space, in the gap between ceilings, behind the walls, behind the ventilation pipes—almost a million dollars in cash. Ian Schrager showed up during the raid, carrying books and papers. He put them on the floor, and because they were now on the premises, they were entitled to be searched. Five packets of what turned out to be cocaine were found, tucked between the pages of the books. Schrager was charged with possession. Agents found $100,000 in cash in the trunk of his Mercedes parked outside. In a safe-deposit box at the 640 Fifth Avenue branch of Citibank, agents found a further $900,000 in cash and the details of how the money was split.

Rubell and Schrager declared a gross income of around one million dollars for 1977, and a taxable income, after expenses, of $47,000 on which they paid tax of $8,000. They were too greedy. Normally, in a cash business, the skim is about 10 percent or, if they can get away with it, as at rock 'n' roll concerts, it might sometimes reach 25 percent. But Schrager and Rubell were skimming about 80 percent of the gross: five million dollars in one year. It was so blatant that the IRS decided to ignore their usual guidelines. Normally no one was prosecuted for less than three years of tax evasion, but they could forget those guidelines for this.

> ## "With us, it was the right thing at the right time—lightning striking. We were a couple of kids holding onto a lightning bolt."
>
> Ian Schrager

It turned out that Schrager had listed every gift ever given to a celebrity, even if it was a bag of cocaine or grass. This did not endear him to many of his erstwhile friends, and there were many. Sometimes it was amusing. Not knowing what to give Andy Warhol for his birthday, they tipped a garbage can filled with 800 dollar bills over his head. He was delighted. As an additional birthday present Steve Rubell let him spend the afternoon looking at a big pile of about $800,000 that he had piled in his living room on W. 55th Street, after pulling it out from its hiding place behind the bookcase. It was not exactly a secret that Rubell and Schrager were skimming. The IRS had a watertight case.

Despite the best efforts of Roy Cohn, on January 8, 1980, Rubell and Schrager received a sentence of three and a half years in prison and a fine of $20,000 each for tax evasion. Their partner Jack Dushey testified against them, and they in turn named other club owners who were skimming cash, and as a consequence managed to get their sentences reduced to twenty months. On February 4, 1980, they went to prison after a going-away party at Studio attended by Andy Warhol, Robert DeNiro, Al Pacino, Diana Ross, Richard Gere, Debby Harry, and a host of other celebrities. Twenty-eight days after they went to jail, the club's liquor license expired. It would take eighteen months to get a new one. It spelled the end of Studio as they knew it. Sylvester Stallone was the last customer to be legally served a drink.

Ian Schrager and Steve Rubell were released on April 22, 1981, ready to start all over again.

Disco No No

AS with any hugely successful musical genre, disco was quickly adopted and adapted by musical performers who were better known for making music that wasn't disco. The term *disco* had earned common usage among both clubbers and the general public via songs with the word in the title. "Trammps Disco Theme" had been included on the band's eponymous album in 1975, the same year that Hamilton Bohannon had a hit with "Disco Stomp" and Isaac Hayes released the instrumental *Disco Connection* album. In May 1976, The Trammps released "Disco Inferno" and while only a minor pop hit (until *SNF*), the temptation to write something with either the word disco in the title or with disco-style musical backing proved too tempting for some failing pop stars, as well as some wannabe pop stars.

Memphis radio DJ Rick Dees claims to have written his novelty song "Disco Duck" in a day. Inspired by a mid-1960s soul song by Jackie Lee that invented a dance called "The Duck," Dees' "dance" number was far less soulful or danceable. It was a much, much bigger hit, though. Crediting the record to Dees and His Cast of Idiots didn't stop people from buying the inane, childish, and repetitive piece of cod-disco trash. Dees used a duck-like "quack-quack" as a rhythm effect throughout the number and had the duck "talk-sing" harmonies in a voice that closely resembled that of Disney's Donald Duck, Clarence Nash (it wasn't Nash, but a friend of Dees). The simple, seemingly never-ending chorus of the title bored its way into millions of people's ears and stayed there for over ten weeks between September and November 1975, making number 1 on the pop charts around the world. It was so successful that Dees attempted a follow-up titled "Disgorilla," which followed pretty much the same pattern musically, lyrically, and stupidly as "Disco Duck" but had nowhere near the same success. However, Dees didn't end his musical career there, going on to record a Barry White parody, "He Ate Too Many Jelly Donuts," backed with "Barely White (That'll Get it Baby)" in 1977, a monster-

Right: The record which did more damage to disco than any other. The ludicrous *Disco Duck* became an international phenomenon and infantilized disco music forever.

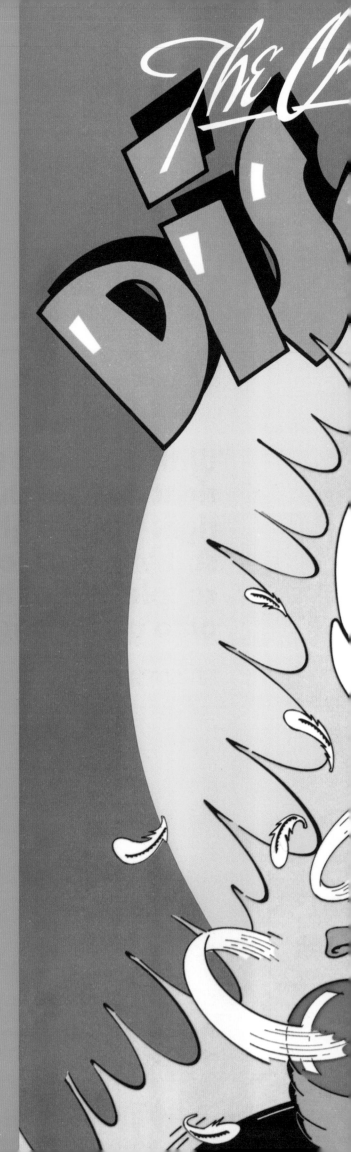

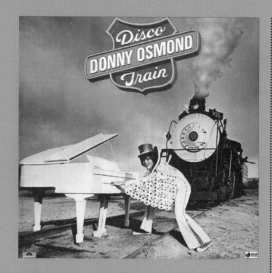

Left: Former pop child star Donny Osmond dons an Elton John–style outfit and attempts to either stop the disco train, or get run over by it.

dance number "Bigfoot" in 1978 (on Stax!), and a Frankie Goes to Hollywood–style parody titled "Get Nekked" in 1984. He's still known as the Disco Duck, though.

When miming to "Disco Duck" on television in 1976, Dees used a duck hand puppet as his singing partner. The makers of Sesame Street were quick to spot an opportunity to get into the disco mood themselves, and hot on the heels of the success of *Saturday Night Fever* in 1977 released *Sesame Street Fever*, with a dance version of "Little Rubber Duckie" being the pick of the tracks. That is, if you have to pick a track.

On the Disco Gravy Train

Donny Osmond had been a teenage sensation in the early part of the 1970s, scoring a number 1 pop hit with "Go Away Little Girl" in 1971, a number 3 pop hit with "Puppy Love" a year later, and as part of The Osmonds (with his four brothers) had a number 1 hit with "One Bad Apple" in 1971 and several other Top 20 hit singles in the following three years. However, the hits had dried up by the end of 1975 for both Donny and the Osmonds, and so he did what many other artists of the time did and made a disco album. Titled *Disco Train*, it has two tracks with "disco" in their title— though neither sound particularly disco-like and the album's title track sounds more like a 1950s-era showtune, featuring a fake audience clapping and shouting along with Donny as he implores us all to "ride the disco train" without a Gamble and Huff riff in earshot. Unsurprisingly, *Disco Train* failed to reverse Donny's failing fortunes, despite its bizarre cover art.

Teen heartthrob actor-turned-singer Leif Garrett made his recording debut with an eponymous album made up of early rock 'n' roll numbers such as Dion's "Runaround Sue" (which made number 13 on the pop chart in 1977), Chuck Berry's "Johnny B Goode," and the Beach Boys' "California Girls." The album failed to storm the charts and sold more modestly than his label, Atlantic Records, had hoped, and they were happy for Garrett to shift his recording contract to a California-based label distributed by them, called Scott Brothers Records. The Scott Brothers promptly brought Garrett into the disco era and had him record the Detroit Emeralds' "Feel the Need" (making it the title track of his sophomore album) alongside some older numbers such as the Beach Boys' "Fun Fun Fun" and Tommy Roe's "Sheila." More importantly they had Michael Lloyd (producer to the Osmonds, among others) write and produce "I Feel Like Dancin'" for Garrett. A pure disco rip-off, it made number 10 on the pop charts and proved to be his sole singing success.

Da Ya Think I'm Sexy?

Rod Stewart was still a major international rock star when he donned tight spandex pants to disco-croon "Da Ya Think I'm Sexy?" early in 1978. Despite fans and critics alike expressing dismay that he'd turned away from his R&B roots, the number 1 spot on the *Billboard* Hot 100 charts helped ease Rod's pain (as if he cared), and set a marker for other singers from disparate musical pastures to try out

> ## "I hate 'Da Ya Think I'm Sexy,' but I have to do it live because it goes down so well."
>
> Rod Stewart

the disco beat. Not long after cashing in the royalty checks Rod claimed that he only recorded the song because his then girlfriend, the Studio 54–attending Swedish former actress Britt Ekland, told him to make a disco record.

Barbra Streisand didn't need disco to rescue her career, but still she scored one of the biggest hit singles of her career when she released a duet with Donna Summer in 1979 titled "No More Tears (Enough is Enough)." It made the top spot on charts around the world, including the United States. The following year Barbra chose to write and record with Bee Gee Robin Gibb, creating the disco album *Guilty*, which quickly became another of her major record release successes. The pair would go on to release a belated follow-up, *Guilty Too*, in 2005.

Ethel Merman, veteran of the stage and screen, was perhaps the most bizarre artist to ever record an album of American showtunes set to a disco beat. On second thought, she could be the only one. Her *Disco Album* beggars description or belief. Yet in 1979 Merman promoted the record with a performance on the *Johnny Carson* TV show—where she sang to a jazz band backing with, oddly, no disco sound at all—at the age of seventy-one and dressed in a swirling, gossamer gown. It didn't help, and the record swiftly became an oddity much discussed and rarely, if ever, heard. At least Ethel only bothered with one take of each song.

Below: So bad it's good? Or just the kind of tacky opportunism which did nobody involved in the project any good?

THE *ETHEL MERMAN DISCO ALBUM*

Fever!!!!

NINE months after the opening of Studio 54, an event occurred that made disco mainstream overnight: the launch in December 1977 of the film *Saturday Night Fever*. Sometimes it takes the distant view from a different culture to capture the universal quality of a scene. Just as The Beatles absorbed American rock 'n' roll and gave it back in a new, more universal form, so Nik Cohn—born in London, brought up in Derry, educated in Newcastle, lived in London—interpreted the Italian disco scene in Bay Ridge, Brooklyn, through his own experience and, astonishingly, turned it into the London Mod scene. *Saturday Night Fever* was based on a piece of reportage called "Tribal Rites of the New Saturday Night," published in *New York* magazine on June 7, 1976. By the time the reader reached the fifth paragraph, it was obvious that what Cohn

Left: The defining image of the movie, the soundtrack, the video, the DVD, the tribute nights.

Stephanie: "Nice move. Did you make it up?" Tony: "Yeah, well, I saw it on the TV first, then I made it up."

Saturday Night Fever

was writing about was not the everyday scene in Bay Ridge, Brooklyn:

"Vincent was the very best dancer in Bay Ridge—the ultimate Face. He owned fourteen floral shirts, five suits, eight pairs of shoes, three overcoats, and had appeared on *American Bandstand*. Sometimes music people came out from Manhattan to watch him, and one man who owned a club on the East Side had even offered him a contract. A hundred dollars a week. Just to dance."

A "Face" was London Mod slang, unknown in Brooklyn. There was a parallel in that the dancers at 2001 Odyssey, like the London mods of the early 1960s, cared passionately about their clothes, but the Brooklyn dancers were, if anything, democratic, communal. There was none of the individualistic virtuoso spins and leaps of dancers who had come to create the "northern soul" scene in the United Kingdom, which is presumably where Cohn took Tony Manero's dance style from. Years later Cohn told the *Guardian*: "My story was a fraud. I'd only recently arrived in New York. Far from being steeped in Brooklyn street life, I hardly knew the place. As for Vincent, my story's hero, he was largely inspired by a Shepherd's Bush mod whom I'd known in the sixties, a one-time king of the Goldhawk Road." He did try to understand what was happening in Brooklyn but couldn't connect with it. He told Steven Kurutz: "I had a few conversations at the club and I couldn't get below the surface. I was out of my depth. It was completely a masculine dominated world. Girls just kind of waited around this dance floor for male pleasures. When the Hustle came on the boys didn't face the girls, they faced forward in a military phalanx." Despite his lack of familiarity with Brooklyn, Cohn knew that he had a good story there. So much so that he gave pre-publication copy of the article to his friend Kevin McCormick, whom he had been working with on a movie project. McCormick gave it to Robert Stigwood, who read it and grabbed the phone to call his lawyer and business partner Freddie Gershon. Anthony Haden-Guest creates the dialogue in *The Last Party*:

ROBERT STIGWOOD: "I see a hundred-million-dollar movie."
FREDDIE GERSHON: "There *are* no hundred-million-dollar movies. You are crazy!"
ROBERT STIGWOOD: "This is a hundred-million-dollar movie. Get the rights."

He got the rights, paying $100,000 for an option. Cohn was offered a crack at the screenplay for $150,000 guaranteed plus, at Nik Cohn's prescient insistence, a percentage of the soundtrack album. Stigwood hired John Avildsen as director after seeing a rough cut of his recently completed movie *Rocky* and recognizing it was going to make a great deal of money. Then, without Cohn knowing, Avildsen hired Norman Wexler to write a script. Stigwood's thoughts turned to casting. Freddie Gershon told Anthony Haden-Guest that he was in the living room of Bungalow Five of the Beverly Hills Hotel when he heard Stigwood screaming in the bedroom, "Quick! Quick!" Stigwood was watching *Welcome Back, Kotter*. Stigwood pointed at John Travolta on the screen. "That's Tony Manero!" he said. Travolta was signed up for a three-movie deal, just like the old days in Hollywood. The day the article came out, Stigwood and Nik Cohn had tea. Travolta was already signed, the movie was already happening.

A Disco Odyssey

THERE were the usual Hollywood problems during the making of what became *Saturday Night Fever*: Cohn's script was dropped, Travolta had to take dancing lessons, and Sylvester Stallone's trainer was brought in to help him lose twenty pounds. The movie was to be shot on location. One of the places under consideration was a huge new disco being built nearby at 254 W. 54th Street, but principal photography was scheduled for January 1977, and Studio 54 was nowhere near ready to be used as a film set. They would have to use the disco that inspired the story: 2001 Odyssey. So Hollywood went to Brooklyn.

The owner of 2001 Odyssey, Chuck Rusinak, told Steven Kurutz, "Two guys from a production company approached us, Milt Felsen and John Nicolella. They said, 'We're going to film a movie on *Saturday Night Fever*. We'd much rather use the original club.' We asked who was in it. Being in the nightclub business, I didn't know who John Travolta was . . . the producers offered us one-tenth of one percent, or a flat rate. We figured we would take a flat rate. I wish I had that one-tenth of one percent."

The huge success of *Rocky* made Avildsen demanding as a director. Robert Stigwood had naturally decided that the soundtrack was going to be by acts that he controlled: everything from "Disco Duck" (*see page 168*), that he'd bought for a mere $3,000, to specially written tracks by the Bee Gees, whom he managed. Just before shooting began Avildsen decided that he didn't want to use the Bee Gees. McCormick told Anthony Haden-Guest that he, Stigwood, and Avildsen had a meeting in the penthouse. Stigwood took a phone call. He turned to Avildsen and told him, "There's good news and bad news. The good news is that you've been nominated for an Academy Award. The bad news is that you're fired."

They quickly hired British-born John Badham, a TV film director whose only motion picture was the 1976 baseball feature called *The Bingo Long Traveling All-Stars and Motor Kings*. Stigwood knew that Badham would do what he asked him to do. Badham was compliant, but Travolta certainly was not. He rewrote his dialogue and, after being forced to take dancing lessons, demanded a dance solo. Stigwood objected but in the end relented, and Travolta's routine, to the Bee Gees' "You Should Be Dancing," turned out to be one of the highlights of the film. Travolta refused to shoot a scripted nude scene, nor would he use a stunt double for the scenes shot on the Verrazano-Narrows Bridge. More seriously, he was in a state of emotional turmoil because his partner, Diana Hyland, was dying of breast cancer. Eventually he had to skip a portion of the principal photography to fly back to California in order to be at her side when she died. This meant that the famous opening sequence of Tony Manero strutting down Ridge Blvd. to the helium vocals of the Bee Gees' "Stayin' Alive" was filmed using his set double, Jeff Zinn. When he returned to Brooklyn, Travolta had to match Zinn's distinctive perambulation for the remaining footage needed to complete the justly famous opening sequence.

> **"The disco community, whatever that was, felt very ambivalent about [Saturday Night Fever]. It brought a lot of attention to disco, it exploded, but once something becomes so big, it has to be over."**
>
> Vince Aletti

Right: John Travolta arriving at the premier of *Saturday Night Fever*, photographed in front of himself as Tony Manero striking the soon-to-be-world-famous pose.

Robert Stigwood got his hundred-million-dollar movie. The film had universal appeal because, as Nik Cohn told Neil Spencer in the *Independent* twenty years later, "I touched on an archetype. Disaffected youth is disaffected youth—that lad standing there in Nowheresville thinking there has to be more to it than this. *Fever* is about that hunger. What was different was that previously people always became rock stars to escape. *Fever* concentrated on tiny stardom, the idea that you could satisfy that hunger on your own turf." Following the enormous success of the movie, there were plenty of people in Brooklyn who claimed to be the *real* Tony Manero. There was one young man called Eugene Robinson who tried to sue Paramount, saying the character was based on him. He walked around 2001 Odyssey wearing a white suit, accompanied by his lawyer, but the hustle didn't come to anything. As Nik Cohn said, "Tony Manero was a complete invention . . . There are models for the characters, but they were West London mods, circa 1965. But anybody who fancied themselves king of the disco for twenty miles around could say, 'They told my story.'" There were plenty of them in discos around the world.

You Should Be Dancing

SATURDAY *Night Fever* sent disco mainstream. All across America and Europe, the metronomic beat of the Bee Gees could be heard as discos opened in their thousands in shopping malls and small towns. And, naturally, as soon as disco was the new "in" thing, all the other record companies rushed to cash in.

The Bee Gees were not your average disco band, though. Born in Malta to British parents and brought up in Australia, the Gibb brothers, Barry, Robin, and Maurice, had been making albums since the early sixties: they had appeared on Australian television shows from 1960 onward and released their first record in 1963. "Spicks and Specks" reached number 1 in Australia in October 1966, just as they were moving back to England. They auditioned for Robert Stigwood in February 1967, who signed them to a five-year contract, and their second British single, "New York Mining Disaster, 1941," entered the UK Top 20. Their first album, *Bee Gees 1st*, reached number 7 in the United States and number 8 in the United Kingdom in 1967. Top 20 songs and albums followed and in 1970 they had their first U.S. number 1 with "How Can You Mend a Broken Heart?" and another in 1975 with "Jive Talkin'," the first time that Barry Gibb had sung falsetto, done at producer Arif Mardin's suggestion. Their next album, *Children of the World*, featured lots more high notes and included the single "You Should Be Dancing" (later included on the *Saturday Night Fever* soundtrack album).

The group had nothing to do with the making of *Saturday Night Fever*; John Travolta was dancing to Stevie Wonder and Boz Scaggs when it was filmed. But Stigwood wanted to keep everything in-house—he had no business interest in either Wonder or Scaggs—and commissioned the Bee Gees to write the songs for the soundtrack. They were already in the Château d'Hérouville, outside Paris—Elton John's "Funky Château"—working on their next album. They wrote the songs "virtually in a single weekend." Essentially, they took the songs they had been working on and used them for the film, losing an album in the process. The result was to change their lives forever.

Three Bee Gees singles, "How Deep Is Your Love?," "Stayin' Alive," and "Night Fever" all reached number 1 in the United States, as well as in many other countries throughout the world. They also wrote "If I Can't Have You," which became a number 1 hit for Yvonne Elliman. *Saturday Night Fever* became the biggest selling album in recording history to that date, selling more than forty million copies, and in April 1978, five songs written by the Gibb brothers

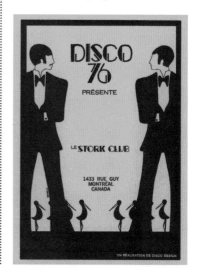

Below: A flyer for an upmarket Canadian disco which, until *Saturday Night Fever*, used an approximation of 1930s-style glamor to sell itself.

April 2, 1979 / $1.25

Newsweek

DISCO TAKES OVER

Donna Summer

Above: When disco went mainstream, Donna Summer was still seen to be the queen of the scene.

Following pages: The *Newsweek* article.

were in the U.S. top 10, tying with The Beatles. Following the movie and sound-track's success disco, which many of the original scenesters thought had run its course, moved from the gay dance underground into the mainstream. The market was swamped with disco records as everyone got in on the act and record companies jostled to cash in on its newfound popularity.

ENTERTAINMENT

Disco hit makers Donna Summer (left), the Village People, Gloria Gaynor an[d]

DISCO

Roll over, rock. Disco is here to stay. Whether they "Do It at the Disco" with Gary's Gang, at the "Y.M.C.A." with the Village People or in "MacArthur Park" with Donna Summer, whether they call it "the weekend two-step," "the bionic boogie" or "le freak," Americans are listening to a different drummer whose message is "shake your booty," "shake your groove thing"—or dance, dance, dance!

Three years ago, disco music was heard only by small urban groups of blacks and Hispanics, homosexuals and Beautiful Insomniacs who turned dozens of off-the-beaten-path discothèques into after-hours shrines. It seemed a good bet that the disco fad would shortly fade, along with platform shoes, pet rocks and the $2 bill. But with the insidious speed of body snatchers, disco has invaded the hearts, minds and feet of all ages and classes. Its method is to reduce melody and lyrics to a minimum and beef up a pounding beat that has the unaccented regularity of a metronome

and the imperative urgency of a war drum.

Disco's ticket to respectability was, of course, last year's smash movie "Saturday Night Fever" and the Bee Gees' all-time best-selling album of the film's sound track. But they simply certified the phenomenon: disco took off—and took over—very nicely on its own. Today, the disco sound has spawned a multibillion-dollar industry.

DISCO PROMS: Billboard magazine estimates that last year 36 million grownups—and not-so-grownups—stepped out on the dance floors of 20,000 clubs, from a spanking $100,000 discothèque in Fennimore, Wis. (population: 1,900), to a bar down the street from the White House called The Buck Stops Here. Discothèques in Detroit and New York open their doors on weekend afternoons to wiggling children. There are disco proms, disco cruises and disco roller-skating rinks; one enterprising club in Dubuque, Iowa, even offers a disco wedding service complete with smoke machine and light effects.

The feverish hustle for new disco products has inspired K Mart stores as well as such *haute-couture* designers as Betsey Johnson and Giorgio Sant'Angelo to bring out their own lines of skintight Lycra jeans, undersize disco bags or disco dresses slit thigh-high. And the beat goes on—into shopping centers and fashion salons via Muzak, into the Steak and Ale restaurants in Atlanta and the dining rooms of New York's Waldorf-Astoria Hotel.

In 1978, disco invaded the home. Now, you can hear Thumpus Uninterruptus virtually nonstop on nearly 200 disco radio stations from Los Angeles to Miami. Television is not far behind. By dialing in such new nationally syndicated dance shows as "Disco Magic" and "Dance Fever," the folks in Cedar Rapids can keep right up with the latest in city shakes and shimmies. Disco has taken over TV's last two strongholds of rock—"Don Kirshner's Rock Concert" and "Midnight Special." Recently, the kinkiest of disco performers, Grace Jones, turned up on the squarest of TV talk

Grace Jones: A multibillion-dollar industry based on a pounding new beat and the public's urge to dance, dance, dance

TAKES OVER

shows. To Merv Griffin's surprise, none of his well-scrubbed, middle-American fans raised a protest when Grace sang "I Need a Man" in a wedding dress exposed to reveal a black garter belt and then playfully turned her leather whip on smiling Merv himself. Disco diplomacy even infiltrated China last December when Chinese guests at the home of a British Embassy official celebrated their country's new ties with the U.S. by doing the Peking hustle.

DRAMATIC TASTE SHIFT: Curiously, nobody has been more surprised by the disco take-over than the major record-company executives. Until recently, they viewed the disco beat as a passing fancy, as dance music by black singers with limited appeal to the white, mainstream pop audience. But suddenly, the handwriting was on the charts: when Billboard magazine toted up last year's top 100 songs, it discovered that 20 per cent of them were disco. Any doubts about its mass acceptance were dispelled when WKTU, a "mellow rock" station in New York City, jumped from relative obscurity to be-

come the most-listened-to station in the country four months after instituting a wall-to-wall disco format. Last month, disco records swept eight of this year's fourteen pop Grammy Awards. "We're going through the most dramatic taste shift in popular-music history," says Rick Stevens, a vice president at Polydor Records. "Disco is the pop music of tomorrow."

Such pop stars of today as the Grateful Dead, Dolly Parton, The Kinks, Paul McCartney, Barry Manilow and Cher are already jumping into the disco pool. Three years ago, jazz flutist Herbie Mann sneered that disco music was "like a porno film [that was] good for five minutes." Two disco hits later, he admits he has changed his tune. "I've come to like pornography," Mann shrugs.

Stewart: Reluctant convert

His current watchword: "Don't let your taste get in the way of reaching a broader audience." Record companies now urge new acts to include at least one disco cut on their albums as a way of getting radio exposure, and disco has revitalized the careers of such fading stars as Peaches and Herb, the Beach Boys and the legendary bluesman B. B. King. "I think in terms of survival," says King.

The most telling sign of disco's power is its effect on two of rock's staunchest loyalists. Last year, the Rolling Stones discovered that a spicy disco single called "Miss You"—a song "disco-fied" by their record-label president without the group's knowledge—could quadruple their album sales by crossing over to the rhythm-and-blues and top-40 charts. The

Roll Baby Roll

WHEN the waiters and busboys at Studio 54 began to use roller skates while working, they were the only ones skating at a disco. Usherettes at drive-in cinemas had used them since the 1950s, likewise waitresses at drive-through diners. Skates (rollerballs at the time) meant that you could move quickly and smoothly through a dancing crowd who were, mostly, static in that they danced in one spot, or a small circle. When dancers saw how fast the busboys at 54 moved, and how they developed "moves" that allowed them to spin, dip, move backwards, and sideways, naturally they also wanted to roller-disco. The craze grew out of the desire to show off and dance. When so many started wearing skates to attend discos, the number of collisions and injuries to dancers increased incrementally. Club owners had to ban them on any but special roller-disco nights, and Studio 54 banned them altogether after Bianca Jagger was left in a cast after a fall in early summer 1979.

Old-fashioned skating rinks that had slowly been going out of fashion in the late 1960s found a whole new life as roller discos. Places like Brooklyn's Empire installed decent sound systems, employed DJs, and instigated a one-way-round-the-floor rule, which helped keep down the number of collisions. One of the first purpose-built roller discos was New York's Roxy, at 515 W. 18th Street, which opened in 1978. The Roxy flourished as both a daytime skating rink and nightclub, and when the disco fad ended, it played a big part in the growth of hip-hop when it hosted MC battle nights, with toasters (soon to be rappers) having turns at the microphone while dancers crowded the floor. The Roxy closed in 2007.

Possibly because clubbers liked to mix dancing with alcohol and drugs, though, roller disco didn't really take long to lose its appeal in the hipper spots. But because it was a popular children's activity, rinks would host roller discos for teens and children too young to get into proper clubs. The fad proved strong enough among teens

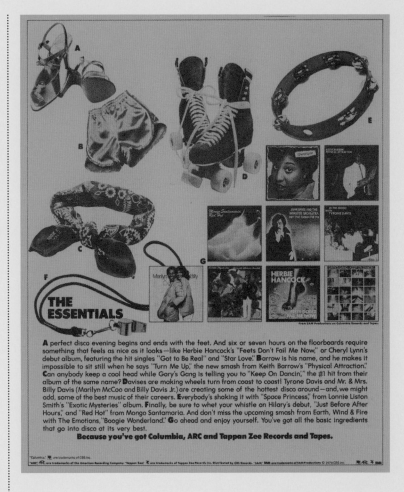

that roller-disco magazines were launched on the back of the 1979 peak in interest in the fad. Celebrities were photographed donning skates to dance at discos from New York to Los Angeles, and there were reports that twenty-eight million Americans had bought a pair by the summer of 1979, according to the July 29 edition of *People* magazine that year, which featured Olivia Newton-John in a white cowboy hat, red blouse, and long white skate boots (plus knee pads). At the end of the decade it seemed as if everyone had gone roller-disco crazy—Hugh Hefner hosted a roller-disco party at the Playboy mansion in November 1979, and an episode of the Scooby Doo cartoon series titled "The Neon Phantom of the Roller Disco" aired in October. Apparently, Jack Nicholson owned a black pair for evening wear.

Christmas 1979 saw the movie *Roller Boogie* open. It was a love story that rolled around Linda Blair (of *Exorcist* fame) and her boyfriend trying to keep their local roller rink open. The soundtrack featured Cher singing "Hell on Wheels" (get it?) and it, like the plot, proved to be prophetic. Released by Casablanca (who else?), the double album soundtrack also included

Left: Roller disco dancers pose for the camera in New York, 1979.

Above: A clever 1978 Columbia Records ad for their disco releases plays on the market for disco paraphernalia, mixing sleeves in with skates and whistle, etc.

WHEELS ON FIRE

By Maryanne Vollers

NEW YORK

VINNIE "VIN-zerilli" Brown would like to put Richard Nixon on a pair of roller skates. In fact, he'd like to strap some wheels onto "everybody who's doing evil in this world and turn them on to the positive energies of roller-disco dancing.

"You see, skating is the ultimate happiness," explains Vin-

zerilli as he demonstrates a toe-wiggling dance step in his bright green skates. "You can't worry about racism or family problems because you're afraid of bustin' your ass on the floor." Vinzerilli knows skating is going to be good for the world, and he knows it's going to be good for him, because the twenty-nine-year-old former family court worker is one of roller disco's most colorful and ambitious performers, and roller disco has become big business.

Most of us remember roller-skating as a squeaky trip down the

sidewalk on clamp-on steel specials, or maybe a Saturday afternoon spin around the local rink with hokey organ music in the background. But these days, legions of teenagers and adults are pouring into rinks that offer flashing disco lights and blaring, pulsing music.

Vinzerilli and partner in full get-up (right); view outside the Empire (below)

In t
the old
have b
disco s
Retaile
sales o
polyu
skates
more a
troduc
cessor
kneepa
skating
with L
Stevie
Queen
"Th
has cha
vice-pr
Skate
est mar
ment.
older c
base."
The
rinks i
date ar
year,
Nearly
effects
of all,
craze st
drome

Left: By 1979 even *Rolling Stone* was writing about Roller Disco.

Earth, Wind & Fire's "Boogie Wonderland" (*see page 189*), and the title theme by Hollywood composer Bob Esty among other, less celebrated tracks. Like the movie, neither Cher's single (highest placing, number 59 on the Hot 100) nor the soundtrack sold well, and that despite Cher making a promotional video for the song in which she roller skates.

Although *Roller Boogie* didn't do well at the box office, it was too late to stop *Xanadu* opening the following year. The film involves a man inspired to open a huge roller disco by a supernatural "muse" who roller skate–disco dances. If only he'd thought of it sooner, and if only the soundtrack had included some disco numbers, rather than just Olivia Newton-John and Electric Light Orchestra songs. But then again, maybe producer Joel Silver saw which way the rollers were headed.

In 1979 *Rolling Stone* magazine devoted a whole issue to disco (only six years after they'd run their first piece about the scene, a long record review column; *see page 103*), and included a spread on roller disco. In it writer Maryanne Vollers concentrated on how disco had "saved" the roller rinks, and made little reference to the music played. It was not just a reflection of the more Rock-oriented magazine's stance, but also a comment on the changing face of American society, equating disco with skating as a fad.

Like any fad, roller disco couldn't last, and like the music, it passed—usurped by a skateboarding fad in the early 1980s. It was fun while it lasted, though, just as long as you could stay upright and moving.

st two years, several of ller-skate distributors to supply rinks with and lighting systems. re reporting increased e new smooth-riding, ane-wheeled roller ced up to $200 and r). Designers have in- nes of roller-disco ac- including sequined nd chiffon tutus. And s gained star appeal, Ronstadt, Joe Walsh, der and even Steve Mc- king up on the trend. nage of roller-skating d," says Joe Shevelson, ent of Chicago Roller pany, the world's larg- cturer of skating equip- co rinks are drawing an now; there's a broader

re about 5000 roller merica that accommo- d 25 million skaters a rding to Shevelson. already have full disco the most famous rink place where the whole d, is the Empire Roller-

As you drive down Empire Boulevard in the Flatbush section of Brooklyn, past Nathan's Famous hot dog stand and a dingy row of warehouses, you can't miss the Empire Rollerdrome's red and green neon sign and the heavy disco bass patterns thumping above the noise of the street. When the door opens, you're clobbered by the full force of the music and the colored lights, sprayed around the room by revolving mirror globes. Before you can even see the skaters, you can pick up the breeze created by dozens of speeding bodies, and with it the odor of sweat and wine and perfume.

As soon as I get inside, I trade in my Pumas for some leather-booted rental skates. I lace them up halfway (I'm told that lacing them to the top is definitely uncool) and wobble over to the guardrail to watch the skaters.

There's Vinzerilli in his daffo-dil-glitter jump suit, skuttle-pumping to the beat up the middle of the rink. Pat the Cat plows along by his side, shooting invisible bad guys with his toy six-guns. Jimmy Jackson and Maurice skate arm in arm, Jersey Bouncing in unison.

"Disco is music for dancing, and people will always want to dance."

Giorgio Moroder

George Clinton: For the Funk of It

Songwriter, band leader, and frontman of Parliament and Funkadelic, George Clinton began his musical career singing doo-wop in the late 1950s. After a spell writing songs at Motown he turned his former doo-wop group Parliament into a funk band by adding some musicians whom he named Funkadelic. Together the singers and musicians created what Clinton termed "P-Funk," mixing rock guitar with soul beats with an extraordinary, visually futuristic look. After eight funk-driven, freeform albums, 1978's *One Nation Under a Groove* made Clinton a disco star.

Left: The Crusaders' break-out album release, the title track of which was a worldwide hit.

Right: Jazz fusion star Grover Washington's fifth album was a laid-back affair.

Funky Fusion

FROM the late 1950s onward, record labels regularly employed musicians to form "house bands" and used them to supply backing for the "stars" of each label: the singers. Some of the musicians had previously been employed in big bands and jazz orchestras; some played jazz music in their downtime. Working jazz musicians picked up un-credited session work at recording studios in New York, L.A., Chicago, Memphis, Miami, and Philadelphia—the Brecker Brothers and David Sanborn supplied horns for Joe Bataan's "The Bottle," for instance, in 1975.

From the 1960s on, some emerging jazz musicians made attempts to move away from the dominant post-bop sound of John Coltrane and Miles Davis and included R&B, Latin, and soul beats in their music. Pianist Les McCann scored an unlikely pop hit in 1969 with a live version of "Compared to What," pushing the live album it was taken from, *Swiss Movement*, into the pop album charts, too. The single featured vocals over an Eddie Harris sax solo and swinging jazz backing and proved very danceable. DJs in the newly emerging clubs found that there were other jazz albums with similarly swinging, danceable, and not too "jazzy" numbers they could spin and keep dancers moving to. "Watermelon Man" from *Taking Off* (1962) and "Cantaloupe Island" from *Empyrean Isles* (1964), both by Herbie Hancock, proved popular, and when Hancock moved from the solely jazz

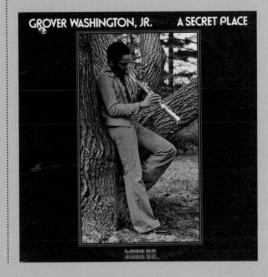

label Blue Note to Atlantic, he began producing soulful jazz, which DJs also loved. "Fat Mama" from *Fat Albert Rotunda* in 1969 was an instant club fave. In 1973 Hancock formed a new band, called The Headhunters, and they produced a classic jazz-funk album titled *Head Hunters* that featured a rerecorded and funkier version of "Watermelon Man" and set the template for other jazz-fusion releases.

Former Blue Note saxophonist Wayne Shorter formed Weather Report with Joe Zawinul in the early 1970s, and in 1974 released *Sweetnighter*, the final track of which, "Non-stop Home," was a true jazz-funk dance number and pointed in the direction the band was to take. They reached full disco fruition with 1977's "Birdland" featuring recently recruited bassist Jaco Pastorius. Former Jazz Messenger Donald Byrd fully embraced jazz funk in the early 1970s with his Blackbyrds (*Street Lady* of 1973 being a stand-out album). Hammond organ player Lonnie Smith and guitarist George Benson produced a great early jazz-fusion album in 1966's *George Benson's Cookbook*, and in the early 1970s Smith began to make jazz-fusion albums as band leader, with 1975's *Afrodesia* being one of the best. Soon a new wave of young jazz artists emerged playing funky jazz, among them Grover Washington Jr., Lonnie Liston Smith, Roy Ayers, Ronnie Laws, Larry Carlton and, although not so young, Ramsey Lewis.

Way of the World

Ramsey Lewis and Larry Carlton had links to two of the most successful jazz-funk or fusion acts of the disco era: Carlton played guitar with The Crusaders (formerly The Jazz Crusaders), and Lewis worked with Maurice White before Earth, Wind & Fire took all of White's time. Having emerged from Houston, Texas, in the early 1960s as the Jazz Crusaders and playing post-bop jazz, Wayne Henderson, Joe Sample, Wilton Felder, and Stix Hooper graduated from pure jazz to a funkier sound in the early 1970s. After adding Carlton and electric bassist "Pops" Popwell, they swiftly became one of the first fusion bands to gain a reputation among club DJs with their blend of soulful jazz and funky grooves. "Put It Where You Want It" (1972), from their second album released as The Crusaders (*Crusaders 1*), was a big dance hit, but "Spiral" (1976) was a bigger disco hit. Featuring Sample's

swirling synthesizer, Carlton's funky guitar, and smooth horns, it was a great portent of things to come, sounding like a prototype of "Street Life," the song that would break the band internationally in 1979. While the album "Spiral" was taken from—*Those Southern Knights*—increased their popularity, it was musically a step further away from what Henderson wanted to play, and he left the band as they began an American tour in support of the Rolling Stones, as did Larry Carlton who signed as a solo artist with WEA in 1977.

Known as an instrumental act until 1979, The Crusaders invited Randy Crawford to sing with them and the resulting album and title track single, "Street Life," made huge stars out of them both. It was an enormous disco hit, and ranks alongside "Young Hearts Run Free" and "I Will Survive" as one of the signature female-sung numbers of the era.

Earth, Wind & Fire began in Chicago where band leader Maurice White was house drummer at Chess Records in the mid-1960s, before becoming an integral part of Ramsey Lewis' jazz trio. In 1969 White formed a band (he was its drumming vocalist) called Salty Peppers, who signed to Capitol, and had a regional hit with "La La Time." After moving to L.A., the band became Earth, Wind & Fire in 1970 and within two years had released two albums and contributed the score to Melvin Van

Below: Earth, Wind & Fire's 1972 issued third album release featured the 8-minute dance floor favorite "Power."

Peebles' seminal movie *Sweet Sweetback's Baadasssss Song*. Earth, Wind & Fire evolved into an eight-piece outfit featuring Ronnie Laws, Maurice's brother Verdine, singers Jessica Cleaves and Philip Bailey, and Larry Dunn. After signing to CBS they released the moderately successful—in sales terms—*Last Days and Time* album. It contained the eight-minutes-plus "Power" which was a dance floor hit.

The band finally broke into the pop charts at the end of 1973 with two singles from their *Head to the Sky* album ("Evil" and the title track). However, it was in 1975 (after Laws' departure and the addition of two other musicians) that Earth, Wind & Fire really made it big, when their "Shining Star" single, taken from *That's the Way of the World*, the soundtrack to a movie of that title, made number 1 on the pop charts.

The album also made the number 1 spot on the pop charts, while two of its tracks— "Africano," which was the B-side of "That's the Way" and "Happy Feelin' (Anatomy of a Groove)"—made the number 1 spot on the disco chart. When the follow-up, double album *Gratitude*, also made the top spot on the pop charts, despite being a live album, Earth, Wind & Fire became a firmly established superstar band.

Between 1975 and 1979 they enjoyed enormous pop and disco hits with, among others, "Sing a Song," "Saturday Nite," "Serpentine Fire," "September," "Boogie Wonderland," and "After the Love Has Gone." They enjoyed hits until 1983 when Maurice "rested" the band to record a solo album. Earth, Wind & Fire reconvened in the 1990s, recording and touring into the second decade of the twenty-first century.

4

Yowsah Yowsah Yowsah!

Disco Underground

DESPITE the disco boom and the commercialization of the music, new clubs continued to open that catered to underground gay disco culture. The early spring of 1977 saw the opening of Paradise Garage at 84 King Street, one block south of Houston Street on the Lower West Side of New York. The Paradise Garage was literally that: a huge concrete truck garage, a discotheque operated by sole owner Michael Brody very much on the classic model introduced by David Mancuso at The Loft. It was a private club with no food or drink, and certainly no alcohol, and so had no need for a liquor license. It was not open to the public. At first Brody could not afford to renovate the whole building, so he began with a series of "construction parties" held in the Grey Room, which would eventually become the entrance area to the club. For the first few months the club was nothing but raw space, with a fantastic DJ in the middle. When the place was finally ready in January 1978, Brody planned a massive A-list party to launch it. But it was a disaster: the sound system, designed by Richard Long, was grounded by bad weather and arrived late. It was an exceptionally cold night, even by New York winter standards, and DJ Larry Levan refused to let anyone in until he had finished setting up the sound system to his liking. Most of the A-listers stormed off, never to be seen again. Michael Brody had to rethink his concept.

When you arrived at the Garage there was a steep ramp leading to the second floor, illuminated only by rows of little red lights. At the top was the Garage logo in neon. The bar was in the enormous parking area, the bleak concrete relieved by immense floor-to-ceiling pornographic murals of Greek and Trojan warriors locked in what Albert Goldman called "sadomasochistic combat." The disco floor was filled with black and Puerto Rican gays, most of them wearing short shorts and muscle shirts. Large handkerchiefs hung from their back pockets, the color and position of which signified the owner's sexual preferences. There were changing rooms; a (non-alcoholic) bar serving free coffee, soft drinks, and fruit and lemon ices in the summer; a chill-out area where movies were shown; and in the summer dancers would sometimes take a break and climb up through the cinema to the enormous roof area, half the size of the club. The roof was lit with colored lights and filled with flowers, and there was even a fountain. It was perfect for embarking on another dance marathon.

But the reason that the Garage is so famous is because it was here that DJ Larry Levan exercised his magic. The club was devoted entirely to picking up sex partners and dancing, and in the center was the high priest, manipulating the atmosphere, reading the crowd, controlling everyone's emotions. Others called him the "puppet master." Levan developed a cult following who referred to his sets as "Saturday Mass." Levan was in a direct lineage of DJs, rather like the transmission of secrets by Tibetan lamas. He told Steven Harvey, "Nicky Siano, David Mancuso, Steve D'Acquisto, and Michael Cappello, David Rodriguez. This is the school of DJs I come from." Nicky Siano and David Mancuso were his main influences, and he had had affairs with both of them. It was a close-knit community, like the Bloomsbury Group or the Surrealists. Levan was a perfectionist; he would sometimes keep people waiting outside until he had changed the EQ levels, or repositioned the speakers, in order to get optimum sound. It was a huge space, holding 2,500 people, yet the sound was crystal clear—and shatteringly loud: Klippschorn speakers, Bozak mixer, and a quartet of JBL tweeter arrays to capture those high notes clearly. He would even change the cartridges in his tonearm throughout the evening, going from a standard model to a $150 Grace near the end of the set.

Chapter opener: Press night at the recently opened Xenon nightclub in New York, 1978. Dancers often wore swimwear for ease of movement—and showing off.

Right: Grace Jones on the cover of the Christmas 1977 edition of *After Dark* magazine, in which you could find the ad below.

AFTER DARK

FANTASY FUN FARE

KENNETH ANGER'S "LUCIFER RISING"

"THE WIZ" AND OTHER FILM FANTASIA

CABARET CAROLERS AND DECKED-OUT HOLLY WOODLAWN

A NEW COLETTE

DISCO SIZZLER GRACE JONES

Disco

by Albert Goldman

Welcome to Paradise

THE club opened at midnight. No one was allowed in after 6:30 a.m. when the doors were closed, and the dancing thundered on until midday or later. It was helped, of course, by drugs. Larry Levan and his close friend Frankie Knuckles had both worked at Nicky Siano's Gallery where their job was to serve the buffet and pop acid tabs into the mouths of clubbers as they arrived. The same happened at the Paradise Garage. For the first three or four years there was acid in the punch: not enough to send anyone on an actual trip, just enough to give them a good time. And after a dozen or more cups through the night, they would be flying high. Like the other clubs, there was also the usual mix of poppers, speed, cocaine, and acid available, with MDA and ecstasy appearing in the early eighties.

There were celebrity visitors to the Garage: Mick Jagger, Stevie Wonder, Boy George, Calvin Klein, Eddie Murphy, Diana Ross . . . but they dressed down, usually turning up in jeans, ready to join the crowd. It was not the same glitzy, showbiz crowd that dressed up to get into Studio 54. At first the Garage only opened on Saturday nights, and in the beginning, Brody tried to make it exclusively gay. After pressure from straight men and women, though, a mixed Friday night was introduced—but Saturday remained the truly wild night. Gaining membership of the Garage was not a simple matter; prospective members were interviewed, but still, lines of hopefuls would form down the block. Levan became a legend—his ability to read a crowd was uncanny, as was his knowledge of his records. He took tremendous risks: he would move from the O'Jays to Yoko Ono and pull it off. He would play the same song three times, or stop a record just before everyone's favorite part came in and then start it again. He was anarchic and often sloppy: his heavy drug use meant that a record would sometimes end, and he would not notice.

Garage music took its name from the Paradise Garage, but for Levan, all music was great: he would play Marianne Faithful and the Clash, Van Halen's "Jump," the Steve Miller Band's "Macho City," and Yazoo's "Situation." He loved reggae and dub, and augmented his sounds using reverb and echo, just like the Jamaican sound system DJs did. Someone once challenged him that he would never play Pat Benatar's "Love Is a Battlefield," but he did, and they loved it. For a decade he was the greatest DJ on Earth, and the Paradise Garage was the best disco on Earth, sticking to the original core values of inclusiveness and equality. It outlived Studio 54 and the death-to-disco movement and only closed when the lease expired. Michael Brody was already weak from AIDS and made no effort to find another space at the time. The club closed on September 26, 1987, with an amazing two-day party. People came from all over the world to attend: graffiti artist Keith Haring, whose work decorated the walls, flew in from Tokyo especially for it. Michael Brody died two months later. Levan died in 1992 and over eight hundred people attended his funeral.

> ## "As a disco DJ the response is immediate. You may drive them off the floor. But it's a wonderful feeling when it works. You get the same gratification as a real performer."
>
> Manny Slali, DJ at Studio One, LA (1979)

Left: Albert Goldman and photographer Sonia Moskowitz produced the first great illustrated (although mostly black-and-white) book about disco in 1978.

Left: Stepping out as Chic, (L–R) Bernard Edwards, Norma Jean Wright, Nile Rodgers, Tony Thompson in 1977.

CHIC was formed by two session musicians, guitarist Nile Rodgers and bassist Bernard Edwards, who first met in New York in 1970. They began making rock music as The Boys and then the Big Apple Band, but had no success because record executives thought that only white musicians could make saleable rock records. Then, in 1977, they brought in drummer Tony Thompson and began to make a living as a cover band. They added singer Norma Jean Wright and recorded a demo tape of their own songs "Dance, Dance, Dance (Yowsah, Yowsah, Yowsah)" and "Everybody Dance," on the strength of which they signed to Atlantic Records. Rodgers and Edwards also began

> "Fifteen years from now, maybe Chic will be thought of as really innovative."
>
> Nile Rodgers (in 1979)

a career as producers, and were delighted when Grace Jones invited them to meet her at Studio 54 on New Year's Eve of 1977–78 to discuss the possibility of them producing her next album. However, when they arrived—Bernard wearing an Armani suit, Nile in a Cerutti jacket, both in black tie and massive afros—it turned out that Grace had forgotten to put them on her list. Doorman Marc Benecke, who normally let them in, was as snotty and difficult as possible and refused them entrance. As the New Year crowd danced to "Dance, Dance, Dance (Yowsah, Yowsah, Yowsah)" they waited outside with the crowd in the falling snow until 1 a.m., in case Grace Jones sent someone to find them. Benecke remained obdurate so Nile and Bernard scored some cocaine and pot, bought champagne, and had their own party at Nile's apartment on

Left: Chic's hugely successful and influential 12" single release of 1979, "Good Times" in a standard Atlantic Records disco sleeve.

Right: The Nile Rodgers and Bernard Edwards-produced Sister Sledge performing live.

nearby 52nd Street. Rodgers told Anthony Haden-Guest: "Bernard and I started jamming, just guitar and bass. We were just yelling obscenities . . . 'Fuck Studio 54 . . . Fuck 'em . . . Fuck off!' . . . And finally it hit Bernard. He said 'Hey Nile! What you're playing sounds really good.'"

They then began to experiment. They changed "Aaaaaaaaah Fuck off" to "Aaaaaaaaa Freak off," but it didn't work. Then it became "Aaaaaaaaah Freak out!" and it jelled. In less than half an hour they had written the biggest song of their lives. "Le Freak" entered the charts on November 18, 1978, and became one of the biggest selling singles of all time, staying at number one for six weeks and selling over six million copies in America alone. In addition, the album it was taken from, *C'est Chic*, which also contained their follow-up single "I Want Your Love," reached number 4 in the charts and topped the R&B charts, selling over a million copies. Chic disbanded in 1980, but Rodgers and Edwards continued to produce hit records: Norma Jean Wright's 1978 album, *Norma Jean*, contained the club hit "Saturday"; the Sister Sledge album *We Are Family* in 1979 contained two Top 10 hits, the title track and "He's the Greatest Dancer," which both made number 1 in the R&B charts; Diana Ross' album *Diana* that contained the chart-topping "Upside Down"; as well as Debbie Harry's solo album *Koo Koo*. After this they went separate ways, with Nile Rodgers producing David Bowie's 1983 *Let's Dance*, and Edwards producing Robert Palmer's 1985 hit *Riptide*. For many people, "We Are Family" was Nile Rodgers' greatest success because it quickly became an all-purpose anthem, used by Black Power activists at demonstrations, by feminists and gay rights demonstrators on marches, as well as by the Pittsburgh Pirates baseball team, who used it as their theme song when they won the 1979 World Series. Rodgers told Peter Shapiro, "When I wrote 'We Are Family' it was a pretty good song to begin with, but when Kathy Sledge came in and heard it for the first time, she got so inspired that her first take was the one that we know and love."

From Xenon to Heaven

■N 1974 there were estimated to be 1,500 discos in America; a year later there were 10,000. By 1978—post-*Saturday Night Fever*—they were impossible to count. Among the most notable was Howard Stein and Peppo Vanini's Xenon, at 124 W. 43rd Street. It opened to a full celebrity A-list in May 1978, but had such technical problems that it closed again until June 7. It was located in the old Henry Miller porno theater and featured a sixteen-channel sound system, said to be the most expensive ever installed in a club and operated by DJs Tony Smith, John "Jellybean" Benitez, Richie Rivera, Bert Bevens, Preston Powell, and Toni "Toni C" Colandreo. There were huge pop art neon tableaux on the walls and also a $100,000 "mother ship" that was supposed to descend from the ceiling

Left: Dancers at Xenon stand
out from the crowd.

Above: A logo for Xenon.

"Disco deserved a better name, a beautiful name because it was a beautiful art form. It made the consumer beautiful. The consumer was the star."

Barry White

and astonish everyone with its whirling mirrored ball. It weighed 7,000 pounds and measured twenty feet across. What they forgot was that in Hollywood, this kind of set only has to work a few times for filming, whereas in a nightclub it has to go up and down several times a night. It never, ever worked properly. Many of the celebrities associated in the public mind with Studio 54 actually spent more time at Xenon, where the atmosphere was less frantic, and they could relax.

In December 1979 London finally got a large-scale gay club, bringing gay culture into the mainstream. It was opened by Jeremy Norman who, in 1978, had previously revived The Embassy, sometimes described as the London equivalent of Studio 54, except with the usual Mayfair emphasis on royalty and fashion: fashion designer Michael Fish was the club's "greeter" and Lady Edith Foxwell its manager—famous for the sex and drugs parties held at Sherston, her country estate. (She was having an affair with Marvin Gaye before he was shot dead by his father.) It was at the height of disco's popularity that Norman decided to open a mainstream gay club, calling it Heaven. It opened in December 1979, in the arches beneath Charing Cross railway station, having previously been the Global Village and later the gay Glades Club in the midseventies. Most recently it had been a roller disco. Until then, gay clubs in London had all been small, discreet, and vulnerable to police harassment and frequent raids.

Heaven was huge (it legally held 1,700 people) and relatively safe from the police because of Norman's background; he was the publisher of *Burke's Peerage, Baronetage & Knightage*, the handbook to Britain's aristocracy, and had many high-level contacts. Despite numerous muck-raking attacks on the club and its clientele by the notoriously reactionary British tabloid press, it survived and in 1982 was bought by Virgin boss Richard Branson who recognized the value in catering to the so-called "pink pound." Many of the best British DJs passed beneath the arches: a former Northern Soul DJ was the first to be hired, followed by Ian Levine, Marc Andrews, Jon Dennis, Marc Monroe, and Wayne G. Live performers included Grace Jones, Eurhythmics, Billie Ray Martin, and Cher. There were evenings featuring gay writers such as William Burroughs, Allen Ginsberg, and Ram Dass. Lady Gaga was a 2009 performer. There were metal walkways surrounding the dance floor, leading to three floors of chill-out rooms, including the "Cruise Bar," where a huge neon star lit the room. The sound system was based on one developed for one of Elton John's tours by Harwell Instruments and incorporated bass horns built right into the floor. Unusual for Britain, there was a $65,000 air-conditioning system. There was a very complicated lighting system involving a 600-square-foot lighting grid, great crystal balls surrounded by neon Saturn rings, and strobes and lasers that followed the dancers' feet as they danced. Heaven opened on December 6, 1979, when DJ David Inches dropped the needle onto Dan Hartman's "Relight My Fire" and London's gay culture came into its own.

Saints

THOUGH there were many gay discos in New York City, there was a need for a truly awesome one that the public could get into, or somewhere membership was at least possible. The answer lay with Bill Graham's old Fillmore East, the classic sixties rock venue that closed its doors in June 1971. This old theater held 2,700 legally, but who was counting? On September 20, 1980, The Saint opened its doors. It was already a success. Saint's owners, Bruce Mailman and his business partner, the designer Charles Terrell, also owned the enormously successful St. Mark's Baths, the center of the downtown gay scene. They distributed membership packs at the Baths and sold 2,500 memberships before they had even opened their doors. The first 700 joined for $150 and the rest paid $250. When it opened there was already a waiting list for membership. But the club cost more than that: it came in $2 million over budget at $4,500,000. The roof needed fixing, no taxes had been paid for six years, and of course it had to be fitted out. Charles Terrell came up with a three-level sex and dance palace. He retained the original lobby and the old marble staircases that rose each side to what was now the dance floor. Leading from the downstairs lobby were several juice bars and a large lounge where people could chill out and make out. Beyond this were the locker rooms, on all three floors, which were rented out to members only for $40 for the season. The dance floor could be accessed from the back of the lounge by two steel mesh spiral staircases. The 4,800-square-foot dance floor was circular, covered by a 38-foot-high planetarium dome, 76 feet wide, that came almost down to the floor and was entered by four doorways. A giant mirror ball could be lowered from the center. In the middle of the dance floor stood a giant, mirrored light tree containing 1,500 bulbs with a rotating hemisphere star projector at its center, ten times brighter than those used in regular planetariums. Hidden behind the dome were 500 speakers, part of the 26,000-watt Graebar Sound system, creating a genuine "surround sound." The dance floor was surrounded by three rows of carpeted bleacher seats and the DJ and lighting booth. Many important DJs occupied these booths in The Saint's eight-year history including Jim Burgess, Roy Thode, Sharon White, and John Ceglia, but the most significant was probably Robbie Leslie, who learned his spinning skills out at the Sandpiper on Fire Island and was responsible for making Jimmy Ruffin's "Hold on to My Love" and "Souvenirs" by Voyage into unofficial Saint club anthems. Also important was Brit Shaun Buchanan who became famous for his "sleaze" sets. On the floor above, surrounding the dome, was the balcony where rough sex was openly practiced as men stared over the balcony to the dance floor below. The Saint was built for sex and music, and when a thousand sweating half-naked men surrounded by 360 degrees of lights and sound were going full blast it was one of the sights of the late twentieth century. Sadly, one of the reasons the club had to close—on May 2, 1988—was something initially known as "Saint's disease," after the club. These buffed, toned, gym-fit young men—mostly white—were among the first to die of the AIDS epidemic that ravaged the New York gay community.

> ## "Too many of these writers in the music papers, they are misunderstanding everything. The disco sound is not art or anything so serious."
>
> Giorgio Moroder

Right: A flyer for gay disco Saint, which opened in the former Fillmore East Theater in 1980.

THE SAINT, THE SPOT

Every Thursday and Friday Night
Dancing, Drinking and Video from 10:00 P.M.

233 East Sixth Street
Just West of Second Avenue

Stayin' Alive

T was arguably the greatest reinvention of a musical act ever. From being lauded in 1967 as the new Beatles and "the most significant new talent" of the year by their hyperbolic manager and would-be musical mogul Robert Stigwood, the Bee Gees were struggling to get singles into the Hot 100 five years later. After enjoying initial success around the world with "New York Mining Disaster 1941" and "To Love Somebody" during the first Summer of Love, the British brothers Gibb, who had been raised in Australia, moved to America's West Coast. They enjoyed several hits throughout the last days of the 1960s and the first two years of the seventies, including "Massachusetts," "Words," "Lonely Days," and "Run to Me" before the hits—and inspiration—dried up. Even Bee Gee Barry Gibb later admitted that "we were virtually dead in the water at that point." Then the head of Atlantic (the U.S. distributor of Stigwood's RSO label) Ahmet Ertegun suggested the brothers try recording some soul songs, and with Arif Mardin producing they came up with *Mr. Natural*, which mixed the sound of Philadelphia horns with rock 'n' roll guitar. It didn't sell well, but was deemed promising enough that a second album with Mardin producing was recorded in the first weeks of 1975. *Main Course* proved to be the turning point in the Bee Gees' career, and helped their reinvention. Mardin encouraged Barry Gibb to sing the whole of "Nights on Broadway" in a peculiarly high, falsetto voice, and to use it as backing for "Jive Talking." The first single from the album, "Jive Talkin'," went to number 1 on the pop charts in the summer of 1975. "Nights on Broadway" made number 7 in September of that year.

The following year, the Bee Gees manager and head of their RSO record label Stigwood demanded that the brothers Gibb contribute tracks to the soundtrack of his new movie, *Saturday Night Fever* (*see page 172*). While the movie had been made with the cast dancing to other disco songs, the Bee Gees' tracks—"Stayin' Alive," "How Deep Is Your Love," "Night Fever," "More than a Woman," and "You Should Be Dancin'"—were written after filming had finished and then dubbed onto the film. The success of the movie and soundtrack album was further enhanced by the Gibb brothers' songs that became hits for other artists, including Tavares's version of "More than a Woman" and Yvonne Elliman's version of "If I Can't Have You." The Bee Gees'

Left: The Bee Gees—reluctant disco knights in silver satin. (L–R) Robin, Barry, Maurice Gibb.

white suits and abundant hair, teeth, and medallions added a whole new look to the disco phenomenon. It was far from original or cool in 1977, but has since unfortunately become the visual shorthand for the crass mainstream appropriation of what had, up to that point, been a hip underground cult.

Dancin' Queen

Just as unhip and decidedly not a part of the original scene, Sweden's pop sensation ABBA were dragged into discos because of their only number 1 pop hit in America, "Dancing Queen." Released at the end of 1976 the song, which co-writers Bjorn Ulvaeus and Benny Andersson based partly on the rhythm section of George McCrae's seminal disco hit of 1974 "Rock Your Baby" (*see page 164*), was an instant hit in Europe, where it was the band's fifth hit release. It took until April 1977 before it reached the peak of the U.S. pop charts, but did so on some extensive club play as well as radio rotation. Renowned "disco mixer" Tom Moulton (*see page 56*) was asked to remix "Dancing Queen," as he later told the Web site disco-disco.com, but apparently felt there was nothing that he could do to make it any better. He told Atlantic Records, "That

record doesn't need me." He went on to say that if he had worked on the multi-track of the single he would have made it "ballsier"; that is, harder and more rhythmically driven. Heard alongside classic disco hits of the day such as Double Exposure's "Ten Percent," The Trammps' "Disco Inferno," or Donna Summer's "Love to Love You Baby," "Dancing Queen" is an odd—and weak—inclusion for any disco compilation. Yet, despite its faults, "Dancing Queen" made ABBA stars in the United States, where "Waterloo," "Fernando," and "Mamma Mia" had failed. The fact that it is a danceable record made all the difference during an era when adopting the disco sound was beginning to make stars out of musical acts who had been trying for years—and ABBA had been releasing singles in America since 1973.

The number of people attending discos had grown enormously by the time *Saturday Night Fever* was released in December 1977. Perhaps If ABBA had managed to get a track onto the soundtrack they would have become much bigger stars in America, where they managed only one more Top 10 hit single ("Take a Chance on Me" in January 1978) and never had a Top 10 album placing.

Above: In hindsight ABBA's "Dancing Queen" has come to be regarded as a great disco track. At the time of release (1976), however, it was considered simply tacky.

Danceteria, FunHouse, & Mudd

THIS was the height of the disco club period, and as mainstream disco became more polyester-clad and plodding, a series of amazing new clubs opened in New York—among them Danceteria and FunHouse—that were more adventurous in their programming. Danceteria was opened by Rudolf Piper and Jim Fouratt in March 1980 at 252 W. 37th Street, but did not survive long. Two years later it reopened at 30 W. 21st Street, the venue that most people associate with the club. It was on three floors, with two dance floors, one of which doubled as a performance space, a video lounge, and restaurant. There was a roof with wonderful views of Manhattan in the summer months, reached by a blue neon-tinted elevator with an operator. At Danceteria they deliberately mixed the downtown avant garde art scene—normally only seen at serious high art venues like The Kitchen—with Latino culture and traditional disco fare, presenting the work of Philip Glass and Glenn Branca alongside Sun Ra, Arthur Russell, and Tito Puente. Jim Fourette told *The New York Times*, "It's all about mixing up these different kinds of people . . . At places like The Kitchen, this work is perceived in a serious, reverential way. At Danceteria, if they like something they cheer; if they don't, they just move on to another floor." The DJs too brought a much wider musical taste to the turntables: Anita Sarko, Johnny Dynell, Bill Bahlman, and Mark Kamins were all familiar with the experimental end of New Wave as well as hip-hop and salsa.

Joe Monk's FunHouse was in a warehouse in the Chelsea neighborhood, at 526 W. 26th Street, between Tenth and Eleventh Avenues. It opened on March 30, 1979, ran until 1985, and is credited as being the birthplace of the electro and break-dance culture, as well as Freestyle. FunHouse was home to DJ John "Jellybean" Benitez, whose combination of disco and hip-hop drew largely Hispanic and Italian-American teenagers from the outer boroughs. There was

Right: Lead singer with Frankie Goes to Hollywood, Holly Johnson at Danceteria in 1984.

Right: Breakdancers pop some moves in and show some key current sartorial styles such as sweatpants, cut-off T-shirts showing bare midriffs, and Chinese slippers. New York, 1983.

a house fashion consisting of sweatpants, cut-off sleeveless T-shirt showing lots of bare midriff, Chinese slippers, and a bandana rolled pencil-thin and tied around the forehead. They were known as "buggas," and the uniform was the same for both boys and girls. One night in 1982, Jellybean's girlfriend persuaded him to play her demo over the sound system. The crowd loved it, and Madonna never looked back. Jellybean went on to produce her track "Holiday."

For some time there had been an alternative club scene, functioning, as Michael Musto called it, as "an amazing antidote to the uptown glitz of Studio 54." This was The Mudd Club, owned by Steve Maas, art curator Diego Cortez, and Anya Phillips. Named after Samuel Alexander Mudd, the doctor who treated John Wilkes Booth after Abraham Lincoln's assassination, it was resolutely downtown, located at 77 White Street and catering to the downtown art crowd. It opened in October 1978 and quickly became the center of New York's underground art and music scene. Talking Heads, Lou Reed, the Ramones, Nico, John Lurie, Lydia Lunch, Kathy Acker, and Glenn O'Brien were all regulars. The club's live music policy centered on New Wave—or No Wave as it was known for a short time—and experimental. The B-52s played their first New York gig there. The DJ was Anita Sarko. But there was also a strong concentration on art, with an ever-changing gallery on the fourth floor curated by graffiti artist Keith Haring, which in turn attracted people like Andy Warhol. As *People* magazine reported: "New York's fly-by-night crowd of punks, posers, and the ultra-hip has discovered new turf on which to flaunt its manic chic. It is The Mudd Club. . . . For sheer kinkiness, there has been nothing like it since the cabaret scene in 1920s Berlin." Like CBGBs, the club had gender-neutral bathrooms, which were crowded with people taking drugs. The door policy was to let in strung-out punks and turn away celebrities. It closed in 1982.

COY
DISCO KID

Get Dancin'!

THE conventions of nightclub dancing had grown out of the first wave of clubs that flourished in the 1920s in America. The Black Bottom, Charleston, and the Shimmy had firmly prescribed steps to follow and everyone did, wobbling their knees and shaking their butts in tandem with a partner. Similarly, in the following decades, as those who could afford it spent evenings dancing and dining, dance steps were formally taught and involved touching your partner—and mostly holding them firmly: the waltz, polka, two-step, and

> ### "The Hustle is an intricate dance. It's more of a ballroom dance than a disco bump thing. There's so much diversification going on that it brings back partner dancing."
>
> Van McCoy

foxtrot mutated into the cha-cha and, when a South American flavor caught the mood of orchestra and band leaders, the tango, mambo, and salsa became popular. Even after rock 'n' roll hit there were formal steps to be learned for the correct way to jive, and then the Twist, the Pony, the Monkey, the Shag, The Hully Gully, and other similarly themed steps evolved from soul and R&B clubs of the 1960s. Until the mid-1960s all dancing pretty much involved dancing with a partner, which meant girlfriends danced together if there were no male partners to be found or to be induced onto the floor from among those men who stood around

Left: Van McCoy's massive, international hit reintroduced to clubs the idea of people dancing with one another rather than separately.

watching and drinking at clubs and bars. (Male-only dancing was confined to private members-only gay clubs in the main.)

When LSD, marijuana, and the whole hippie-psychedelic culture turned dancers' focus inward, dancing solo became the norm, even for people who didn't want to "turn on, tune in, drop out." Since the "tuning in" became a matter of hipness among the predominantly white population, by the time that disco began its inexorable rise, the dance steps that had evolved naturally among the working class and newly emerging black middle class of America were there to be discovered, just as they had been in the early 1960s when Motown, Stax, Sue, Chess, and assorted other soul and R&B labels issued vinyl singles encouraging listeners to do a dance with a great name.

One of the simplest contact dances to be seen in the early days of disco was "The Bump," in which partners bump hips, thighs, and bottoms together in time to the music. In 1975 veteran Memphis soul legend Rufus Thomas—who made his name with the dance step anthem "Walking the Dog" in 1963—had a minor hit with "Do the Double Bump," but by far the biggest hit for the dance-step came in 1977 when Joe Tex (not to be confused with Disco-Tex and the Sex-O-Lettes) scored a number 12 pop chart hit with "Ain't Gonna Bump No More (With No Big Fat Woman)."

The Body Language

Fittingly it was the small Avco label of New York that issued the first major disco dance-step instructional single: "The Hustle," by veteran soul songwriter and producer Van McCoy. Released in 1975 and credited to McCoy and his Soul City Orchestra, the song—which became an international number 1 pop hit—had been written after he watched dancers at the Big Apple nightclub in New York doing a line dance known as the Hustle. McCoy's opportunism paid off big time, and the subsequent largely instrumental album that included "The Hustle," titled *Disco Baby*, also became an international hit. Following hot on the stacked heels of McCoy's dance-inspired song was the Fatback Band's "(Are You Ready to Do) The Bus Stop," another line dance in which dancers take steps back, clap, and step forward; the single was an international dance hit. In 1976 the Fatback Band—a great New York instrumental funk

act who scored dance hits with, among others, "Street Dance" in 1973, "Keep on Steppin'" in 1974, and "Yum Yum (Gimme Some)" in 1975—released another version of the dance song with "(Do the) Spanish Hustle" in 1976. It proved to be one of many derivations of the step that became ubiquitous at discos around the world following John Travolta's showcasing the steps in *Saturday Night Fever*.

After choreographer Lester Wilson had finished with John Travolta, he was almost a better dancer than he was an actor. A former pupil of the great jazz choreographer Bob Fosse (famous for choreographing *Sweet Charity*, his biopic is titled *All That Jazz*), Wilson toured New York and L.A. nightclubs gaining the knowledge of how dancers were performing on dance floors alone, in lines, and with partners. He then reinterpreted—or mimicked—the steps for Travolta and the rest of the cast. Following the movie's huge success there was naturally a demand for dance classes everywhere, and instructors learned the names—or invented them—and the steps that went with them.

In 1978 L.A.-based dance instructor Karen Lustgarten published the first and most successful disco dance manual, titled *The Complete Guide to Disco Dancing*. It featured no less than six variants on the Hustle (including the intriguingly titled Lust Hustle), and moved pupils from preparing their body for "the disco dance experience" through the "Disco Dynosoar," the "Roller Coaster," "Special K," "Sway and Swirl," and "Jackson 5 Shuffle" before tackling the "City Swirl," "Night Fever," "Turning Point," and "Breakdown Hips," and then graduating to the various Hustles. Among the main section headings are "Line Dances" and "Partner Disco Dances," which highlighted the fact that, after a decade of solo, free-form dancing in clubs being the norm, an element of social interaction had returned to the dance scene—although it was to prove short-lived.

However, while the contact, partner-dance craze swept the floors of discos around the world in the wake of *Saturday Night Fever*, in the hip clubs and bars where disco music didn't involve white men in white suits singing in falsetto voices, dancing retained an edge of individuality. When Chic (see *page 197*) hit the number 1 spot in December 1978 with "Le Freak," the song caused a dance revolution.

Right: *Rolling Stone* magazine gets down on the dance floor in 1975.

THE GROUP-GROPE, SNAKE-DANCING BUTTERMILK MACHINE... ...CHURNS ITS WAY DOWN THESE MEAN RECESSION S

DANCING MADNESS

IN WHICH A SUBURBAN PROLE DECADENT DOES BATTLE WITH A HOT MIDTOWN MANHATTAN DISCOTHEQUE—TWO OUT OF THREE FALLS, NO CURFEW

By Ed McCormack

New York—"Never go to Le Jardin on the weekends," say the jaded, hipper-than-thou Wednesday night regulars—the boys who cut hair at Cinandre and the girls who readily confess to being "professional fag hags." After all, that's when all the novice prole decadents in platform heels and marshmallow clodhoppers come pouring in from the suburbs like some raging epidemic, and you need a tube of K-Y jelly to ooze into the penthouse-bound elevator of the gone-to-seed Diplomat Hotel on Manhattan's West 43rd Street. "Forget about the dance floor, honey," they warn, unless you're willing to risk the pumping, thumping, gang-banging glitter trash and hoi polloi who think that true art deco decadence can be purchased at the closest unisex boutique. "Believe me, baby," they advise, "your best bet is to try to talk your way into one of the private clubs"—because, they feel, even on these Wednesday nights the commuters from the outer boroughs have you surrounded, and no matter that Barry White is breathing in your ear like an obscene phone caller turned up to 110 decibels.

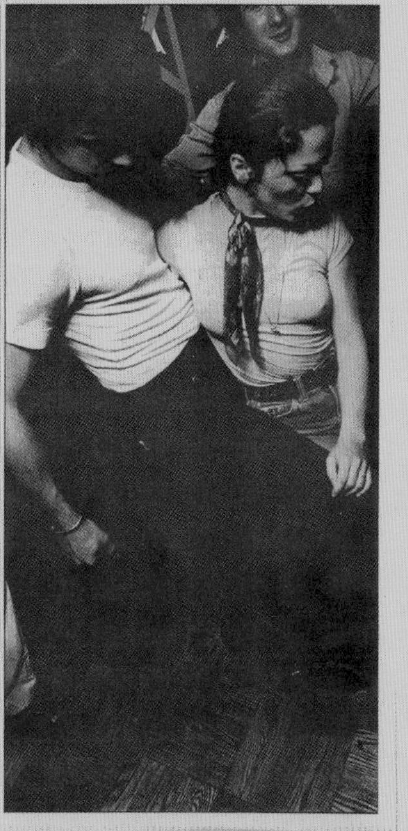

But if you chance the elevator's housing-project urine-odor ride upstairs and pay your $6 ($2 more if you're unhip enough to attend on weekends), you enter a totally other environment, the kind of place that Truman Capote gushingly told a chin-in-hand Johnny Carson, has "these art deco couches all along the room, these palm fronds drooping down everywhere—and out on the dance floor this terrible churning, the whole place churning like a . . . buttermilk machine." At Le Jardin, the music commands a snaking daisy chain of dancers through pelvic puppet paces as the atmosphere grows heady with the adrenalin incense of Brut cologne and a thousand amyl nitrate poppers, each lending its queasy aphrodisiac rush to the whole mind-boggling, switch-hitting group grope going on out there on the floor. After all, this is the place where the gamut of dress runs from Pierre Cardin suits to silver cosmic clothing, from Halston originals to backless halters, through all the shades, cycles and fetishes of chic, camp and queer, until it culminates in the truly bizarre ensemble of one muscular young madman who sports a leather aviator's cap, smoked Captain Midnight goggles and red plastic clothespins clamped onto his bare nipples, squeezing them out into two little ouch-drops of excruciating S&M ecstasy while he goes limpidly gazonkers out on the dance floor.

The crowd at Le Jardin is a mix of jaded Manhattan scenemakers like Hollywood DiRusso, a publicist in the New York office of famous Mod fashion figure Mary Quant, who checks out the disco action as soon as business takes her to a new city; mucho macho types like lightweight contender Chu Chu Malave, the Puerto Rican Mick Jagger of pugilism, who can frequently be spotted going through some Rudy Nureyev moves with his girlfriend, German model Uschi Odermier; boys who affect the smug upwardly mobile suave of Geraldo Rivera and girls who look like Carmen Miranda as drawn by *Interview* illustrator David Croyland and shake a spacey spice into the sometimes predictable syncopations of Soul Dancing; David Jo Hansen, former lead singer of the New York Dolls; Cyrinda Foxx, platinum-tressed sweater-girl starlet of the Seventies; Arthur Bell, who introduced gay activism to the New Journalism; and the members of a prole decadent generation weaned on cave-chested, Beardsleyesque Englishmen who shook their satin little buns like the swishiest of queens while bellowing as though the testicles of Muddy Waters had been grafted where their tonsils used to be, and who now find their way here, even on Wednesday evenings.

Take a kid like Tony Pagano, from Dongan Hills, Staten Island. They have more Civil Service people, minor Mafioso and beat cops per square inch in Tony Pagano's home borough than in a 300-page Jimmy Breslin novel. These folks, mostly Irish and Italian drinking-class people, take a certain pride in having provided their offspring with modest, pastoral preserves that feature plaster saints on the mantle and pink flamingos on the lawn; you can imagine what Tony's poor parents must think when he puts on his Lou Reed T-shirt, his Mick Jagger pajama bottoms and his corkscrew wedgie sandals and lights out for 43rd Street.

"What my old man doesn't understand is that you don't have to be a fag to be into this scene," Tony says as he sips a tequila sunrise at the big, white leather bar behind which guys in basketball uniforms bound back and forth filling orders for drinks (the first test for the hetero male who wishes to be in tune with at least the basics of bisexual chic is to not feel threatened when addressed as "baby" rather than "sir"). "My old man doesn't understand that dancing is not a tight-assed, uptight sex role scene. It's just a way of communicating with people you might not have anything to say to if you sat down to talk. It doesn't mean you want to fuck a broad or a guy if you dance with them. You're just doing what comes natural."

But not to some. Le Jardin was "une discothèque pour monsieur" when it opened four or five years ago, and it stayed that way until Steve Ostrow, one of the more visionary gay entrepreneurs, came to terms with the specter of bisexual chic and set a precedent by opening his Continental Baths to women. Even today, this New Chicness remains as puzzling to older gays as it does to older straights. One vested, white-suited, Carl

[Continued on 60]

Ed McCormack is currently working on a book, 'New York Satyricon.'

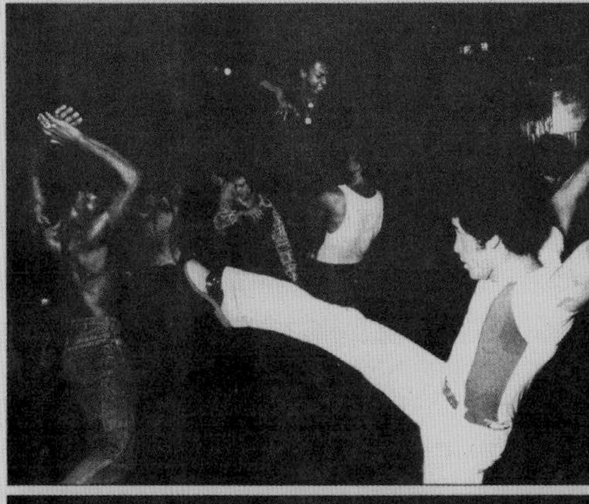

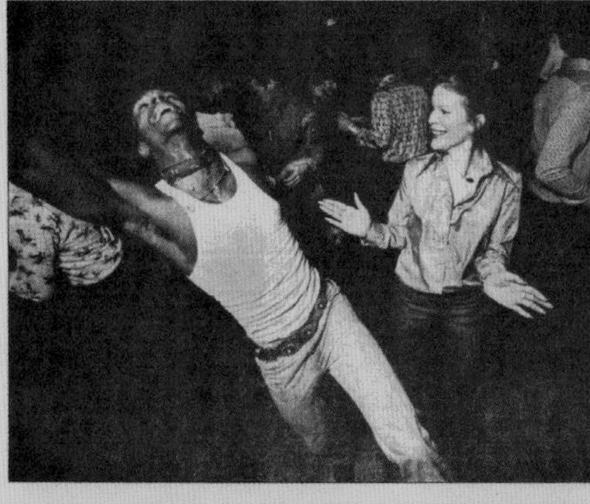

DISCO MADNESS ANALYZED . . . THE DISCO SOUND REVEALED . . . TRENDY PLATTERS

By Vince Aletti

NEW YORK—It's not easy to pin down the disco craze with figures. As one independent mixer of disco singles explained, "The numbers are growing so fast. Every day I get four or five invitations to grand openings of new clubs." But even the rough estimates of disco scene observers are revealing: 2000 discos from coast to coast, 200 to 300 in New York alone—the uncrowned capital of dancing madness, where an estimated 200,000 dancers make the weekly club pilgrimage. And when disco people like a record, it can become a hit—regardless of radio play. Take Consumer Rapport's "Ease On down the Road." Released on tiny Wing and a Prayer Records, it sold more than 100,000 copies in New York in its first two weeks before it was picked up on the radio.

Discos and what has come to be known as disco music have turned out to be, if not the Next Big Thing everyone in the music business was waiting for, then the closest thing to it in years. Discos have opened in old warehouses, steak restaurants, unused hotel ballrooms and singles bars . . . any place you could stick a ceiling full of flashing, colored lights, a mirrored ball, two turntables, a battery of speakers, a mixer and a DJ. In a recession economy, they're a bargain both for the club owner—who has few expenses after his initial setup investment and an average $50-a-night salary to the DJ—and the patrons, who can dance nonstop all night for a fraction of the cost of a concert ticket.

But the spread of disco music, especially in the last year and a half, has outpaced even the growth of discos themselves. Though the new disco music evolved from the hard dance records of the Sixties—primarily Motown and James Brown—the direction has been away from the basic, hard-edged brassy style and toward a sound that is more complex, polished and sweet. If one style dominates now, it's the Philadelphia Sound, which is rich and elegant, highly sophisticated and

Vince Aletti began cataloging the disco scene for ROLLING STONE *in 1973.*

tightly struc punch. The ducers are th strings energ well as softer and they've p sound with the Blue No Trammps, th and Blue Ma and the oth working out excelled in k lyrically sha while much has reduced words or sim co music nov different per Jackson 5 t and so man tied together ent danceable nition has to

The discos fluence on n length of rec co music is f breaks, whic shifts of mo one song an long instrum the break wo pivot and ar the song—lik and gradual by instrume dricks's "C Change of M the best da made. It's ha fective build short record. is tight and texture of th diverting, a s ten minutes, mood on da

So "disco mix" means record is lon released for it may also r specifically ter," brighter are much mo the technica ords they pl counterpart erwise danc cause of the mix or their at high volu for quality Both Atlanti put selected inch discs at production a

AT LAST, A PERFECT ANTHEM FOR THE FIVE BOROUGHS

In New York, dancers get all decked out in fancy dresses and expensive suits to do the Hustle. You can wear anything you want, but it should be either highly absorbent or well ventilated because you're going to sweat a lot.

We're presenting one of several versions of the New York Hustle. Different and more complicated versions exist, and about all that's agreed upon is that the N.Y. Hustle is done with a partner in the Social Dance Position. This may have been before your time: The man and woman (or any modern combination) face each other, the woman's left hand resting on the man's right shoulder, the man's right hand on her waist. Their other hands are extended to the side and clasped. This is just the starting point, but the constant factor will be that your extended hands remain clasped.

The version we present is similar to the Swing or Lindy, except the rhythm is slow-quick-quick. The basic step is a triplet or three-step combination. Standing with feet apart, the woman would begin by stepping on the right foot; touch the ball of the left foot behind the right foot; and step again on the right foot. In four counts, that would be right-pause-left-right or step-pause-step-step. That's one triplet. The directions should be reversed for the man (i.e., left-pause-right-left) since he is facing the woman, so they're both moving in the same direction. Then the triplet is repeated in reverse, with the woman stepping on the left foot, touching the ball of the right foot behind the left and stepping again on the left foot in place. That's the basic step, the foot story. Regardless of what you're doing with your arms and body, turning, rocking back and forth, flipping your partner over your back, your feet maintain this two-triplet pattern.

There are a couple of corollaries to this. If you forget what your feet are doing while you're executing a turn, you'll be stepping all over your partner when you return to the normal position. Then you'll have to stop feet while you try to get the step again, and the humiliation will be unbearable. Also, turns, twists, etc., must be carefully timed so that when you end up in the normal position facing your partner, you will still be moving in unison. This you'll have to work out by practice because, frankly, it's too complicated to explain.

Unlike the L.A. Hustle (see next page), there is no set pattern of steps other than the basic triplets. The movements illustrated here are classic movements of the Very Hip, but you don't have to do them in order and you can and should add your own variations.

Loosen up by getting in the Social Position and rocking toward your extended hands for the first triplet (1), then second triplet (2). Repeat this entire pattern from one to 20 times or until you finally catch on (3 and 4). Get ready to release the shoulder-and-waist hands, to draw back from your partner for a turn, keeping the extended hands together.

To turn, the man lifts his left arm for the woman to pass under (5). Then the woman has miraculously passed under (6). She continues turning around (7), ultimately facing her partner again (8). This whole turn should take two triplets. Her partner, obviously, has continued dancing in triplets while she has been turning, and since she has made the turn doing an even number of triplets, they are again moving from side to side going in opposite directions. For dummies, this means that if you do the turn in three triplets, you're going to be screwed up when you face your partner again. Do it in increments of two. Those with a vivid imagination will also realize that the man can do a turn instead of the woman. When the turn is completed, return to steps 1 through 4.

Onward to the double turn, where both partners go under the arms at the same time. On the triplet where you would ordinarily be rocking forward, raise the extended arms (9), allowing both partners to go under (10), rotating until you face completely away from each other (11) and continuing around to a

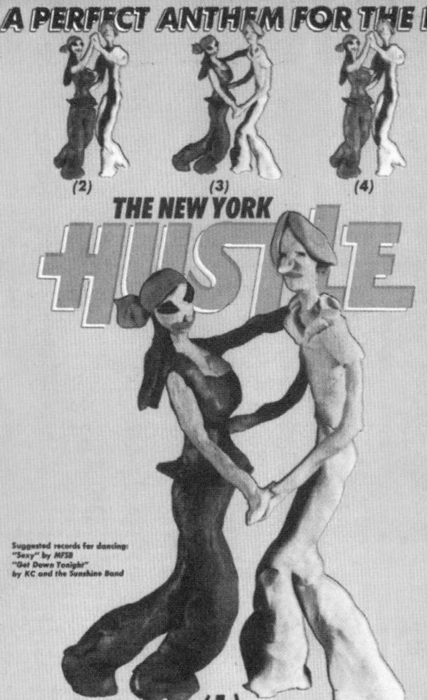

Suggested records for dancing: "Sexy" by MFSB "Get Down Tonight" by KC and the Sunshine Band

Again, this should take two or four (or six, etc.) triplets. A snazzy variation on this is to keep ahold of both pairs of hands (13) and do a double turn without releasing your hands. This may land one of you with a dislocated shoulder.

Now, for a peaceful interlude, keep doing the triplets, facing your partner with one hand still clasped, rocking subtly side to side and wondering what to do next (14). Gradually exaggerate this motion until you are rocking, facing the clasped hands (15). When you are facing your right arm, you should be leading the triplet with your right foot. On the second triplet, the partners turn away from the clasped hands (16). Try it a couple of times. Then take your partner's other hand, bop style, and stretch away from your partner (17) before coming together with both hands still clasped. This pattern can be repeated until you're bored and ready to move on.

Here's a tricky step, in which the woman should find herself leaning back against the man with her arms crossed strait-jacket style. Beginning with both pairs of hands clasped, bring one pair of hands up. The woman will turn in toward her partner (18) as she passes under her partner's arm (19). If you've made it this far without letting go, the woman has her back to the man. They then lower their clasped hands in front of her (20) so that her arms are crossed, his are around her and they are still holding hands (21), rocking back and forth. If you are facile enough to get yourselves into this, you can bloody well get yourselves out of it and back to a somewhat normal position (22), after which you will probably be content to assume once again the Social Dance Position (23)

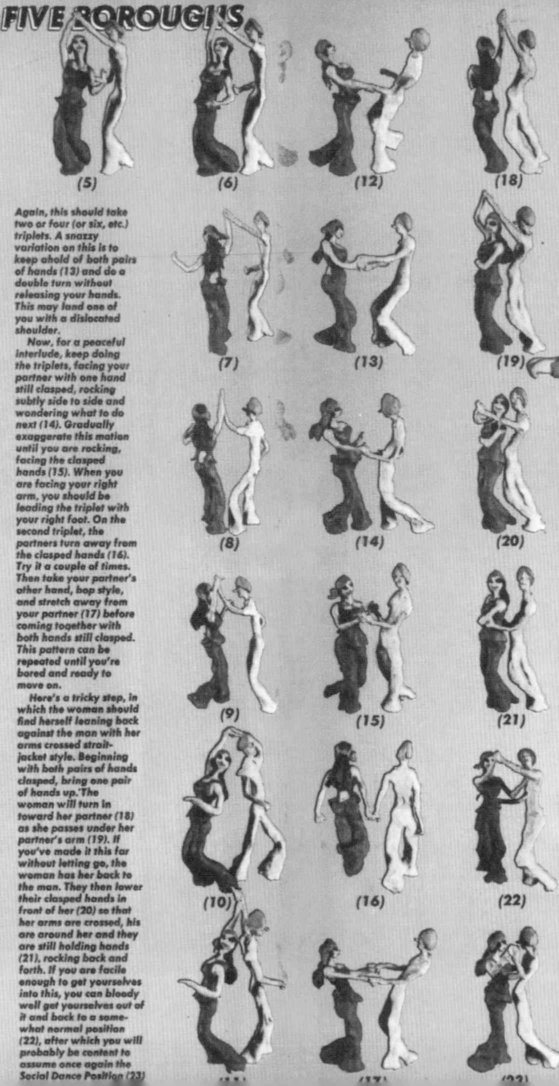

WHAT HAS FOUR HIPS AND GRIN

The idea is to bump against your partner on the onbeat and swing around or away from your partner on the offbeat.

There are no "steps": The feet are comfortably separated and pretty stationary, except when you need to move them to turn or keep your balance. The knees should be bent, the parts of the body not bumping should swing in the opposite direction from the part that's bumping, the whole body should be loose as a goose and it helps to be drunk. Only by coincidence should you be bumping with the same thing your partner bumps with, but for the sake of simplicity we've begun this sequence with both partners bumping the same thing in unison. Position "X" indicates the swing away from the partner that comes after each bump; hopefully, it will encourage your natural sense of rhythm.

Okay, let's begin with hip bumping. With knees slightly bent, bump hips (1), swinging arms and torso away from partner. You can also bend your knees deeply and bump hips low (2). Another variation of hip bumping is back to back (3), sticking your ass out behind you toward your partner, and throwing your arms out in front of you. If you don't feel stupid doing this, then you're not doing it right.

Then, of course, you can bump shoulders (4), elbows (5) or knees (6 and 7). Knees should be bumped (a better term might be brushed) on the outside of the knee—actually the outside of the thigh—rather than head-on, in order to avoid painful accidents. When bumping your knee, throw your arms back.

If you want to vary things a bit, surprise your spinning around on the offbeat and bumping his or her hip with your shoulder (8). Try turning around a lot (don't worry about how you make the turn) and bump whatever is handy when you get there.

You're probably wondering by now why you've heard this is a dirty dance. That's because there are more body parts than we've mentioned so far. One variation of the hip bump (9) ought to set your mind at rest. Again, don't expect always to bump the same parts as your partner—sometimes he or she won't even have one (10). But that can work both ways.

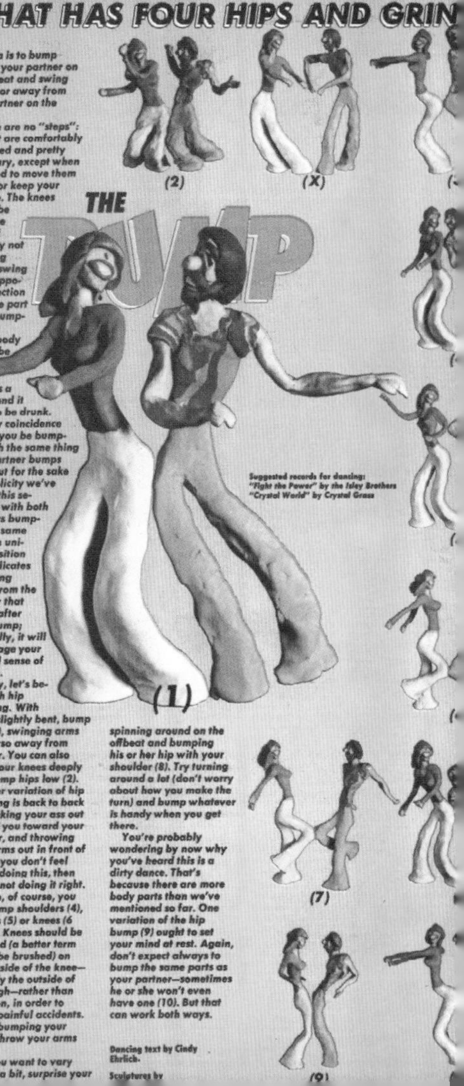

Suggested records for dancing: "Fight the Power" by the Isley Brothers "Crystal World" by Crystal Grass

Dancing text by Cindy Ehrlich.

Sculptures by

In the Area

ICKING up where Steve Maas left off, Area opened in September 1983 at 157 Hudson Street, downtown. It was opened by four Californians: Eric and Christopher Goode, Shawn Hausman, and Darius Azari, who only intended to keep it open for two years. Area was a 13,000-square-foot space housed in an 1866 redbrick former stable block, and for a few years it was one of the hottest clubs in New York. It had three bars, a swimming pool, and a tank filled with real live sharks. There was a large dance floor and a long, glass-topped silver bar. The sound system was by Kenny Powers, of Richard Long Associates, operated by Johnny Dynell and Anita Sarko, both from Danceteria. But though the music was important, the art was even more so. Eric Goode—now owner of the Bowery Bar—told Glenn O'Brien, "Area was purely visual. It was based on 'happenings,' on what Allan Kaprow and Jim Dine and Claes Oldenburg did." Their approach could be seen from day one: for people on their mailing list, the club's opening was announced by a pharmaceutical capsule, housed in a jeweler's box together with instructions to "Place capsule in glass of hot water and allow to dissolve," revealing the

Left: Area was where Art came to dance and to pee in homage to Marcel Duchamp, underneath Chuck Close's painting.

R. COURI HAY

INVITES YOU TO WELCOME

Colette

BACK FROM BERLIN

(POST OPENING PARTY IN HONOR
OF HER EXHIBITION AT THE
DANIEL NEWBURG GALLERY

THURSDAY, JANUARY 9, 1986
OPEN BAR 10 — 12 PM

DRESS ARTISTICALLY

A R E A

157 HUDSON ST. • N.Y.C. • 226-8423

PRESENTED BY ALAN RISH

PHOTO: "FROM SILK TO MARBLE" ©COLETTE 83   PHOTO: T. GUDNASSON

**Above: An invite to an arty
party at Area, 1985.**

message. Their "Suburbia" installation was announced by a slice of plastic-looking Velveeta processed cheese. The installation itself incorporated more than one hundred boxes of cereal, pink plastic flamingoes, astro turf, cleansing products, and an oak-veneer bedroom suite. The invite for "Disco" was on a record, and "Confinement" was announced by a Chinese finger trap. Jennifer Goode, sister of Eric and Christopher, was responsible for the club's themes, which changed every six weeks or so. One of the most elaborate invitations was for "Gnarly," which came in a corrugated box containing a mousetrap. When the box was opened the mousetrap was set off, smashing an ammonia capsule. The U.S. Post Office had a few things to say about that one, not all of them complimentary. They invited real bikers to the club for "Gnarly," because everything had to be as authentic as possible. They came with their own naked "old lady" and enjoyed the attention—surrounded by monster trucks, a skateboard ramp, a speedboat in the pool, and a strobe-lit electric chair. For their "Sex" theme they had real perverts.

Another time David Hockney flew to New York to supervise the pool, and Andy Warhol was part of an art installation. The long hallway leading to the dance floor had large window displays on each side, like a shopping arcade or a zoo. In one sat Andy, in his fright wig, absolutely still, while everyone wondered if it was really him or just a wax model. Then he blinked. Keith Haring painted on the walls and floor. The bathrooms were huge and acted like a VIP room. Photographer Stephan Lupino set up a studio there and photographed people naked, while Chuck Close exhibited his notorious big penis painting there. One of the waitresses, Karen Finlay, first performed her signature act in which she stripped naked and did unusual things with canned yams. Artists loved Area and it was not unusual to find Jean-Michel Basquiat as temporary DJ, spinning his favorite cuts by Miles Davis, Charlie Parker, and Duke Ellington. After twenty-five different and very costly installations, the club closed early in 1987.

Disco Movies

WHILE *Saturday Night Fever* continues to stand stack-heeled and flared-trousered above the genre, there are other disco movies of note—and some were even made before *Saturday Night Fever*. The first movie to earn the respect of disco dancers was *Car Wash*. Not because of what happened on screen, which was a mish-mash of set pieces revolving around a car wash (naturally), its staff, and oddball customers, but because of its soundtrack. Written and produced by former Motown writer/producer Norman Whitfield, the title track was an international number 1 hit for Rose Royce, an L.A.-based funk band fronted by Gwen Dickie aka Rose Norwalt. Released in the fall of 1976, both movie and single did well, but long after the theaters stopped playing the film, Rose Royce enjoyed hits from the soundtrack album, including "I Wanna Get Next to You" (number 10 pop hit in 1977) and "I'm Going Down" (number 10 R&B hit) the same year.

Somewhat different in content to *Car Wash*, the movie adaptation of Judith Rossner's best-selling novel *Looking for*

Mr. Goodbar didn't get people doing the Hustle, but the movie soundtrack is a fantastic disco taster for 1977. Songs include Boz Scaggs' "Lowdown," the O'Jays' "Backstabbers," Donna Summer's "Prelude to Love/Could it Be Magic," and the Commodores' "Machine Gun" among others. They provide the aural background to the story of a schoolteacher (played by Diane Keaton) searching for the perfect man among New York's clubs and bars. Like *Cruising* (1980), starring Al Pacino, the disturbing story finds a perfect setting among the nightlife of the day. Pacino plays a straight cop who goes undercover as a gay man cruising bars in order to catch a serial killer who picks up his victims in the bars and clubs of New York. The soundtrack album for *Cruising* is not filled with disco classics, however, favoring instead the junkie strut of Mink DeVille and post-punk band The Germs.

As disco became a social phenomenon and familiar place of entertainment for much of the Western world, so more and more movies had scenes set in clubs, and more movies included disco tracks on their soundtrack. Three Jackie Collins novels were made into movies between 1978 and 1980 that exploited the disco boom: *The Stud* and *The Bitch* both "starred" Joan Collins (the latter as an owner of a disco), while *The World Is Full of Married Men* starred Anthony Franciosa and Carroll

Below: A scene from the Village People movie *Can't Stop the Music*, 1980.

Baker, although its soundtrack out-grossed the movie. A double collection, it's a veritable best-of-disco, including "Shame" by Evelyn Champagne King, "Take That to the Bank" by Shalamar (the act who invented the moonwalk), "You Make Me Feel Mighty Real" by Sylvester (*see page 230*), "Copacabana" by Barry Manilow, and the title track by Bonnie Tyler. Both *The Stud* and *The Bitch* were similarly supported by a best-of-disco soundtrack, the former featuring Odyssey's "Native New Yorker" to great effect, the latter using Gloria Gaynor's "I Will Survive" and Gonzales' "I Haven't Stopped Dancing Yet." In both cases the soundtrack compilations were far better than the movies they were named after.

Thank God . . .

Post-*Saturday Night Fever*, there were attempts to emulate its success by slightly reworking the idea, none too successfully. *Xanadu* and *Roller Boogie* (*see pages 181, 183*) slipped by painlessly enough, but *Van Nuys Boulevard* (1979) barely left the blocks, thankfully. The soundtrack didn't include any original disco hits but pale imitations with titles such as "Discoliope" and "Boogie on Down the Boulevard," instead. Since the movie was about cars you'd have hoped for some decent upbeat tunes, but there were few to relieve the tedium. A year later, the German-American co-production titled *The Apple* (aka *Star Rock*) was set in the music business of the future (1994). Judging by the soundtrack it sounded a lot like things hadn't progressed past disco—but then, why would they? The songs were written for the movie and sung by the cast, none of whom you'd ever heard of. Naturally the movie now has a cult following—it's that bad.

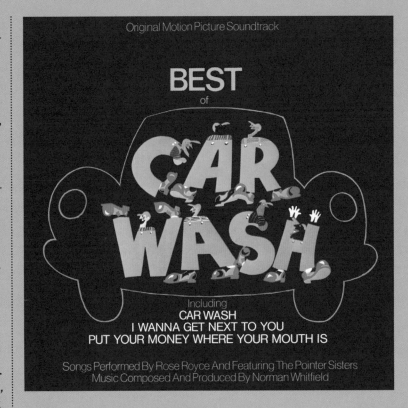

However, released before *Saturday Night Fever* in the summer of 1978, *Thank God It's Friday*, made by Casablanca Records (*see page 98*), has an interesting and mixed soundtrack, which includes an early Cameo track ("Find My Way"), the Commodores' "Too Hot to Trot," and several Donna Summer numbers, including a remake of Serge Gainsbourg and Jane Birkin's "Je'taime." A triple album, it kept listeners entertained for longer than the convoluted goings-on at The Zoo, the disco in which all the "action" takes place.

In 1980 a biopic of The Village People, titled *Can't Stop the Music*, proved that actually, you can. Starring the VP as themselves, it sought to tell a version of how they came to form a band and make it big-time. *Newsweek* called it "the first all-singing, all-dancing horror film; the *Dawn of the Dead* of the disco era," and it won no less than seven Golden Raspberry Awards (including one for worst film of the year). Even the soundtrack album by the VP only managed to reach a paltry number 47 on the pop charts (despite containing their 1979 hit "YMCA"), although the title track did make number 10 on the singles chart. After that, movie makers moved away from disco pictures for a while, although the era was successfully revisited in the 1990s with *Boogie Nights* (1997), and *The Last Days of Disco* (1998) did fair business. They had great soundtracks, too.

Above: The soundtrack album for one of the better disco movies.

Left: A soundtrack album for one of the less better disco movies.

They Want You, They Want You

THE Village people were a French idea and were not a gay group. At least, the original voice of what became The Village People, Victor Willis, isn't gay. In 1977 Frenchman Jacques Morali, a producer for Philadelphia's Ritchie Family —"Brazil" being their first and biggest hit with him producing (1975)—made a visit to a Greenwich Village, New York, gay bar and witnessed a procession of theatrically attired "macho men" pass him, which gave him an idea. Having recently been impressed by a demo tape sent to him at Can't Stop Productions by an unsigned singer-songwriter named Victor Willis, Morali decided to create an act to back Willis, dress them in various gay stereo-typical outfits, and call them The Village People. His idea was enough to persuade Neil Bogart to license a deal with his Casablanca Record label (*see page 98*).

At first the "band" did no more than dance and pose behind Willis as he pro-moted *The Village People* debut album on TV shows and made personal appearances

Below: This original single sleeve shows the change in market direction for The Village People from the moody, street-cred band of the debut album release (see opposite).

'GO WEST'
VILLAGE PEOPLE

in clubs. While Morali and his business partner Henri Belolo had created the music for the band based on the swiftly evolving Eurobeat disco sound (*see page 230*), they naturally employed English-language lyricists for the first album, which contained only four tracks, side one being a medley of "San Francisco (You've Got Me)"—their debut single release—and "In Hollywood (Everyone Is a Star)." Side two contained "Fire Island" and "Village People." It was obvious from the beginning that here was an act designed to take what was at the time an underground scene and make it very, very mainstream.

Dressing the band in outfits of a highway patrolman (Willis), a Native American in headress (Felipe Rose), a soldier (Alex Briley), a cowboy (originally Dave Forrest but replaced quickly and permanently by Randy Jones), a construction worker in a hardhat (Mark Mussler, replaced in 1978 by David Hodo), and a mustachioed, macho leatherman (Lee Moulton, replaced by former toll collector Glen Hughes) gave the act an appeal to people blissfully ignorant of the homosexual stereotypes, but who liked the theatricality of it all. The simple, catchy choruses of their hit songs—"Macho Man" (number 25 pop hit in Spring 1978), "Y.M.C.A." (number 2 pop hit early in 1979), "In the Navy" (number 3 pop hit 1979)—made them a pre-teen sensation, too.

Sold as a disco act at a time when disco's popularity was peaking, The Village People enjoyed enormous success for two years. They also earned plenty of dance floor play with a series of remixed 12" versions of their hits—and misses, such as "Go West," which would later prove a huge pop hit for the British band Pet Shop Boys (in 1993). However, when Willis, the lyric

"When Jacques Morali first approached me, I couldn't understand him because his [French] accent was so thick. He said, 'We're going to put a disco group together, a gay disco group.' I didn't get it, and I thought, Oh great, this is going to go over like an atom bomb."

Felipe Rose

writer for many of their hits, left the band because of personal reasons just before filming began on their biopic *Can't Stop the Music* (*see page 219*), it marked the beginning of the end of their chart success. Willis was replaced by Ray Simpson, and the movie was made and duly bombed. As did the soundtrack release in 1980, whereas its predecessor *Go West* had made number 2 on the same list the previous year. The title track was released as a single and made it to number 10 on the pop chart, but it was the last Village People single to make any kind of impression.

The movie title proved to be sadly inappropriate. After struggling through an album with Simpson as lead singer, and despite luring Willis back to front them for another flop album—*Fox on the Box* (1982)—The Village People stuttered to an end in 1985 after a ninth and final album release titled *Sex over the Phone* (with Ray Stephens as lead singer) failed to sell well even in the dance charts. And that despite the album being a pure HI-NRG production (*see pages 230, 233*) when it was all the rage.

Left: The grainy black-and-white photo of an unsmiling Village People on the band's debut album release was to prove unique. Soon it would be all smiles (see opposite).

Palladium

WHEN Steve Rubell and Ian Schrager got out of jail they found it hard to make a comeback, at least at first. Many of their old clients from the Studio 54 days now shunned them as ex-jailbirds. However, they soon found backing to open Morgan's, a mid-price, midtown hotel that quickly became popular with young Europeans and celebrities. In the mid-1980s Rubell and Schrager returned to the night-club business, looking to do something completely different from Studio 54. In 1985, they took the old Palladium at 126 E. 14th Street and employed Japanese architect Arata Isozaki, who was later commissioned to do the Barcelona Olympics, to create a new club. He built a huge, angular, gridlike structure within the shell of the 1926 building at the original orchestra level, contrasting with the building's original ornate architecture, which was left more or less intact. The theater was so huge that this new building within was contained without seeming cramped, creating a total of seven floors of mezzanines and balconies overlooking Isozaki's dance floor. The discotheque and the upper balconies were reached from the vast lobby by a spectacular hi-tech double staircase. Its floor, and the floor of a huge landing, was made up of 2,400 round lights set in round glass blocks. To walk up it was to walk on light, angling its way into the heavens. Video was the in-thing and huge banks of television monitors, each with twenty-five of the largest screens available, dominated the walls. Each could operate separately or one large image could be shown on the grid. Each bank could be raised or lowered three floors, so the dance floor always looked different. The actual size of the room also changed. When the dance floor became too crowded, the surrounding walls were raised to enlarge it. And at the height of the evening, a small four-sided room was lowered into the middle of the floor, so people would be dancing in a small room with a window and door.

Steve Rubell said, "It will be a club for the eighties. I want a different kind

Below: A collage of various Palladium flyers and invites from the mid-1980s (author's own collection).

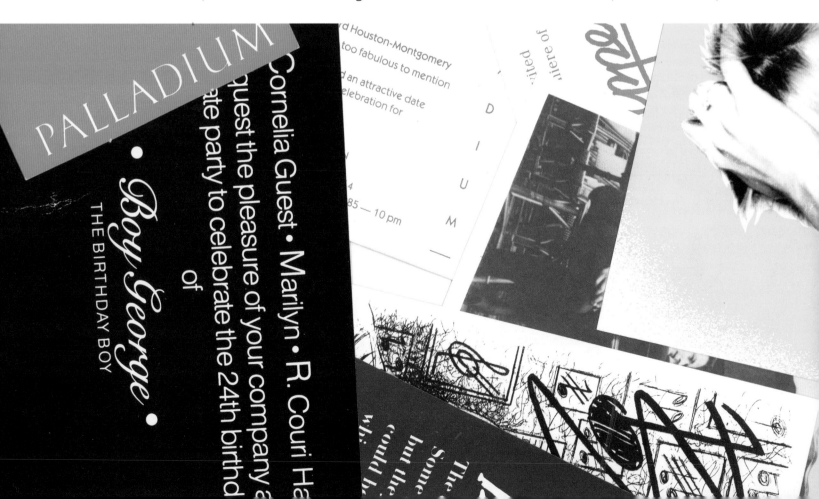

Above: There was no uniform identity for Palladium, and different events had different flyer and invite designs.

of environment now. No blinking lights. In the end clubs are about magic—you never know if it is going to work until the opening night and then you know. You always know." Rubell and Schrager were listed as "conceptual consultants," because convicted felons are not permitted to hold liquor licenses. Taking their cue from Area, Rubell and Schrager employed artists to design the interior: a stage backdrop by Keith Haring two floors high that changed color with the lighting, a huge canvas behind the bar in the Mike Todd room by Jean-Michel Basquiat—who sometimes acted as DJ, playing Miles Davis, Dizzie Gillespie, and Charlie Parker as he did at Area—ceiling frescos by Francesco Clemente above one of the theater's old vestibules, work by Laurie Anderson, and a fantasy fairground basement by graffiti artist Kenny Scharf, with neon-lit fur walls, mirrors, and dinosaur-embellished public telephones, everything heavily encrusted in globs of paint and graffiti. All of it curated by Henry Geldzahler, the Curator for American Art at the Metropolitan Museum of Art in New York. It was really several clubs in one; the exclusive Mike Todd Room upstairs, run by Anita Sarko, could hold 700 at a pinch and even had its own VIP section in addition to the main one backstage in the dance floor (and of course there were even more exclusive, shabby back rooms where the top elite gathered to snort cocaine).

There were special events and parties in the Mike Todd Room virtually every day, each one of which was announced by sending out thousands of invitations, but even with one of those you had to get past doormen Haoui Montaug and Sally Randall; Sally became so famous in her own right that she had her own gossip column. Once inside, the Mike Todd Room continued the Studio 54 tradition of mixing celebrity with money and everyone from Boy George to Tony Bennett would be there, mingling with the rich and the political. Naturally Palladium employed top rank DJs: Richard Sweret and Junior Vasquez both spun discs there, also Dwayne Holt and Robbie Leslie. But with Palladium, the visuals were in some ways more important than the music, and areas like the crowded Mike Todd room were devoted mostly to networking and picking up.

Except on Saturday night, that is, where from 10:30 p.m. until midday on Sunday thousands of people danced the night away, celebrating being in, what was for them, the most fabulous club in New York.

It was to prove the last hurrah for the original disco euphoria, though.

Madonna: the last disco diva?

When she moved to New York in 1977 disco was a staple of all the hippest clubs. Her first experience of the music business came in 1979 when she performed as a backing singer for the HI-NRG disco star Patrick Hernandez. As a dancer at Electric Circus and FunHouse she got to know DJs, musicians, and producers who were remixing, creating, and promoting disco music. Her solo career took off after persuading Danceteria DJ Mark Kamins to play an early demo recording of "Everybody" in 1982. Here she's dancing at Palladium in 1985, as confetti hearts fly.

5

When the music stops

Death to Disco

T'S hard to see what all the fuss is about now, but at the end of the 1970s and in the wake of the all-conquering *Saturday Night Fever* movie and soundtrack album, there arose in America a grassroots, rock-music-led movement that was vociferously and violently against disco. Not since evangelical Christian leaders had mobilized their kids against the Beatles in 1966, following John Lennon's assertion that the Beatles were "bigger than Jesus," had America witnessed the kind of rabid anti–pop cultural backlash culminating in riots and the burning of disco records as the "death to disco" movement provoked.

The original inspiration for the movement probably owes something to a Long Island punk band named Jimi LaLumia and the Psychotic Frogs, who released "Death to Disco" in late 1977. It took a while to reach a wider audience, but the title itself seems to have spread much further and faster than the record ever did.

From the distance of more than three decades, the furor created over disco records, the clubs, fashions, and the lifestyle that went with it in 1979 seems more than simply hysterical. As the new decade loomed, however, if you were not a fan of disco then you were part of a minority, or so it seemed. Disco music was to be heard everywhere—on TV, in ads selling everything from cars to candy, in clubs and bars, in stores selling clothes designed for a Saturday night spent doing the Hustle (whether it be Latin, New York, L.A., or Lust—*see page 214*), on movie soundtracks, in TV shows, and—crucially—on the majority of music format radio stations.

Across America DJs who had spent years spinning rock records found themselves being ordered to play disco and only disco records. Some complained but did it anyway, others complained, refused to play it, and were fired. One of the latter, a Chicago-based rock DJ named Steve Dahl, was fired by WDAI when he refused to play disco records instead of the album-oriented rock (AOR) he preferred. He was swiftly hired by rival station WLUP, though, and began a personal, on-air, anti-disco vendetta, ridiculing the music and lifestyle. He even recorded a version of Rod Stewart's—admittedly woeful—disco hit "Da Ya Think I'm Sexy?" titled, "Do Ya Think I'm Disco?"

A favorite on-air trick was to "blow up" a disco record (playing a snatch of the track before hitting the SFX button).

The explosion gave an idea to a friend of Dahl's who was equally affronted by the popularity of disco music: Mike Veeck, son of the owner of the Chicago White Sox baseball team. Along with WLUP promotions director Dave Logan, the two men hatched a plan for people to gain free admittance to a Detroit Tigers–White Sox double-header on July 12 in exchange for a disco record, which Dahl would add to a crate and then blow them all up on the field between games. The radio station set about advertising their Disco Demolition

> **"'Disco sucks' has become the catchphrase of the intransigent rocker (when work on this supplement got under way, T-shirts with that motto began appearing in the Rolling Stone office)."**
>
> Mikal Gilmore, Rolling Stone magazine, 1979

Chapter opener: Dancers at Manhattan's Limelight club take a breather during the Dog Days of Disco.

Above: Anti-disco protesters invade the field at Comiskey Park, Chicago, following the explosion of a crate of disco records, July 12, 1979.

Night and hoped to get about 12,000 people there. In the event an estimated 90,000 anti-disco demonstrators overfilled the stands and surrounding area, hanging banners that read "Disco sucks" along the rails of the bleachers and barely managing to contain themselves with chanting "disco sucks" until the explosion of the discs. The big moment was amateurishly staged, the timing of everything off, and the resulting wreckage burned a hole in the grass and set off a small fire. After leading the crowd in a version of his "Do Ya Think I'm Disco?" Dahl left the field—which was instantly invaded, leading to a riot with people setting new fires, ripping up the batting cage, and fighting. The game was abandoned and the riot police had to clear the stadium, with the result that the event was reported everywhere and came to be a defining moment in the anti-disco movement (prompting Dahl to hold two other events with similar, though less well reported, results).

Footage of the riot at Comiskey Park shows that the majority of the "protesters" were white, long-haired, and young—too young for disco, too uncool for anything but Album Oriented Rock. Those rioters were self-professed rock and metal fans naturally inclined to want their favorite music to be the dominant sound of the day. Ironically, of course, rock music was derived from the same sources as disco—not that the "death to disco" dolts understood that.

Naturally, disco musicians were both astounded and somewhat frightened by the event, which was exacerbated by numerous editorials in music magazines and newspapers supporting the "death to disco" ethos and the widespread condemnation of their music. It wasn't stretching things too far when Chic's Nile Rodgers made an analogy with Nazi book-burnings.

As is the way with any fad, disco came and went, largely unaffected by the "death to disco" unpleasantness, its demise not hastened by it.

HI-NRG

T started in Germany and was of Italian descent. While there are some who would have you believe that it began with Kraftwerk, those teutonic man-machines who liked to drone and repeat electronic beats forever, don't believe them. The idea of there being a direct line from the band's "Autobahn" (1974) to the swirling, ecstatically electronic disco storm that is Sylvester's "You Make Me Feel (Mighty Real)" in 1978 is preposterous. Certainly both records are made with human voices laid over processed, synthesized, electronic musical backing, but that's as far as any connection goes. Sylvester's sound is classic HI-NRG, defined by its fast beat (120 bpm-plus) and drum machine-driven backing. Kraftwerk's sound is generally referred to as Krautrock, and fans, if not the band themselves, took it very seriously. HI-NRG is all about fun.

Sylvester, a gay drag performer who worked under his real name, sang in a falsetto voice, wore flamboyant dresses, and began his career as a member of the drag troupe the Cockettes in San Francisco in the early 1970s. After trying various musical styles, and on hearing Donna Summer's "I Feel Love" Sylvester must have realized that his time was coming. Giorgio Moroder's production on Summer's records (see page 69) was an easy one to mimic, given the right setup. The Italian Moroder built a studio in Munich, which proved to be the maternity ward for HI-NRG. So successful was the electronic disco sound that his sound was adopted by fellow Europeans and soon traveled around the world, after conquering Europe completely. In Germany Frank Farian, a producer with ambitions similar to Moroder's, created a disco act that was almost as big as Donna Summer in Europe: Boney M. Farian also scored hits with Silver Convention (and, controversially in the 1990s, with Milli Vanilli).

In America HI-NRG was sometimes called Eurobeat (or Eurodisco) because many of the acts that scored disco hits with the HI-NRG formula were from France (Cerrone, Ottawan, and Grace Jones—indirectly), Italy (Macho), Spain (Baccara), and England (Pet Shop Boys, and everything produced by Stock, Aitken, and Waterman).

In 1977 Sylvester met a young musician and producer named Patrick Cowley and originally asked him to join his backing band. Soon, though, Cowley was producing instead, and together they came up with "Dance (Disco Heat)" and "You Make Me Feel (Mighty Real)," which became instant dance hits and pop chart hits, too, in 1978. Their unique sound worked well, enough for Sylvester to have hits in 1979 with a version of "I (Who Have Nothing)" and "Can't Stop Dancing." Further minor hits followed in 1980 and '81 before, in 1982, they scored their last big dance hit with "Do You Wanna Funk." It was originally credited to Cowley as the lead artist, with Sylvester "guesting" because Cowley had scored dance hits the previous year with "Menergy" and "Megatron Man." Sadly Cowley died at age thirty-two in November 1982 of complications arising from undiagnosed AIDS, one of the disease's early victims. Sylvester died in 1988, also from AIDS-related illness, at the age of forty-one.

> "I have everything it takes to be a disco star; personality, charisma, special powers, and a voice that really works for disco."
>
> Sylvester

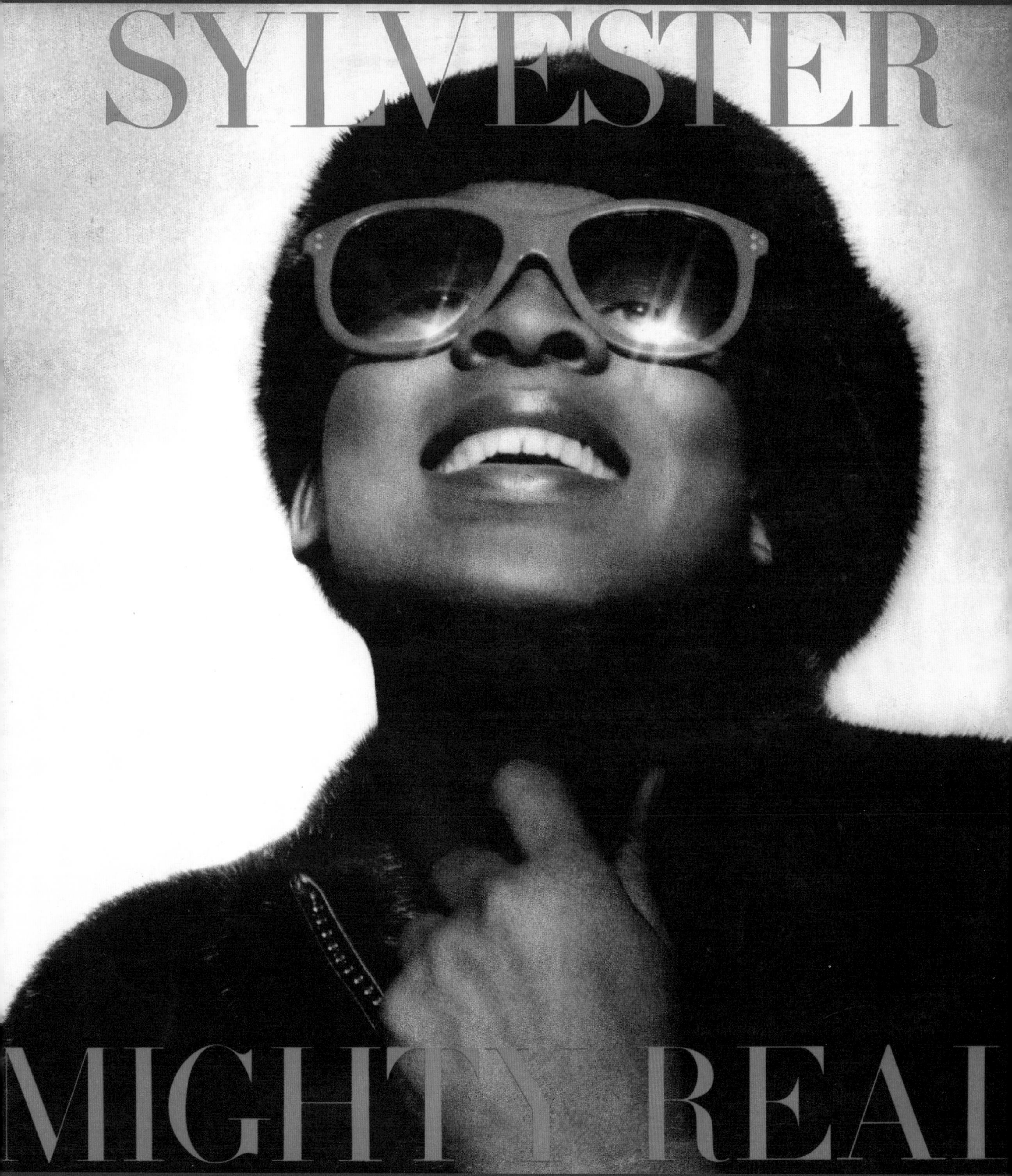
SYLVESTER
MIGHTY REAL

West End Boys

HARDCORE HI-NRG became a staple of gay disco from the late 1970s, and by the end of the decade it had broken out into the mainstream—France Joli's "Come to Me" (1979), Claudja Barry's "Radio Action" (1981), The Weather Girls' "It's Raining Men" (1982), Miquel Brown's "So Many Men, So Little Time" (1983), and Evelyn Thomas' "High Energy" (1984) were all pop chart successes that spread the beat further into "straight" clubs and kept pretty much to the Moroder-inspired recipe for HI-NRG. However, during the eighties the HI-NRG beat was expanded on and buffed up by British acts Yazoo ("Don't Go" made number 7 on the U.S. dance charts in 1982), Pet Shop Boys ("West End Girls," their first U.S. pop number 1 in 1986), Bronski Beat ("Small Town Boy," U.S. dance number 1 in 1984), Dead or Alive ("You Spin Me Round," made number 2 in the U.S. dance chart in 1985), and Erasure ("Oh L'amour" made number 3 on the U.S. dance chart in 1986). But they, too, stuck pretty close to the all-electronic high-bpm formula laid down by Moroder.

At the same time, though, there was a growing cross-over movement beginning in UK clubs, which saw former punks, post-punks, and Goths adding electronic beats and dance melodies to their sound. New Order had originally been Joy Division, a somber, post-punk, black-clad rock fourpiece from Manchester. After their lead singer Ian Curtis committed suicide in 1980, the rest of the band released "Blue Monday," an electronic beat and synth-driven seven-minute-long dance track that became an enormous hit in the United Kingdom and Europe, as well as making the top spot on the American dance chart.

As disco died, some clubs went electronic and raised their bpm to the HI-NRG beat. It was just a different kind of disco.

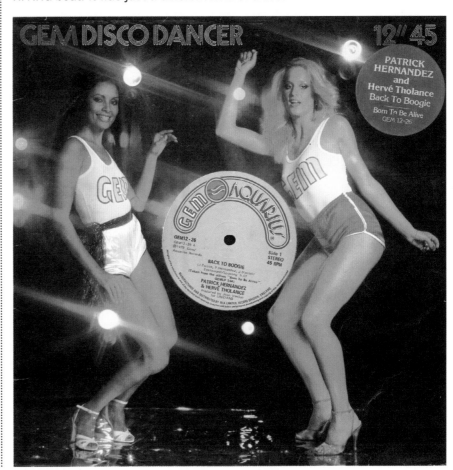

Left: Chris Lowe and Neil Tennant, The Pet Shop Boys, in the mid-1980s.

Right: Gem Records' generic 12" single sleeve containing Patrick Hernandez's "Back to Boogie," 1979.

What You Hear Is Not a Test . . .

WHILE disco was being done to death across America in the early days of the 1980s, in high schools, parks, and community halls of New York's five boroughs a new dance sound was being distilled. Inspiration for the emerging hip-hop scene had come from Jamaican "toasters" or "MCs," who would set up sound systems playing records through huge speakers at either end of a hall and then talk-sing over the top and at each other. They were competing to see who could get more people dancing and would drop in personal jibes at their "opponent" as they improvised over ska, reggae, and dub, backing tracks and singles. By the end of the 1970s some New York rappers, such as Afrika Baambaata, Grandmaster Flash, Melle Mel, Kurtis Blow, and Fab 5 Freddy had graduated from free-styling over records at clubs in the Bronx and Brooklyn to making records themselves.

Being a grassroots movement, hip-hop hadn't made its way into the offices of the major record companies until a small label in Englewood, New Jersey, put out "Rappers Delight" by the Sugar Hill Gang, in 1979. Sugar Hill Records had started in 1974 as a vehicle for owners Joe and his wife Sylvia Robinson (who'd had a couple of R&B hits as half of Sylvia and Mickey) to put out records by local soul, funk, and disco acts. They were among the first people to acknowledge the growing hip-hop scene in their neighborhood and heard a hit record in "Rapper's Delight." To be fair, what they heard first was the bass line of a true international disco hit: Chic's "Good Times." But on top of that was a whole new way of putting across a song. Boasting, playful, talk-chanting by Big Bank Hank, Wonder Mike, and Master Gee told a story of macho romancing and dance-enhancing beats, while the Sugar Hill house band played a funky—disco— backing beat. It was new, but familiar enough to become a huge dance floor hit in seven-minute and fourteen-minute versions, as well as a radio hit in a 3:45-minute edit. Sugar

Right: Wonder Mike out front as Big Bank Hank (left back) and Master Gee (far right) give directions to dancers during a Sugarhill Gang performance in 1979.

Hill only released it in a 12" format, but it still sold over 100,000 copies, making it to number 36 on the pop charts. Hip-hop had its start, and the last days of disco as it existed were marked.

Don't Push Me I'm Close to the Edge

Following the success of "Rapper's Delight," another local hip-hop act, Grandmaster Flash and the Furious Five, who had not enjoyed the same success with their debut release "Superrappin'" on the small Enjoy label, moved to Sugar Hill hoping for some of that magic to rub off on them. Plenty of other acts made the switch, too, including Positive Force, whose "We Got the Funk" was a big disco hit in 1979; New Guys on the Block, who gave ex-Philadelphia Records man Bunny Sigler a last stab at filling dance floors; West Street Mob, who featured Joe and Sylvia's son Joey Jr. and had a hit with "Let's Dance (Make Your Body Move)" in 1981; Spoonie Gee, who is now recognized as one of the pioneers of what would become known as Gangsta rap; and the first female rappers to release a record, The Sequence, whose "Funk You Up" was released on Sugar Hill in 1979.

However, Grandmaster Flash and the Furious Five began their ascent of the pop and dance charts with "Freedom" in 1980 which made number 19 on the R&B charts, and followed it with the first scratch 12" single to make a big impression, "The Adventures of Grandmaster Flash on the Wheels of Steel," later the same year (which sampled, among others, tracks by Queen, Blondie, and Spoonie Gee).

In the first two years of the 1980s discos began to play more and more hip-hop, and less "classic" disco music. Acts who had not previously been heard in discos began adding rappers and hip-hop beats to recordings and getting played at clubs across America. Blondie's "Rapture" was considered a rap-rock hybrid and enjoyed enormous dance floor success in 1981, and Tom Tom Club, an offshoot of art-punks Talking Heads, had a huge dance hit with "Wordy Rappinghood" in 1981, following it later that year with the chart and disco hit "Genius of Love"—now one of the most sampled records in rap. British punk pioneers The Clash released the hip-hop/rock/reggae crossover single "This Is Radio Clash" in 1981 and gained their highest club play chart placing of number 17. In June 1981 The Clash put Grandmaster

Flash on the bill for their record-breaking seventeen-night sell-out residency at New York's Bond's Casino. The crowd was not wholly receptive to hearing the rappers, but The Clash continued to promote the act and their music in interviews with the almost wholly rock-oriented music press.

In 1982 Grandmaster Flash and the Furious Five (plus Grandmaster Melle Mel) released the single that would revolutionize hip-hop and add another dimension to the music. "The Message" combined politics with dance break beats in such style that it was an immediate smash hit, selling over a million copies in a month. Unlike earlier hip-hop, "The Message" does not have a fast bpm, and it uses a swirling synthesizer sound over a clearly electronic beat and a drum sample from Tom Tom Club's "Genius of Love." It was fresh, new, and made it possible to stretch the boundaries of hip-hop beyond the disco floor.

As rap began breaking into the mainstream, former rock-oriented artists who liked to dance began experimenting with rap. While New York's premier art-rock ensemble Talking Heads took a break from it in 1981, married rhythm section Tina Weymouth and Chris Frantz put together Tom Tom Club, and scored dance hits with "Wordy Rappinghood" and "Genius of Love." Rockers began to dance at last. . .

Left: Grandmaster Flash (front left), Melle Mel (left center) and The Furious Five in 1982.

Above: Tom Tom Club's debut 1981 album *Wordy Rappinghood* featured former members of The Talking Heads.

The Hot 100 Disco Trax Part II (1977–1984)

Roy Ayers Ubiquity: Running Away (6:57/12" single/Polydor/1977)

Cerrone: Supernature (10:20/album title track/1977)

Heatwave: Boogie Nights (4:49/single/Epic/January 1977)

Chic: Dance, Dance, Dance (Yowsah, Yowsah, Yowsah) (8:21/12" single/Atlantic/September 1977)

Detroit Emeralds: Feel the Need (7:04/12" single/Westbound–Atlantic/May 1977)

Yvonne Elliman: If I Can't Have You (2:57/single/RSO/December 1977)

First Choice: Dr Love (7:35/12" single/Gold Mind Records/May 1977)

Loleatta Holloway: Hit and Run (6:01/album track on Lolleatta/Gold Mind Records/1977)

Grace Jones: I Need a Man (7:30/12" single/Beam Junction/April 1977)

Odyssey: Native New Yorker (5:35/12" single/RCA/November 1977)

Below: Progressive disco? Cerrone's third album from 1977.

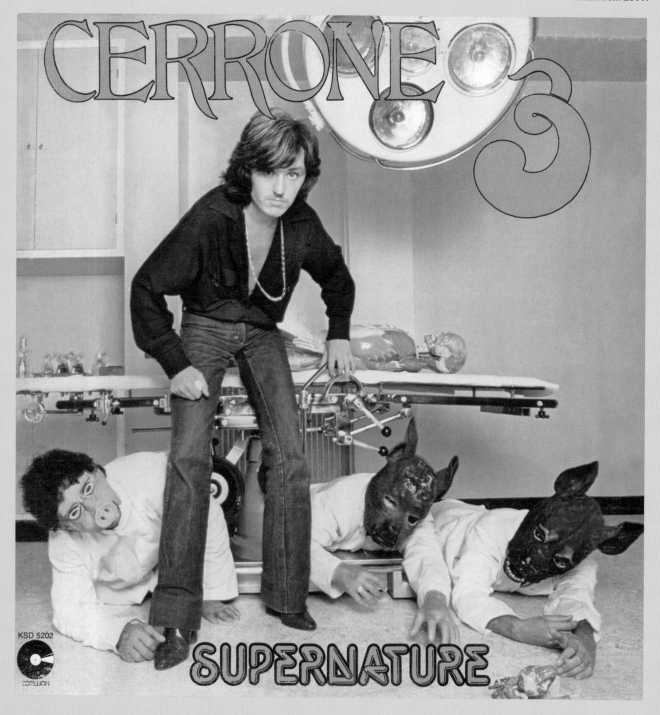

Donna Summer: I Feel Love (8:15/12" single/Casablanca/August 1977)

The Trammps: Disco Inferno (10:54/12" single/Atlantic/April 1977)

T-Connection: Do What You Wanna Do (7:15/12" single/TK Disco/June 1977)

KC and The Sunshine Band: Boogie Shoes (2:17/single/TK Records/January 1978)

Voyage: Voyage (32:27/LP/Marlin/May 1978)

Evelyn "Champagne" King: Shame (6:35/12" single/RCA/June 1978)

Hamilton Bohannon: Let's Start the Dance (5:50/12" single/Mercury Records/July 1978)

Sylvester: You Make Me Feel Mighty Real (6:17/12" single/Fantasy/July 1978)

Alicia Bridges: I Love the Nightlife (Disco Round) (5:37/12" single/Polydor/August 1978)

Third World: Now That We Found Love (7:37/12" single/Island Records/August 1978)

Musique: Keep on Jumpin' (7:02/12" single/Prelude Records/September 1978)

Dan Hartman: Instant Replay (8:15/12" single/Blue Sky–Epic/September 1978)

Chic: Le Freak (5:30/12" single/Atlantic/October 1978)

Above: Evelyn King's debut album release, 1977.

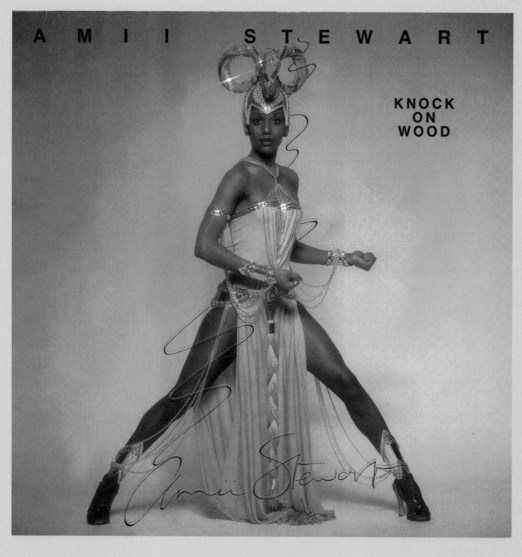

A M I I   S T E W A R T

KNOCK
ON
WOOD

Left: Futuristic,
space-age disco with
Amii Stewart, 1979.

Below: Luther Vandross'
seminal 1981 debut
album release,
Never Too Much.

Gloria Gaynor: I Will Survive (8:02/12"
single/Polydor/October 1978)

Funkadelic: One Nation Under a Groove
(11:26/12" single/Warner Bros/
November 1978)

Chaka Khan: I'm Every Woman (4:22/12"
single/Warner Bros/November 1978)

Bombers: (Everybody) Get Dancin'
(9:24/12" single/West End
Records/1979)

Tom Browne: Funkin' for Jamaica (4:43/
album track on Love Approach/GRP
Records/1979)

Gibson Bros.: Cuba (7:48/12" single/
Mango/1979)

Amii Stewart: Knock on Wood (6:10/12"
single/Ariola/March 1979)

Sister Sledge: We Are Family (8:06/ 12"
single/Cotillion/April 1979)

Anita Ward: Ring My Bell '79 (8:08/12"
single/TK Disco/April 1979)

Earth, Wind & Fire: Boogie Wonderland
(9:21/12" single/ARC/May 1979)

McFadden & Whitehead: Ain't No
Stoppin' Us Now (10:45/12" single/

Philadelphia International/May 1979)

Michael Jackson: Don't Stop 'Til You
Get Enough (5:45/12" single/Epic/
July 1979)

Crusaders feat. Randy Crawford: Street
Life (11:18/album title track/MCA/
September 1979)

France Joli: Come to Me (9:39/album
title track/Prelude/September 1979)

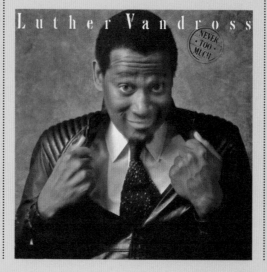

The Sugarhill Gang: Rapper's Delight '79 (15/12" single/Sugar Hill Records/October 1979)

The Gap Band: Oops Upside Your Head (8:39/12" single/Total Experience-Mercury/December 1979)

Lipps Inc.: Funkytown (7:51/12" single/Casablanca/January 1980)

Loose Joints: Is It All Over My Face (female vocal) (6:56/12" single/West End Records/1980)

The Jones Girls: Nights over Egypt '81 (4:34/single/Philadelphia International/1981)

Luther Vandross: Never Too Much (5:36/12" single/Epic/October 1981)

Tom Tom Club: Genius of Love (7:24/12" single/Sire Records/March 1982)

Grandmaster Flash & The Furious Five: The Message (7:10/12" single/Sugar Hill Records/May 1982)

Fat Larry's Band: Zoom (4:11/single/Omni Records/July 1982)

The Weather Girls: It's Raining Men (5:24/12" single/CBS/September 1982)

Marvin Gaye: Sexual Healing '82 (5:30/12" single/CBS/October 1982)

The Valentine Bros.: Money's Too Tight To Mention (6:00/12" single/Bridge Records/April 1983)

Evelyn Thomas: High Energy (7:40/12" single/TSR Records/August 1984)

Above: Gap Band mixed old style funk with disco and hip-hop on 1983's *Strike a Groove*.

Lucky Star

MADONNA'S showbiz career began as a dancer, and thanks to the HI-NRG disco smash "Born to Be Alive" by Frenchman Patrick Hernandez in 1979 she began her journey from chorus line to superstar. Following European success for Hernandez's single, in July 1979 the song made the number 1 spot on the dance chart in the United States, and he moved to America to further his career. After a sell-out tour of the States at the end of 1979, Hernandez toured the rest of the world in 1980, and among his retinue of dancers was Madonna Ciccone, traveling abroad for the first time in her life. While on tour she met and romanced Dan Gilroy, who, while playing guitar for Hernandez, also fronted a band called the Breakfast Club. Madonna joined him briefly as drummer and co-vocalist, but she soon moved on to a new band called Emmy with an old boyfriend from Michigan, Stephen Bray, who had joined Breakfast Club as drummer (Bray would return to Breakfast Club and eventually get a Top 10 pop hit in 1987 with "Right on Track").

In 1982 Madonna's new boyfriend, a DJ at New York's Danceteria named Mark Kamins, introduced her to Sire Records boss Seymour Stein, who had signed both The Ramones and Talking Heads. He saw star potential in the singer on hearing the demo produced for her by Kamins, who wanted to become a producer. On hearing the slow-tempo, electronically driven disco number (in which Madonna name-checks the "DJ"), Stein was impressed enough to initially give her a singles deal only. "Everybody" was not a pop success, but it was a club hit, and Madonna wisely concentrated her efforts in that direction for promotion. Her first magazine cover shoot was for *Dance Music Report*'s December 1982 issue. That month, in an attempt to get Stein to make a video of the song to help promote it, Madonna arranged to mime to the record and choreographed a dance routine herself (wearing top hat and tails) at Danceteria. It worked and Stein paid $1,500 for a video shoot at Paradise Garage.

The ever-savvy Madonna realized she could build a career as a pop artist emerging from the hip New York club scene, and was arguably the last great disco star to make it. "Everybody" did well enough to persuade Stein to make an eponymous album with Madonna, and the second single taken from it, "Burning Up," was a more upbeat, almost HI-NRG disco number. Madonna made countless PAs at clubs in the United States and United Kingdom promoting it, and while it failed to get into the pop charts, it was another great dance hit.

A year later she finally made it into the pop charts with "Holiday," a song written by Curtis Hudson and Lisa Stevens of disco act Pure Energy, and produced by

> "I am my own experiment. I am my own work of art. I stand for freedom of expression."
>
> Madonna

another Madonna boyfriend, John Jellybean Benitez. It was an immediate club hit (becoming her first number 1 Hot Dance Club Play hit), and although it took more personal appearances by the singer to promote it, "Holiday" made number 16 on the *Billboard* pop charts. Her career then took off big-time. "Lucky Star," the fourth track from *Madonna* to be released as a single, made number 4 on the pop charts and was another number 1 dance hit. Although "Borderline," the final single from the debut album, wasn't quite as successful (making number 10 on the pop chart and number 2 on the dance chart), by 1985 Madonna was a pop star and no longer a club act. She left the disco behind, although her music continued to be dance-oriented.

Dancing out of the Limelight

T is said that a properly run discotheque made roughly a 40 percent return on expenditure, which is an enormous profit margin in any business. Once the knowledge of how much money there was to be made in one club became public—the Studio 54 IRS case being the first indicator of such—it didn't take long for serious business to take notice. If just one fabulous club made so much profit, what would a chain of them manage to do? Canadian Peter Gatien started out selling jeans and running rock music clubs in his homeland before opening the first Limelight in Hollywood, Florida. After it burned down, in February 1980 he opened another one in Atlanta, housed in a strip mall. It was successful, but not loved. The locals called it "Slimelight." Wary of losing public approval, he sought out better sites for further Limelights and got the idea of housing his

LIMELIGHT

Left: Original flyer for New York's Limelight.

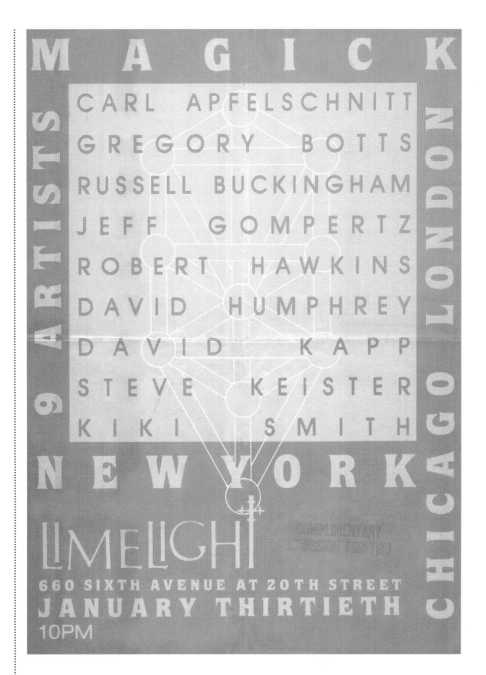

Right: The printing of locations for all the Limelights on this early flyer contributed to the idea of it being a commercial enterprise.

clubs in historical buildings after opening the Limelight in Chicago, which occupied the listed former home of the Chicago Historical Society.

In November 1983 Gatien opened a Limelight in New York on 660 Sixth Avenue at 20th Street, in the 12,000-square-foot former Church of the Holy Communion, built in 1844. This was followed by a Limelight in London, which was also housed in a former Victorian Welsh Presbyterian church on the corner of Shaftesbury Avenue and Charing Cross Road in Soho. By this time disco music was all but dead, and the Limelights switched to playing rock and emerging techno dance music. In London the club hosted regular Goth nights and gigs.

The Limelight chain did well enough and, perhaps inevitably, in the mid-1990s Gatien was investigated for possible tax fraud in the United States. He was eventually sentenced to sixty days in jail and fined $1.9 million in 1999. When he got out he was deported back to Canada, where he opened a club called Circa in Toronto (which went out of business in 2010).

Perhaps the main reason why Gatien's chain of clubs failed to become places of pilgrimage for disco dancers in the way The Loft, Paradise Garage, and similar other clubs had been was that they opened too late. By 1983 disco had blown itself out as a vibrant, important grassroots movement.

WHEN THE MUSIC STOPS **245**

Hip-hop, rap, and technobeat had replaced the sound of swirling strings, snappy snare, horns, and uplifting, swooping choruses interspersed with instrumental breaks on dance floors everywhere. As disco music faded, new trends emerged among the young who wanted their own nightlife culture. In Europe the Rave scene grew rapidly and established itself as the dominant alternative culture among clubbers (fueled by the new drug Ecstasy). In America, House music played in enormous, industrial sites to increasingly segregated crowds. Rap became the sound of the new urban culture on the East and West coasts, and even if much of it sampled the sound of James Brown or Philly, it wasn't the same kind of dance music as disco. Nightclubs across America began mixing up dance nights with Goth, Punk, and even Country events (line dancing became a popular fad) in order to stay in business. The "Death to Disco" movement (*see page 228*) rejoiced as radio splintered into genre-specific sections, allowing listeners to ignore anything that they didn't already know. The emerging college radio network established itself on a diet of "alternative" rock music (*Billboard* magazine invented a new category for it in 1988), which fed into nightclubs who'd play REM, Sonic Youth, and The Cure instead of Chic, Kool & The Gang, or Gloria Gaynor. By the time Madonna became an international star in 1984 she was regarded simply as a pop artist, despite having made her reputation with music that came out of New York's gay disco scene.

From the 1990s onward, clubs would occasionally host retro disco nights and invite people to dress up, but "serious" nightclubs stuck to a diet of the new R&B (which used to be called soul or disco), Techno, and dance-pop to get people dancing. Disco became a dirty word for serious clubbers.

"Discos belong to the people. The public invented it and now business has capitalized off it."

Clarence Satchell, The Ohio Players

Right: New York's Limelight was a former church, as can be seen from this 1984 photo of a packed dance floor.

Below: Generic Limelight flyers could be used at any of the clubs.

Disco Stick

TWENTY-FIVE years after Madonna first hit the big time, there has been a change in attitude to disco. In 2008 another female singer-songwriter emerged from the New York East Side gay scene with a thrilling new take on disco, rekindling an interest in what it was all about in the process, as well as showing what it might still be: Lady Gaga sought to recreate a night at Studio 54 or 2001 Odyssey with her Monster Fame Ball tour of 2009–2010. Her Moroder-like, Eurobeat-driven pop proved hugely successful among an audience that mixes people who came of age before she was born and their children alike. Gaga's constant use of the mirror ball in videos and onstage—even in her costumes—offers a constant visual reminder of the fun, frolics, and fancy footwork that was to be had in the original discos.

By the time Stefani Germanotta was born in 1986, Madonna was America's premier female pop star and discos had all but disappeared, replaced by "clubs," at which a range of music was played, not all of it dance-oriented. So it's kind of odd that as Lady Gaga, Stefani not only created a retro-disco sound in her music—which is admittedly more Eurodisco than funky, but still disco-centric—but also stated that she wished to create the atmosphere of a New York club circa 1979 at her *Fame Monster Ball*.

Lady Gaga proved to be something of a musical genre collector from the start of her career, mixing glam rock and metal drum sounds with HI-NRG beats and synthesized backing. She wrote songs for Pussycat Dolls and New Kids on the Block, which sounded like a twenty-first-century version of how disco might have progressed had it not been done to death at the beginning of the 1980s. Her own music, produced by RedOne, a Moroccan who learned his trade in Sweden, employs a HI-NRG beat with classic pop hooks. Gaga expressed her admiration for a wide range of artists, performers, and musicians, among them Grace Jones, one of disco's great individual talents with whom Tom Moulton worked (*see page 56*) and Boney M, Frank

Farian's classic Eurodisco outfit.

Not only is Gaga's music created to get people dancing, but her shows also worked hard at getting her fans moving and enjoying a night out in the way that—as she heard from her parents who lived in New York during the classic disco era—disco dancers used to. In many ways Gaga resurrected "disco" and helped introduce a new generation of music fans and dancers to the genre. YouTube videos of promotional films from the classic disco era received enormous numbers of hits, as did videos that showed a hand lowering a stylus onto a spinning vinyl record, the disc going round and broadcasting rare and classic disco numbers in their original 12" format as they played.

While Gaga became a worldwide superstar by selling huge quantities of MP3 downloads, she also understood the benefits of a great dance remix of her songs. She ensured that the best remixers of her day worked with her songs, just as those classic disco tracks were remixed for the dance floor. Gaga also sold a high number of vinyl records to the growing army of DJs who preferred to spin vinyl and not just data files at clubs in the second decade of the twenty-first century.

It didn't exactly add up to a disco revival, but it reignited interest in the original scene, and made Gaga almost a new disco diva.

Left: Lady Gaga in her mirror ball-inspired outfit performing live in 2010.

What the *!#* Was That All About?

AS Albert Goldman, the greatest chronicler of disco who ever shook his ass at Studio 54 wrote, "Disco music is not meant to be confronted head on as something you sit down and listen to. Disco is meant to be experienced subliminally, not so much in the mind as in the body—which it exhorts ceaselessly to dance, dance, dance." Professor Goldman knew of what he wrote. Having been a detached but wholly committed chronicler of the counterculture in the 1960s, he put himself into whatever he wrote about. His fabulous and cruelly unsuccessful book *Disco* came and went in one brief print run in 1979, wrecked on the shores of mass acceptance of the bland brand of disco as promoted by *Saturday Night Fever*, the movie, soundtrack, and pop phenomenon. Not that the movie wasn't good, because it was, and is. It was just that, while Professor Goldman wrote thrillingly and chillingly about the sex, drugs, snobbery, and ecstasy of the true disco experience, the people who got dancing ten years after it had first started didn't want to read about it, they wanted to do it.

So they did, in their millions—right up until the music stopped. Ultimately, Disco danced itself dizzy. After a decade of musical innovation and excellence—with a few unfortunate opportunistic interludes involving farm animals and the terminally unhip—disco musicians and producers became stuck in the runout groove. By the early 1980s all disco music had become formulaic, and had to include repeated whistle blasts, be driven by the same electronic drum beat and feature familiar lyrical clichés. Just as the original scene had begun privately and quietly, with rent parties advertised by word-of-mouth from among an underground scene, so it was replaced by another in New York: hip-hop from the South Bronx moved across the river and kicked disco out of clubs. Meanwhile in L.A., rappers from South Central moved into Midtown clubs and fantasised over guns, not go-go. In the Mid-West racist, uncool, long-haired rockers blew up vinyl disco records and demanded the return of interminable drum solos played by Neanderthals wearing headbands on their radios.

By the mid-1980s, with the horror of AIDS ravaging the original disco crowd, musical tastes changing, and society focusing on greed and not good times, disco was soon all played out. Maybe, too, some of the original disco crowd got too fat, tired, and old to dance anymore. Whatever it was, disco died in the mid-1980s, becoming just another part of pop culture's colorful past ripe for nostalgic revaluation when the time was right. When would that time be? Maybe when another worldwide recession hit an America busy fighting an unwinnable foreign war which had been ramped up by a dishonest Republican president? Maybe in an America that had put faith in a rookie Democrat whose idealism clashed with a pragmatic and largely Republican Congress? Kind of like this second decade of the twenty-first century.

The truly great thing about the original disco scene was that it allowed everyone who ventured onto the dance floor to become—just as Tony Manero demonstrated—a star, at least for the duration of the dance. That is something which, more than thirty years after Professor Goldman wrote about it in 1978, makes disco ripe for revival: "Everybody sees himself as a star today . . . The one thing they lack—talent—is precisely what is most lacking in those other, nearly identical young people whom the world has acclaimed a star. Never in the history of showbiz has the gap between amateur and professional been so small. And never in the history of the world has there been such a rage for exhibitionism. The question is, therefore, what are we going to do with all these beautiful show-offs? Disco provides the best answer to date. Every night the stage is set, the lights are lit, and the audience assembled; the floor will clear magically for anyone who is really intent on getting out there."

Right: Invites to the opening of the completed Tunnel in New York at the end of 1986 came in the form of this manuscript. There was no mention in it of disco.

TUNNEL
220 12TH AVENUE
NEW YORK, NY 10001
212.244.6444

New York City, Christmas 1986

Dear Trendie:

An Abandoned waterfront. Decaying piers. Echoes of forgotten
gang wars. Dark warehouses, speakeasies, and ladies of the
night. A frozen river and windy avenues...
Manhattan's Wild West!
The perfect setting for a new club.
<u>Tunnel!</u>
Endlessly mysterious...

And now, the last segment is finally completed:
<u>Basement!</u>
A dungeon below ivory towers...
<u>Private Opening</u>
Monday, December 29, 1986
10PM
DJ: Jody Kurilla
<u>This manuscript admits two</u>

PS: Tunnel is now a completed project.
Open to the public seven nights a week.
Monday, Tuesday, Wednesday: Basement only
Thursday, Friday, Saturday: The open-ended club
Sundays: Steven Cohn's Evenings

All Aboard!

Choo! Choo! Choo!   Rudolf

Index

Note: Page numbers in bold indicate illustrations.